Contents

E X T E N D I N G
ArcView GIS

Teach yourself to use ArcView GIS extensions

Network Analyst

Spatial Analyst

3D Analyst

self-study workbook
for ArcView GIS users

Tim Ormsby • Jonell Alvi

ESRI PRESS

Published by
Environmental Systems Research Institute, Inc.
380 New York Street
Redlands, California 92373-8100

Environmental Systems Research Institute, Inc.

Extending ArcView GIS
ISBN 1-879102-05-6

Editors: Michael Karman, Lisa Godin, Suzanne Boden
Contributors: R.W. Greene, Heather Kennedy, Pat Breslin, Maggie Ruan, Jamil Alvi
Cover design: Amaree Israngkura
Book design and production: Michael Hyatt

Acknowledgments

THE SPATIAL DATA
used in exercises and images in this book was provided by the organizations listed below. Internet addresses have been given where these may be useful for further research.

Africa elevation data was provided by the EROS Data Center of the United States Geological Survey.
http://edcwww.cr.usgs.gov/landdaac/gtopo30/gtopo30.html

Atlantic hurricane data was provided by Weather Services International.

Big Bear, California, elevation data was provided by the California State University, Northridge, Geography Department.
http://www.csun.edu/~hfgeg003/index.html

Boston, Massachusetts, street data was provided by Geographic Data Technology, Inc., and is used herein by permission.

California earthquake data was provided by the Southern California Seismic Network, a cooperative project of the Pasadena office of the United States Geological Survey and the Caltech Seismological Laboratory.
http://maps.esri.com

Curry County, Oregon, elevation and vegetation data was provided by the Oregon State Service Center for Geographic Information Systems and is used herein by permission.

Gillette, Wyoming, digital orthophoto was provided by the University of Wyoming Spatial Data and Visualization Center.
http://www.sdvc.uwyo.edu/index.html

Idaho vegetation data was provided by Space Imaging Corporation.

Mount Rainier elevation data was provided by the University of Washington Libraries' Map Collection and Cartographic Information Services.
http://wagda.lib.washington.edu

National parks data, including data for Canyonlands National Park, the Mississippi National River and Recreation Area, Tallgrass Prairie National Preserve, and Yellowstone National Park was provided by the National Park Service (NPS). Thanks to the following NPS employees for research assistance: Laura Ball, Project Reviews/GIS, Mississippi National River and Recreation Area; Peter J. Budde, Midwest Region GIS Coordinator; Sandy Griffith, Information Specialist, Canyonlands National Park.

http://www.nps.gov/gis

Oregon rainfall, U.S. snowfall, and U.S. temperature data was provided by the PRISM Climate Mapping Program. The agencies supporting the program are the Oregon Climate Service at Oregon State University, the National Resource Conservation Service of the United States Department of Agriculture through its Water and Climate Center and its National Cartography and Geospatial Center, and the PRISM Model.

http://www.ocs.orst.edu/prism/prism_new.html

Ozone density data was provided by the Office of Air and Radiation of the United States Environmental Protection Agency.

http://www.epa.gov/airsdata

Redlands, California, satellite image data was provided by Emerge, a division of TASC, and is used herein by permission.

Santa Barbara, California, and Washington, D.C., street data was provided by the United States Census Bureau.

Seattle baseball stadium, building, elevation, and street data was provided by the City of Seattle and is used herein by permission.

Siuslaw National Forest elevation and soil data was provided by the Pacific Northwest Research Station of the United States Department of Agriculture Forest Service.

Space shuttle images of Clear Lake, California; Kauai, Hawaii; and Miami, Florida, were provided by the National Aeronautics and Space Administration.

Vegetative index image was provided by the National Oceanic and Atmospheric Administration.

Additional image data was provided by ERDAS.

The United States Geological Survey is in many cases the original source of geographic data that was obtained from another provider.

Many data sets used in the exercises came from the ArcView GIS sample data and the *ESRI Data & Maps* CDs. The data providers are credited in the ArcView GIS online help.

Introduction

EXTENDING ARCVIEW GIS

is the companion workbook to ESRI's best-selling *Getting to Know ArcView GIS*. Taking up where that book leaves off, it explores the three most popular ESRI® ArcView® GIS extensions: ArcView Network Analyst, ArcView Spatial Analyst, and ArcView 3D Analyst™. You'll complete dozens of step-by-step exercises in the course of solving a variety of GIS problems. Concepts are presented concisely and in context, while color graphics reinforce your progress at every stage.

The exercises in this book require that you have ArcView GIS 3.1 software. To complete each of the three sections, you'll also need the appropriate extension software—ArcView Network Analyst 1.0b for the Network Analyst section, ArcView Spatial Analyst 1.1 for the ArcView Spatial Analyst section, and ArcView 3D Analyst 1 for the 3D Analyst section. Each section is self-contained and uses only the extension software it describes. The accompanying CD contains 90 megabytes of spatial data used in the exercises.

ArcView Network Analyst solves problems of network traffic on streets, rivers, railroads, pipes, or any interconnected set of lines. It finds the shortest route, or the fastest, from your origin to your destination, including all the stops you have to make along the way. It tells you whether one place (a stream segment, for example) is or isn't linked to another hundreds of miles away. It finds the closest facilities to a location—this may be the nearest hospital to the scene of an accident or all the shopping centers within a fifteen-minute drive of a housing development. It identifies service areas, such as the total territory that a delivery business can reach in half an hour or less. Network Analyst also lets you build sophisticated models of traffic flow that incorporate speed limits, prohibited turns, closed or one-way streets, underpasses and overpasses, and more.

ArcView Spatial Analyst solves problems involving geographic surfaces. Rainfall, soil acidity, elevation, sun exposure, land use, vegetation type, noise, population density, wildlife diversity, incidence of disease, and distance to the nearest stream are all examples of geographic surface phenomena. With ArcView Spatial Analyst you can overlay different surfaces to find areas that meet particular conditions. Which land has the best combination of slope, soil type, and rainfall for a vineyard? How closely do areas of ozone concentration correspond to areas of poor tree growth? Which urban neighborhoods combine high population density with limited access to city parks? ArcView Spatial Analyst creates geographic surfaces as well as analyzing them. From a set of sample elevation points, you can estimate the elevations of every location in the area. You can also create surfaces of feature density, variety, proximity, and many other measurements.

ArcView 3D Analyst displays data in three-dimensional perspective to show you what a landscape really looks like—from the contours of hills and canyons, to a city skyline, to a cave or lake bed. You can view data from any direction, angle, or distance, and change the sun position to see the effects of light and shadow. 3D Analyst also solves problems of three-dimensional geography. Does one building have an unobstructed view of another? If a contaminant is spilled at a certain point, which way will it flow? What's the volume of earth that will have to be moved for a construction project?

Extending ArcView GIS includes comprehensive descriptions of the dozens of other extensions that work with ArcView GIS, as well as a preview of ModelBuilder, the automated spatial modeling system that's part of ArcView GIS 3.2.

Every exercise in the book provides detailed instructions, but you'll be on firmer ground if you're already familiar with basic GIS concepts and ArcView GIS operations. If you're new to GIS, you'll benefit by reading *Getting to Know ArcView GIS* first.

Some of the exercises use modified or fictional GIS data. And while most of the problems you'll solve are less intricate than those you might face in the real world, the approaches and methods you'll employ are the same. Of course, it can't be said that *Extending ArcView GIS* will teach you everything there is to know about ArcView Network Analyst, ArcView Spatial Analyst, or ArcView 3D Analyst. The curvature of the earth limits the distance you can see on even the clearest day, and this book, too, is a kind of curved surface. By the time you finish it, however, you'll have seen a good deal. And you'll be ready to climb higher, and see farther, on your own.

1

Introducing ArcView Network Analyst

Network Analyst applications

Understanding travel costs

Exploring Network Analyst

Imagine a stream

flowing from a mountain to the sea. It doesn't take the most direct route on its journey; it follows the course of least resistance, which often means changing direction to avoid obstacles. It follows, in a word, the most efficient path.

Now imagine yourself traveling from your home to a place you've never been. You don't have gravity to choose your path for you. While you drive through the city, the most efficient path takes the least amount of time or distance and avoids obstacles like one-way or closed streets. Unfortunately, the map in your hand only shows you the multitude of possibilities. The route you choose may turn out not to be the most direct, because the map can't tell you where traffic is most congested or where construction has closed a lane. Network Analyst can help you find the best route through a network of streets.

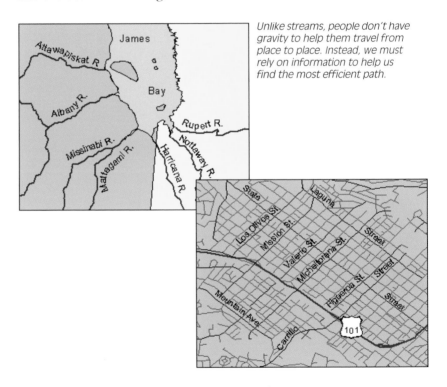

Unlike streams, people don't have gravity to help them travel from place to place. Instead, we must rely on information to help us find the most efficient path.

If you run a delivery business and have to make a few dozen deliveries each day, you want to know the most efficient route to follow. If you dispatch emergency vehicles, you want to get them to the accident quickly and then just as quickly to the nearest hospital. If you're opening a restaurant, you want to put it where the largest number of people can reach you within a ten-minute drive.

ArcView Network Analyst can solve all these types of problems. In the real world, networks are systems of roads, rivers, pipelines, and so on. In a GIS, networks are sets of interconnected line features that represent these systems. You don't need specialized data sets to solve problems in Network Analyst—all you need is a data set of interconnected lines. These line themes, when used for network analysis, are called network themes.

Network Analyst applications

With Network Analyst, you can find the best route, the closest facility, or a service area. A pizza restaurant that guarantees deliveries in thirty minutes would want to find the quickest route. Network Analyst can find the route that will enable the driver to reach all customers within thirty minutes.

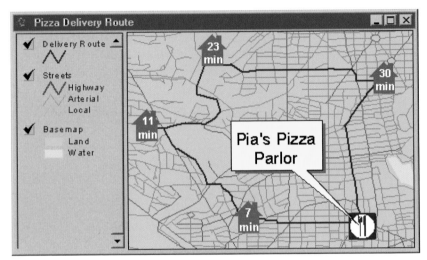

Network Analyst finds the most efficient delivery route.

In case the driver isn't familiar with the neighborhood, Network Analyst can create and print a list of directions.

At the scene of a traffic accident, help needs to get there and then get somewhere else, quick—tow trucks to remove damaged vehicles to the nearest garage, ambulances to get people to the nearest hospital. Network Analyst can get them to the scene and to the other places they need to go, via the quickest route.

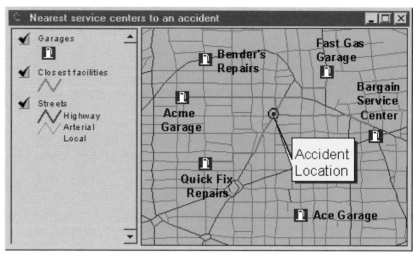

Network Analyst finds the closest garages and the best way to reach them from the accident scene.

A service area contains all the streets of a network that lie within a certain distance or driving time of a location. Both distance and time are measured along roads, so a fifteen-minute service area is defined as the area that can be reached within a fifteen-minute drive of a location. A business considering three different sites for a new branch could use Network Analyst to find the service areas for each site. The service areas can then be used to find out which site has the most customers within a certain driving time to the site and how close its competitors are.

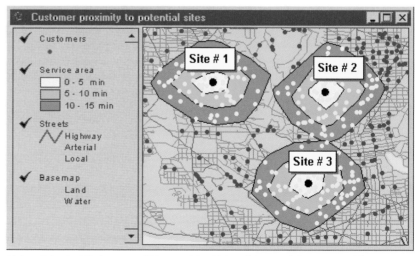

Network Analyst finds areas within a certain driving distance of three potential sites. With this information and a customer database, you can find how many customers are close to each location.

Understanding travel costs

A fundamental concept in network analysis is "travel cost," which is most commonly distance or time. When you find the shortest route between two points, you're using distance as a travel cost. When you find the fastest route between two points, you're using time as a travel cost. These are often not the same. Typically, you can drive 10 miles on a freeway in less time than you can drive 9 miles on surface streets. Travel cost is the unit of measure you use to define the best route between or among points on a network.

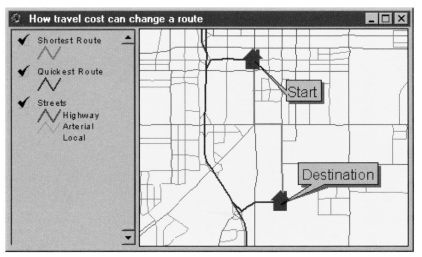

Here, the red line represents the shortest path (distance) between the two houses, and the blue line the quickest (time). The route you choose depends on whether time or distance is more important.

Other impediments, such as one-way streets, closed streets, and prohibited turns, can affect travel times. The more information you have about a network and can store in your network theme's attribute table, the more accurate your analysis becomes.

Exploring Network Analyst

Now that you have some familiarity with networks, travel costs, and routes, you're ready to start working with Network Analyst. This exercise shows you how to set up and solve a simple network problem.

These exercises assume that you're using Network Analyst 1.0b (incremental patch version). If you're using Network Analyst 1.0b (unpatched version), you can download the patch at no extra cost from the following ESRI Web site:

www.esri.com/software/arcview/extensions/netext.html

When you download the patch, an executable file is copied to your computer's hard disk. Double-click on the executable to install the patch.

If you're using Network Analyst 1.0a, you can download Network Analyst 1.0b at no cost from the ESRI Web page. You'll then need to install the incremental patch.

◆ *E x e r c i s e   1 a*

1   If necessary, start ArcView GIS. In the Welcome to ArcView GIS dialog, choose "Open an existing project" and click OK. (If ArcView GIS is running and you've already dismissed the Welcome dialog, open the project from the File menu.)

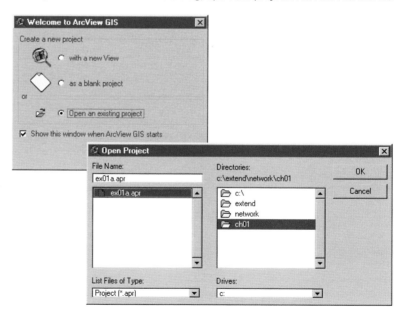

2   In the Open Project dialog, navigate to the \extend\network\ch01 directory
and open the project "ex01a.apr."

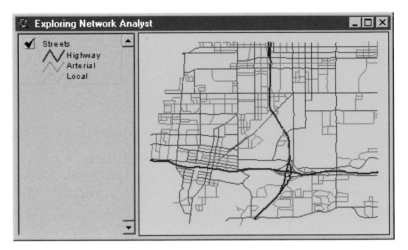

When the project opens, you see a view of San Bernardino, California, that contains a line theme called *Streets*. This is the network theme.

Now you'll load the ArcView Network Analyst extension and see
how the ArcView GIS interface changes.

3   From the File menu, choose Extensions. In the Extensions dialog, scroll
down until you see Network Analyst. Click on its check box to turn it on,
then click OK.

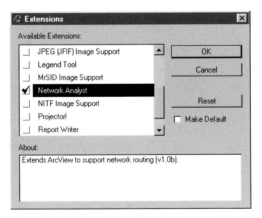

In the remaining exercises in this section, the Network Analyst extension will already be loaded when you open a project. If the extension is loaded when a project is saved, ArcView GIS loads it automatically whenever the project is opened.

When the extension is loaded, the ArcView GIS interface adds the Network menu and three new controls. (The controls are disabled because you haven't defined a network problem yet.)

You'll learn about the Network menu and each control as you encounter them in the exercises.

4 From the View menu, choose Properties to display the View Properties dialog.

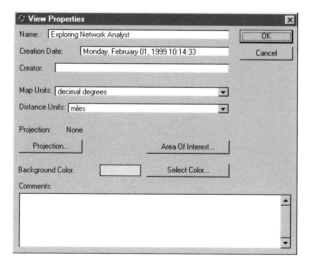

The map units are set to decimal degrees, meaning that the source data is unprojected. The distance units are set to miles. Network Analyst makes its calculations with the source data units (decimal degrees) and reports the results in distance units (miles).

Now you'll add a theme that contains the locations the route will visit.

5 Close the View Properties dialog, then click the Add Theme button. If necessary, select the drive where you installed the data for this book, then navigate to the \extend\network\ch01 directory. Double-click on "twopoints.shp" to add it to the view. In the view's Table of Contents, click on the check box next to the *Twopoints.shp* theme to turn it on.

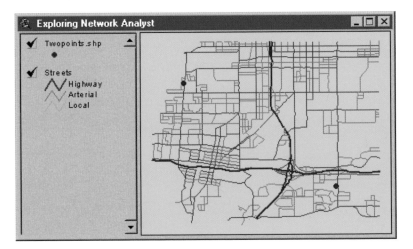

The point theme that contains the locations that a route will visit can be either an ArcView GIS shapefile, an ArcInfo™ coverage, or an ordinary text file. The two points in this shapefile will mark the beginning and ending of the route. By default, the first point listed in the theme table is the origin, the beginning location of the route.

6 Make the *Twopoints.shp* theme active and click the Open Theme Table button.

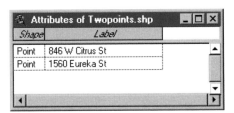

The table has two fields, Shape and Label. Label can contain any sort of description—store names, customer names, or addresses. The Label field isn't required, but, as you'll see later, the labels help identify the stops in the Problem Definition dialog.

7   Close the table. Select the Identify tool, then click on the upper left point.

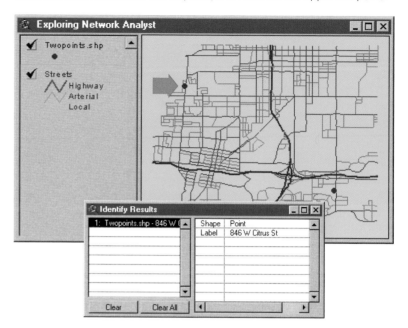

In the Identify Results window, the Label field tells you that the address of this point is 846 W. Citrus St., which you know will be the origin.

8   Identify the other point, the destination. When you've finished, close the Identify Results window.

Now you're ready to define the network problem.

9   Make the *Streets* theme active again.

The active line theme will be the theme Network Analyst uses to solve a problem. If no line theme is active, network analysis can't be performed.

10 From the Network menu, choose Find Best Route. This displays the Problem Definition dialog called Route1 and simultaneously adds a result theme, also called *Route1,* to the view.

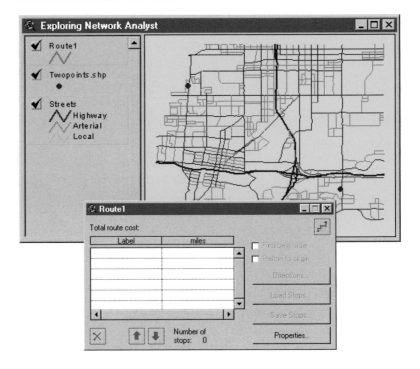

The *Route1* theme is active and turned on by default, but contains no features until Network Analyst finds the route.

Network problems are defined in the Problem Definition dialog. The name of the result theme appears in the title bar of the Problem Definition dialog. The Problem Definition dialog is used to provide Network Analyst with the details of a network problem, such as what data to use, which stops to visit, and what travel cost to use. After Network Analyst solves the network problem, the result theme is updated with the solution.

Understanding result themes. When you open the Problem Definition dialog, Network Analyst creates a new theme in the view, called *Route1* (or *Route<n>,* where <n> is the number of result themes in the project). Result themes are created in your temporary directory, typically c:\temp, and are deleted if you close the project without saving changes. Although result themes consist of the same three files as other ArcView GIS shapefiles (with the extensions .dbf, .shp, and .shx), they can't be edited. To edit a result theme, you must first convert it to a shapefile. In the online help, use the Find tab to locate the topic *Network Result Theme Contents.*

Even though you've added the point theme *Twopoints.shp* to the view, you still need to tell Network Analyst that you want to use these points as stops along the route.

11   In the Problem Definition dialog, click the Load Stops button to open the Load Stops dialog.

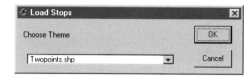

12   *Twopoints.shp* is the only point theme in the view and thus the only choice in the drop-down list. Click OK. If the Problem Definition dialog is blocking the view, move it out of the way.

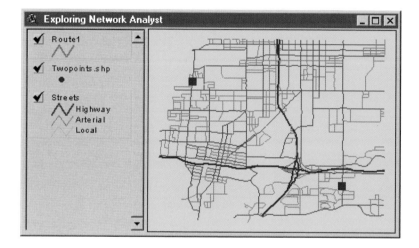

When the features in *Twopoint.shp* are loaded as stops in the Problem Definition dialog, their symbols in the view are covered by green squares, called graphic flags.

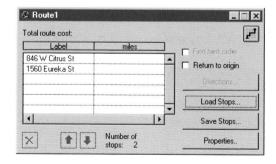

In the upper left corner of the dialog is a field where the total cost of the route will appear (in this case, that means its total distance). The number of stops is reported at the bottom of the dialog. The Label field displays the label information from the *Twopoints.shp* theme table. The stops are listed in the order they'll be visited— by default, this corresponds to the order of records in the network theme's attribute table. The incremental cost of visiting each stop on the route will be listed in the miles field. In this case, the travel cost is reported in miles because the view's distance units are set to miles. You'll learn how to use different travel costs in chapter 3, "Defining travel costs."

13   In the Label field of the Problem Definition dialog, click on "846 W Citrus St" to see its location in the street network.

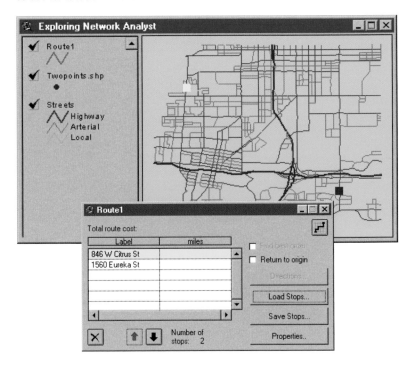

Highlighting the label in the dialog highlights the corresponding graphic flag in the view. You can use this technique to identify stops in the view without having to open the theme table. Here you can see that the upper left square is 846 W. Citrus St.

14   In the Problem Definition dialog, clear the selected stop by holding down the Shift key and clicking on the address.

15   In the Problem Definition dialog, click the Solve button.

As Network Analyst processes the problem, it reports its progress in the status bar at the bottom of the ArcView GIS window. When the problem has been solved, both *Route1* and the Problem Definition dialog are updated with the solution. (The theme is assigned a random color that you can change in the Legend Editor, if you like.)

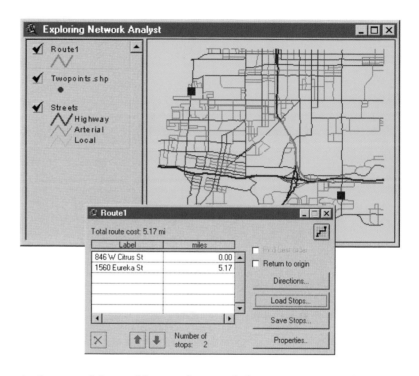

At the top of the Problem Definition dialog, you now see that the route's cost (its total length) is 5.17 miles. The miles field displays the cost of reaching each stop; in this case, that's equal to the total route cost.

When you solve a network problem, you can use either the Solve button in the Problem Definition dialog, or the Solve button on the ArcView GIS button bar.

Network Analyst writes additional information to the result theme's attribute table. Now you'll open it to find out what information it contains.

16   In the view's Table of Contents, click on *Route1* to make it the only active theme. Click the Open Theme Table button. Resize the window so you can see all six fields.

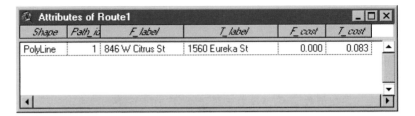

Shape	Path_id	F_label	T_label	F_cost	T_cost
PolyLine	1	846 W Citrus St	1560 Eureka St	0.000	0.083

The Shape field shows that the result theme is a PolyLine theme. Path_id is an identifier. F_label (the "from" label) contains the address of the first stop in the Problem Definition dialog and T_label (the "to" label) contains the address of the last stop. F_cost contains the cost of reaching the F_label point (0.000); T_cost contains the cost of reaching the T_label point (0.083).

You may wonder why the travel cost value reported in the table is 0.083, when the cost in the Problem Definition dialog was 5.17. These values reflect different units. The result theme table stores travel costs in the source units of the data, in this case, decimal degrees, while the Problem Definition dialog reports them in the distance units of the view.

17   From the File menu, choose Close All. Again from the File menu, choose Close Project. Click No when you're prompted to save your changes.

If you're going on to the next chapter, leave ArcView GIS running. Otherwise, choose Exit from the File menu.

2

Finding the best route

Visiting several locations

Ordering stops on a route

Adding and deleting stops

I<small>N</small> CHAPTER 1,

you solved a network problem with two stops. In this chapter, you'll work with network problems that have several stops. When you have several stops, Network Analyst can determine the shortest or quickest order in which to visit them. You can make a route return to the origin, so that it's a round trip. You can add or remove stops from a route, or move a stop to a different location on the network.

Visiting several locations

Most routes include a number of stops. In this exercise, you'll create the shortest route that visits nine stops.

◆ *E x e r c i s e   2 a*

1   If necessary, start ArcView GIS. Navigate to the \extend\network\ch02 directory and open the project "ex02a.apr." When the project opens, you see a
view that contains two themes.

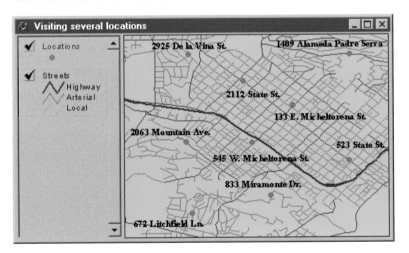

Locations is a point theme of addresses and *Streets* is a network theme of the streets of Santa Barbara, California. You'll create a route that visits all the points in the *Locations* theme.

2 From the Network menu, choose Find Best Route to open the Problem Definition dialog and create a new result theme.

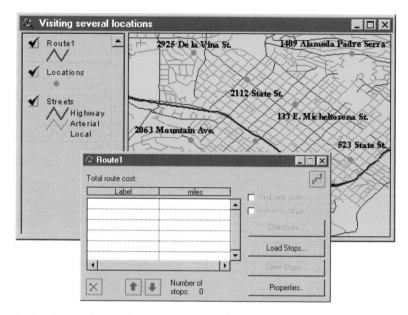

3 In the view, make *Route1* the only active theme. From the Theme menu, choose Properties to open the Theme Properties dialog.

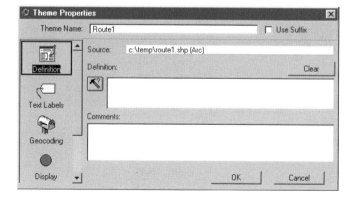

The default theme name, *Route1*, matches the name of the source data, route1.shp. You'll change the theme name to something more descriptive.

4   In the Theme Properties dialog, change the name to **Multi-stop route** and click OK.

The result theme is now called *Multi-stop route* in the view and in the title bar of the Problem Definition dialog.

5   In the Problem Definition dialog, click the Load Stops button. In the Load Stops dialog, the *Locations* theme is selected by default. (It's the only point theme in the view.) Click OK to load the theme. Resize the dialog so that you can see all nine stops.

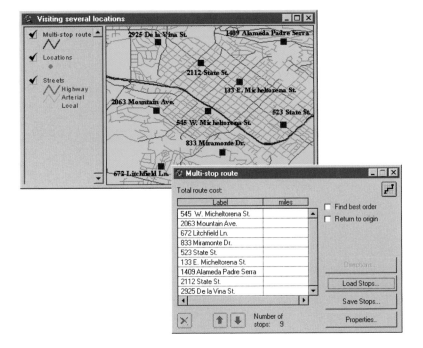

6   Click the Solve button.

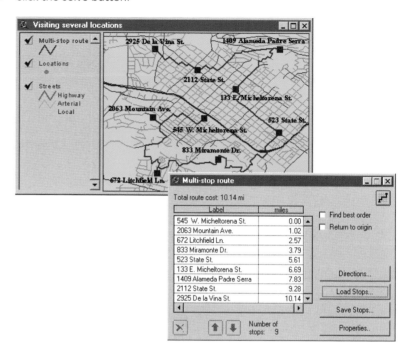

Network Analyst calculates the shortest route. The Problem Definition dialog lists the cumulative cost of reaching each stop in the
miles field and shows the total cost of the route at the top.

Network Analyst uses Dijkstra's algorithm to find the least-cost path
between stops. For more information, see appendix A, "Network Analyst
pathfinding algorithm."

By comparing the labels in the view to the order of stops in the
Problem Definition dialog, you can see where the route begins and
where it goes. You can make the route even easier to follow by
using a line symbol with an arrow.

7   Double-click on the *Multi-stop route* theme to open the Legend Editor. In the Legend Editor, double-click on the line symbol to display the Pen Palette. In the Pen Palette, scroll down and click on one of the arrow symbols to select it.

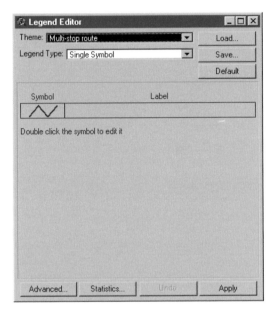
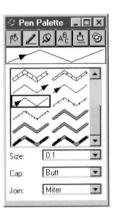

8   In the Legend Editor, click Apply. Close the Symbol Palette and the Legend Editor.

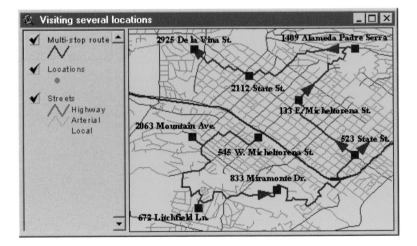

The arrows show the direction of travel.

9   With the *Multi-stop route* theme active, click the Open Theme Table button.
     Resize the table so you can see all the fields and position it so that both the
     table and the view are visible. (You may need to make the application win-
     dow larger.) Make the Select tool active and click on the first record in
     the table.

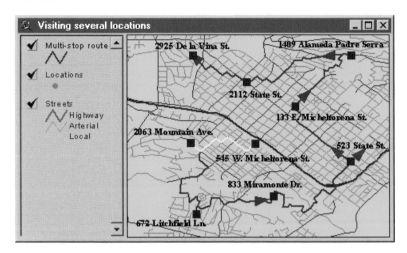

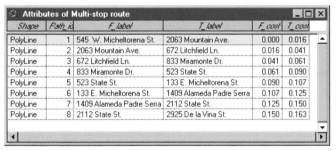

This table has the same six fields as the one in the previous exercise,
but instead of one record there are eight (one for each segment in
the route). Segment 1 starts at 545 W. Micheltorena St. (the F_label
value) and goes to 2063 Mountain Ave. (the T_label value). The cost
of the route at the start of this segment is 0.000 (the F_cost). The cost
of traversing the segment is 0.016 (the T_cost). As before, the source
data units are in decimal degrees (that is, they're unprojected) and
the results are reported in miles.

10   Select the next record.

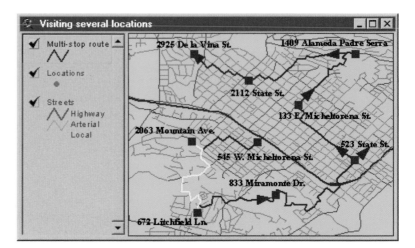

Shape	Path_id	F_label	T_label	F_cost	T_cost
PolyLine	1	545 W. Micheltorena St.	2063 Mountain Ave.	0.000	0.016
PolyLine	2	2063 Mountain Ave.	672 Litchfield Ln.	0.016	0.041
PolyLine	3	672 Litchfield Ln.	833 Miramonte Dr.	0.041	0.061
PolyLine	4	833 Miramonte Dr.	523 State St.	0.061	0.090
PolyLine	5	523 State St.	133 E. Micheltorena St.	0.090	0.107
PolyLine	6	133 E. Micheltorena St.	1409 Alameda Padre Serra	0.107	0.125
PolyLine	7	1409 Alameda Padre Serra	2112 State St.	0.125	0.150
PolyLine	8	2112 State St.	2925 De la Vina St.	0.150	0.163

2063 Mountain Ave. is now the F_label and 672 Litchfield Ln. is the T_label. The T_cost for segment 1 becomes the F_cost for segment 2. The cumulative cost from the origin on Micheltorena St. to 672 Litchfield Ln. is listed in the T_cost for segment 2. This process continues until the destination is reached.

11   From the File menu, choose Close All. Again from the File menu, choose Close Project. Click No when you're prompted to save your changes.

If you want to go on to the next exercise, leave ArcView GIS running. Otherwise, choose Exit from the File menu.

Ordering stops on a route

In this exercise, you'll change the order in which stops are visited. When Network Analyst loads stops from a point theme, they appear in the Problem Definition dialog in their order in the point theme's attribute table. This order may not be the one that you want.

You'll also make a round-trip by returning a route to its origin. Finally, you'll let Network Analyst determine the most efficient order in which to visit the stops.

◆ *E x e r c i s e   2 b*

1   If necessary, start ArcView GIS. Navigate to the \extend\network\ch02 directory and open the project "ex02b.apr." When the project opens, you see a view of Redlands, California, containing a point theme of historic sites and a network theme of city streets.

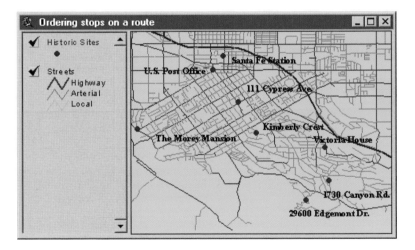

You'll use these points to create a driving tour.

2   From the Network menu, choose Find Best Route to open the Problem Definition dialog and create a new result theme named *Route1*. When the *Route1* result theme is added to the view, open the Theme Properties dialog and change its name to **Tour Route**. Click OK.

3   In the Problem Definition dialog, click the Load Stops button and choose the *Historic Sites* theme. Click OK to load the stops. Resize the dialog so you can see all eight stops.

4   Click the Solve button.

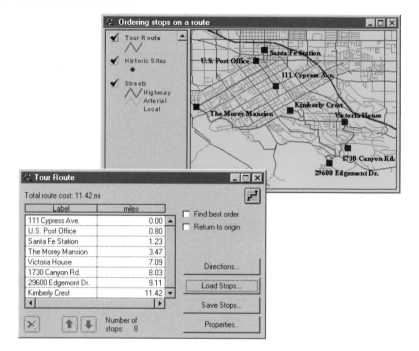

Network Analyst finds the shortest route that visits the stops in their default order. The total cost of the route is 11.42 miles.

The routes you've looked at so far have not returned to their point of origin. You'll change the route to make it a round-trip.

5   In the Problem Definition dialog, click the "Return to origin" check box to turn it on.

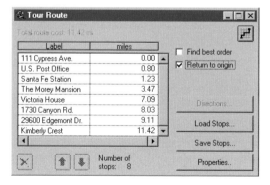

The cost values for the route turn gray, indicating that the dialog settings have been changed since the route was created.

6   Click the Solve button.

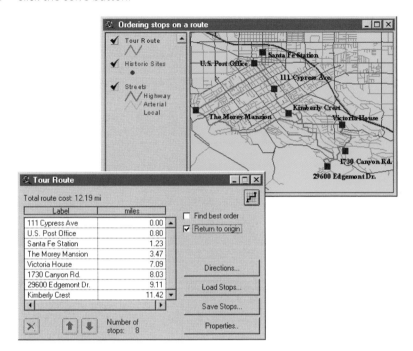

In the view, the route is now a round-trip. A route segment connects Kimberly Crest (previously the destination) with 111 Cypress Ave. (which is now both the origin and the destination). In the Problem Definition dialog, the cost of reaching the Kimberly Crest stop hasn't changed—it's still 11.42 miles—but the total route cost is now 12.19 miles. The difference between these values is the distance from Kimberly Crest back to 111 Cypress Ave.

Both the Cypress Avenue and Kimberly Crest stops are in a residential area of Redlands. You'll change the origin so that the route starts and ends downtown, at the Santa Fe Station.

7   In the Label field of the Problem Definition dialog, click on "Santa Fe Station" to highlight it. Click the Up Arrow button twice to move the label to the top of the list.

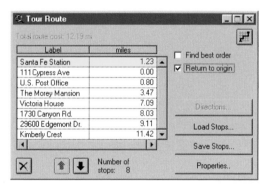

Once again, the cost values turn gray, signifying that the dialog settings have been changed since the problem was solved.

8   Deselect the Santa Fe Station stop by holding down the Shift key and clicking on it. Click the Solve button.

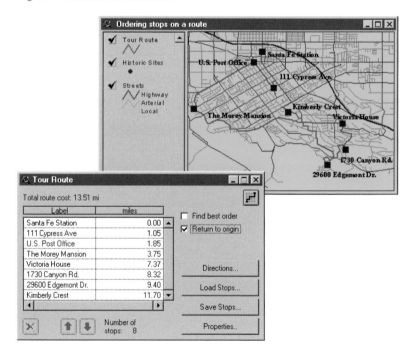

Network Analyst calculates the route, visiting stops in the new order.

The route seems unnecessarily complicated. It starts at the Santa Fe Station, goes to 111 Cypress Ave., then backtracks to the post office. It crosses itself near the Kimberly Crest stop and, as it returns to its origin, passes by a stop it has already visited (111 Cypress Ave.). Unless the stops must be visited in a set order, you can have Network Analyst find the best order.

9 In the Problem Definition dialog, click the "Find best order" check box to turn it on, then click the Solve button.

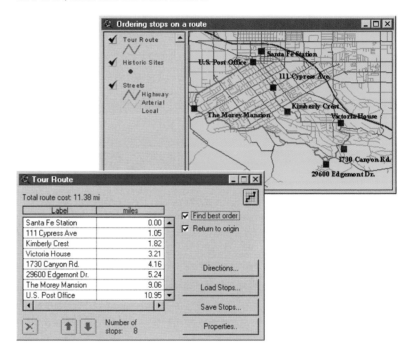

Network Analyst rearranges the stops to create the shortest possible route. The total travel cost has decreased from 13.51 miles to 11.38 miles, and the route forms a simple loop.

The "Find best order" option rearranges all stops, except the origin and destination, into the order that results in the lowest total route cost. The origin and destination stops aren't changed. (If the "Return to origin" option is used, the origin is also the destination and is the only stop that can't be reordered.)

---

10 From the File menu, choose Close All. Again from the File menu, choose Close Project. Click No when you're prompted to save your changes.

If you want to go on to the next exercise, leave ArcView GIS running. Otherwise, choose Exit from the File menu.

Adding and deleting stops

If you don't have stops stored in a file, you can add them interactively by specifying an address or simply by clicking on a location in a view. Stops can also be removed from a route, either by deleting them or by excluding them without deleting them.

◆ *E x e r c i s e   2 c*

1   If necessary, start ArcView GIS. Navigate to the \extend\network\ch02 directory and open the project "ex02c.apr." When the project opens, you see a view that contains the *Historic Sites* theme and the *Streets* theme from the previous exercise.

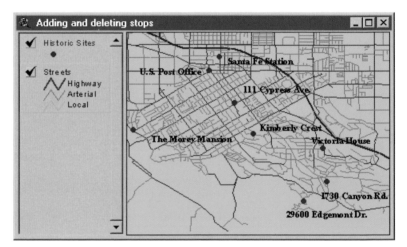

2   Make sure the *Streets* theme is active. From the Network menu, choose Find Best Route. When the result theme is added to the view, open the Theme Properties dialog and change its name to **Tour Route**. Click OK.

3   In the Problem Definition dialog, click the Load Stops button and choose the *Historic Sites* theme. Click OK to load the stops. Click the "Find best order" and "Return to origin" check boxes so that they're turned on. Click the Solve button.

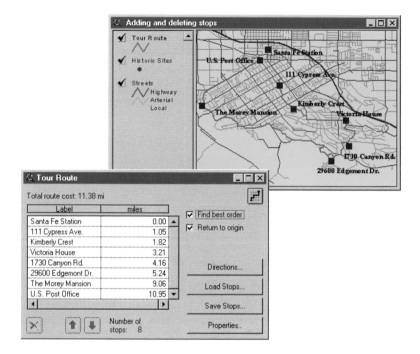

Restoration has just been finished on a historic home at 699 Fern St. You want to add this location as a stop on the route, but the *Historic Sites* theme doesn't have a point feature for it. You'll add this stop using its address.

4 Make sure the *Tour Route* theme is active. Click the Add Location by Address button on the ArcView GIS button bar to display the Locate Address dialog. In the input box, type **699 Fern St.** Click OK.

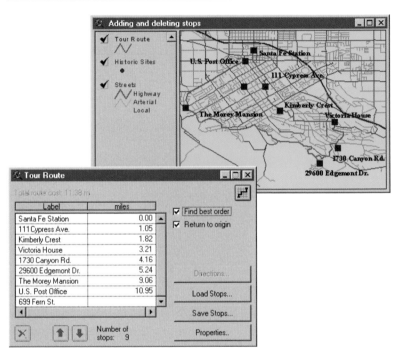

In the view, Network Analyst puts a graphic flag at the new address. The address is also listed at the bottom of the Problem Definition dialog. (You may need to resize the dialog to see it.) The cost values turn gray and the number of stops changes to 9.

The Add Location by Address button is enabled only when the result theme is active in the view and the network theme is geocoded. In the online help, use the Find tab to locate the topics *What is geocoding?* and *Overview of address geocoding.*

Although the address is now a stop on the route, it's not a point feature in the *Historic Sites* theme. (If you need to use the stop again, you can create a new point shapefile of all stops in the Problem Definition dialog by clicking the Save Stops button.)

5   In the Problem Definition dialog, click the Solve button.

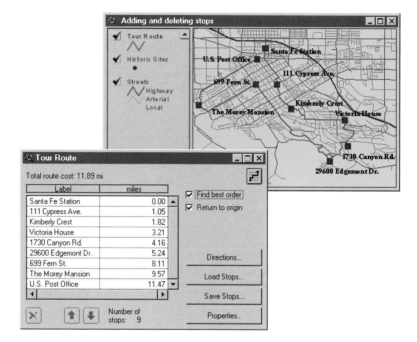

The route is updated to include the new stop. If you want to label it in the view, use the Text tool to add the text "699 Fern St." (The font is 10-point Times New Roman bold.)

Because the "Find best order" option is turned on, Network Analyst moves the Fern address from the bottom of the list to its best position.

Adding a location by address works as long as you have an address to use. Many locations, however, either don't have addresses (landmarks, for instance) or are easier to recognize by their position on a map than by an address. When you don't have an address, you can add a stop by clicking directly on the view.

A fresh-squeezed orange juice stand has opened for business on San Timoteo Canyon Road. Redlands is famous for its oranges and you'd like to include the stand on the tour. Being a stand, however, it doesn't have an address. You'll add it as a stop by clicking on the network.

6   With the *Tour Route* theme active, select the Add Location tool on the ArcView GIS toolbar. Move the mouse pointer over the view and click on the location shown by the arrow in the following graphic. (Your location doesn't have to match exactly, but you do have to click directly on the street feature.)

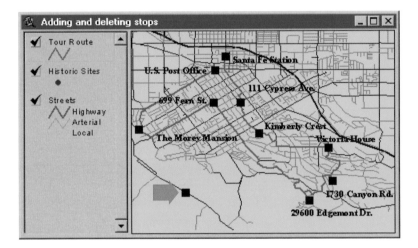

Network Analyst places a graphic flag at the location you picked, and the Problem Definition dialog lists the stop as "Graphic pick 1" (not a very descriptive label). In the Problem Definition dialog, the number of stops changes to 10.

7   Resize the Problem Definition dialog so you can see all ten stops. In the Label field, double-click on "Graphic pick 1" and type **Juice Stand**, then press Enter.

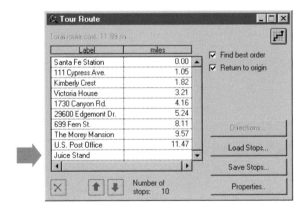

Label the stop in the view if you want to.

8   Click the Solve button.

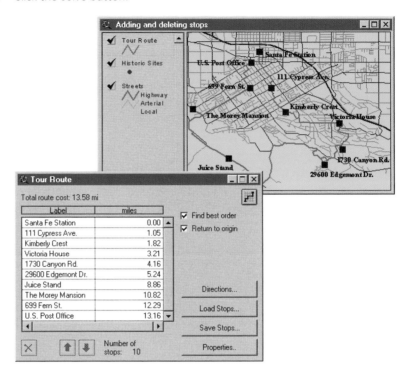

Your cost values may differ slightly from those shown here, depending on where you put the juice stand. (Even the order of your stops may be different, though the total route cost should be the same.) In the Problem Definition dialog, Network Analyst puts the stand at its best position in the list of stops.

You've just seen two ways to add stops to a route; now you'll see two ways to remove them. The owner of one of the historic homes wants to be taken off the tour route.

9   In the Problem Definition dialog, click on "29600 Edgemont Dr." to select it, then click the Delete button to remove it from the list of stops. The number of stops changes from 10 to 9. Click the Solve button to find the new route.

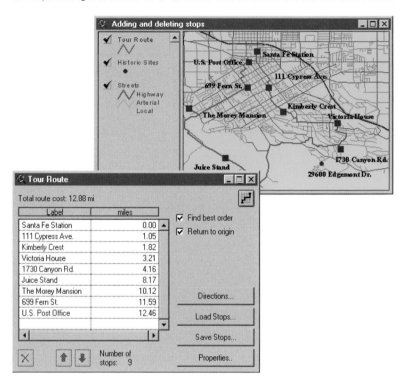

Although the graphic flag is deleted from the view, and the address "29600 Edgemont Dr." no longer appears in the Problem Definition dialog, the point feature from the *Historic Sites* theme remains to mark the stop's location.

Deleting stops. When you delete a stop that has been added interactively, nothing remains to indicate the original location of the stop. When you delete a stop that was loaded from a point feature in a theme, you delete the graphic flag in the view and the label in the dialog, but not the point feature itself. To restore a deleted stop, you can either click on its location in the view, specify its address, or load it from a point theme. If you load it from a point theme, select the point feature that you want in the view before loading stops. Only the selected feature will be loaded.

Victoria House is being renovated. During the renovations, it's closed to visitors, so you'll temporarily remove it from the route.

10 Select the Pointer tool and click on the Victoria House graphic flag. Drag it to a place where there aren't any streets, then deselect it.

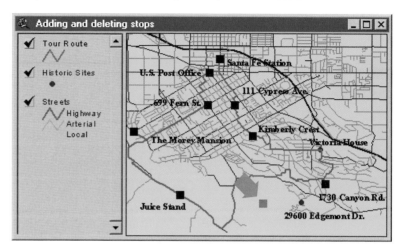

The graphic flag turns red, indicating that the stop is no longer on the network and won't be included in the route calculations. The point feature from the *Historic Sites* theme is unaffected.

If a stop isn't placed within a certain distance of the nearest line feature (1/100th of the horizontal or vertical extent of the network theme, whichever is greater), it will be marked with a red graphic flag and will be ignored when you solve the problem.

The Problem Definition dialog now reports Victoria House as "Not on network." The cost values turn gray, but the number of stops is still 9.

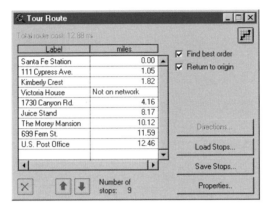

 11   In the Problem Definition dialog, click the Solve button.

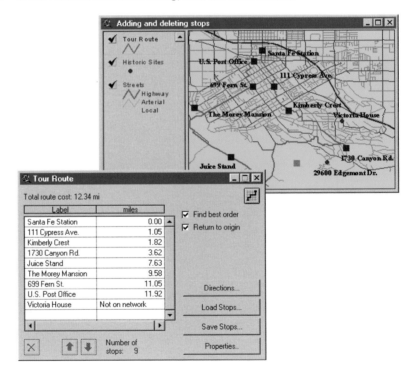

Network Analyst recalculates the route, without Victoria House. The label for the stop moves to the bottom of the Problem Definition dialog.

Once the renovations are complete, you'll include Victoria House on the tour again.

12 With the Pointer tool selected, click on the red graphic flag. Drag it to its original location, then deselect it.

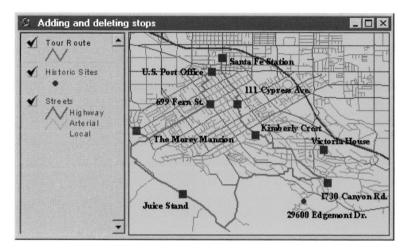

The graphic flag turns green to show that the stop is once again on the network. In the Problem Definition dialog, Victoria House is now listed as "Not reached," rather than "Not on network."

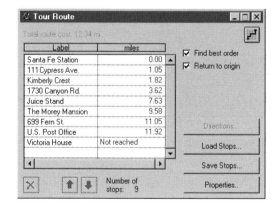

13 Click the Solve button.

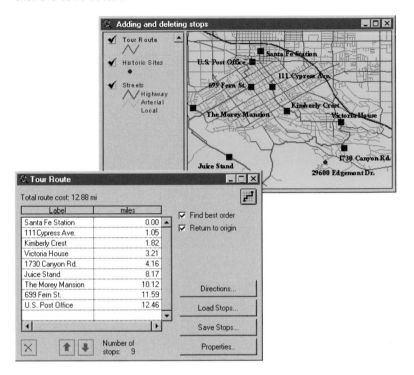

Network Analyst again includes Victoria House on the tour. Your results may differ from those shown here, depending on where you placed the graphic flag. To make sure the graphic flag is placed at the original location, you can zoom in on Victoria House.

14 From the File menu, choose Close All. Again from the File menu, choose Close Project. Click No when you're prompted to save your changes.

If you're going on to the next chapter, leave ArcView GIS running. Otherwise, choose Exit from the File menu.

3

Defining
travel costs

Using distance as a travel cost

Using time as a travel cost

BY DEFAULT,

Network Analyst calculates routes in the source data units of the network theme, using the length of each line segment as the travel cost. This works well when the length of each line segment is stored in a constant unit of measure, such as meters or feet. However, with unprojected data, line length is stored in decimal degrees and the default is less reliable. That's because decimal degrees are not constant, as you'll see shortly.

With unprojected data, Network Analyst calculates a route using decimal degrees, then converts the results to miles and reports them in the Problem Definition dialog. If you convert your data to a constant unit of measure (such as feet or meters) before you calculate the route, you may get different results.

The following graphics show two identical routes that begin in Winnipeg, Canada, stop in Vancouver and Yellowknife, and end in Deadhorse, Alaska. In the first case, the route is solved in decimal degrees and then converted to miles (the Network Analyst default). In the second case, although the source data remains unprojected, the decimal degrees values were converted to a constant unit of measure before the route was solved.

The results aren't dramatically different, but they're different nonetheless.

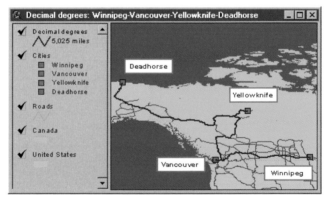

The route that's solved using decimal degrees is 21 miles longer than the same route solved in constant distance units.

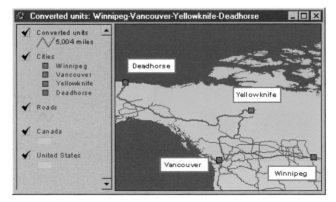

Although the effects of converting decimal degree values to a constant unit of measure aren't always noticeable, conversion is recommended practice and you'll learn how to do it in this chapter. But first, it may be interesting for you to know exactly why decimal degrees are not a constant unit of measure.

A degree is simply 1/360th of a circle (0.002777… when converted to a decimal). If you have circles of different sizes, you'll have degrees of different lengths. In the spherical coordinate system, on which unprojected data is based, locations on the earth are measured in degrees of latitude and longitude. Lines of longitude run north–south around the globe, meeting at the poles. The circles they make are all the same size (approximately—the earth isn't perfectly smooth). Lines of latitude, however, which run east–west, make parallel circles that are large at the equator and become smaller as they get closer to the poles.

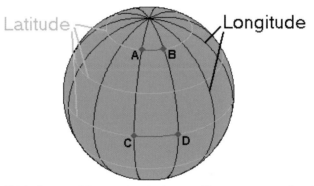

Thirty degrees at the equator (CD) is 3,339 kilometers (2,075 miles), but only 1,673 kilometers (1,040 miles) at the 60th parallel (AB).

When you solve a network problem and the line length is stored in decimal degrees, Network Analyst will find the shortest route—in decimal degrees. For example, a route that's 30 degrees "long" will be chosen over a route of 31 degrees. The problem is that the route of 30 degrees may not actually be shorter. It all depends on where you are and how far you go and in which direction.

So, to get accurate results with unprojected data, you need to use a travel cost other than decimal degrees. You can do this by converting the decimal degree values to a constant unit of measure and storing the results in a field of your network theme table. You can then tell Network Analyst to use the values in this field to solve network problems.

Using distance as a travel cost

In this exercise, you'll see a striking example of how decimal degrees can lead you astray in solving network problems. The routes you'll create, along lines of latitude and longitude, aren't ones you'd likely follow in the real world, but this is a travel opportunity for your mind.

◆ *Exercise 3a*

1 If necessary, start ArcView GIS. Navigate to the \extend\network\ch03 directory and open the project "ex03a.apr." When the project opens, you see a view of Alaska. The data is unprojected.

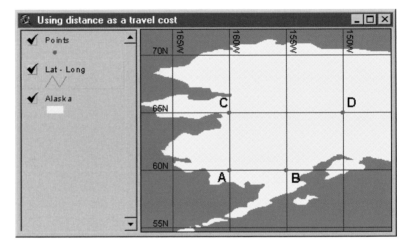

The *Points* theme shows the locations you'll use to create a route along the lines of latitude and longitude in the *Lat - Long* theme. The theme has interconnecting line features, so you can use it in a network problem.

By default, when your data is unprojected, Network Analyst solves problems using decimal degrees but reports the results in miles. You're going to see what it looks like when the results are also reported in decimal degrees.

2   From the View menu, choose Properties. In the *Distance Units* drop-down list, choose "unknown." Click OK.

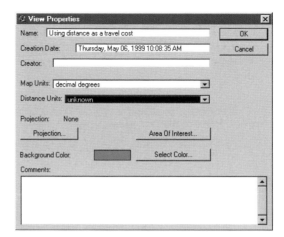

There's no decimal degrees option in the *Distance Units* drop-down list, but if you set the distance units to "unknown," Network Analyst will use the Map Units setting as the reporting units.

Now you'll find the best route among the stops, starting at point A.

3   From the Network menu, choose Find Best Route to create a result theme and open the Problem Definition dialog. When the *Route1* result theme is added to the view, open the Theme Properties dialog and change its name to **Test Route**.

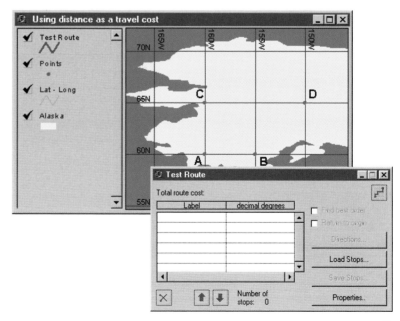

4   In the Problem Definition dialog, click the Load Stops button and choose the *Points* theme. Click OK to load the stops.

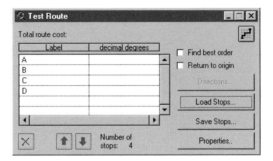

5   Click the Solve button.

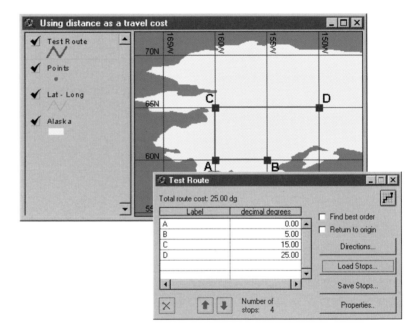

The route that Network Analyst calculates, from A to B to C (passing by A again) to D is 25 decimal degrees. This makes sense because the lines in the *Lat - Long* theme are 5 degrees apart, and the route traverses five line segments.

If your result doesn't match the one in the graphic, you're probably not running the patched version (1.0b) of Network Analyst. See chapter 1 for instructions on downloading this patch from the ESRI Web site.

Now you'll reverse the position of points B and C and solve the route again. The new route will go from A to C to B to D, and should also be 25 degrees, because it will again traverse five line segments.

6   In the Label field of the Problem Definition dialog, click on "C" to select it. Click the Up Arrow button once to move "C" so that it comes after "A" and before "B." Press the Shift key and click on "C" so that it's no longer selected.

7   Click the Solve button again.

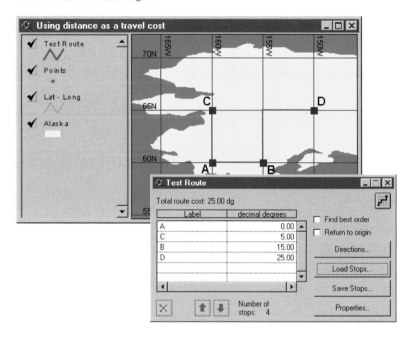

This time, Network Analyst finds a different route, from A to C to B (passing by A again) to D. The two routes are the same from Network Analyst's point of view—they're both 25 decimal degrees "long." But, as you know, decimal degrees are not a constant unit of length. So, are these two routes really the same distance?

8   From the View menu, choose Properties. In the *Distance Units* drop-down list, choose "miles."

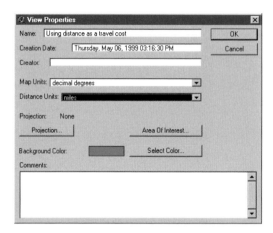

9   Click OK to apply the new distance units.

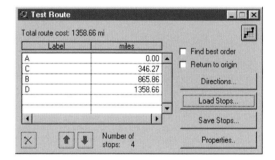

The route from A to C to B to D is 1,358.66 miles long. This length is correct: after solving the route in decimal degrees, Network Analyst made an accurate conversion from line length to miles, taking into account the number of miles per decimal degree for each different segment of latitude and longitude.

10 In the Label field of the Problem Definition dialog, click on "C" to select it. Click the Down Arrow button once to move it below "B" and above "D." (This is the same order of stops from the original route.) Press the Shift key and click "C" so that it's no longer selected. Click the Solve button again.

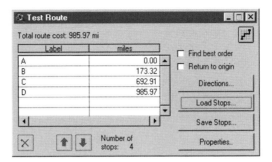

And now you see why decimal degrees are problematic. The route from A to B to C to D is only 985.97 miles long—and this distance is accurate, too. Route ABCD is 372.69 miles shorter than ACBD, because degrees of east–west distance are shorter the farther you get from the equator.

The solution to this difficulty is to convert decimal degrees to a constant unit of measure before you solve a network problem and to tell Network Analyst to use the converted units instead of decimal degrees. Fortunately, there's an Avenue script that does this for you. The script is available in the online help under the topic *Long distance routing on decimal degree data*. In this exercise, you'll use a slightly modified version of this script, which has already been loaded in the project. The script creates a field called "Meters" in the network theme table and populates it with the length in meters of each unprojected line segment.

Using projected data. An alternative, and equally valid, solution is to use projected data. Map projections are mathematical methods for representing the earth on a flat surface. In so doing, they replace spherical coordinates with map units that are stored in a constant unit of measure, such as meters. There's no need to project your data to solve network problems: the solution presented in this exercise is just as effective. But if you're working with data that's already in a map projection, using the default settings will provide you with reliable results. In the online help, use the Find tab to locate the topic *Setting the map projection.*

11 In the Project window, click the Scripts icon. Double-click on "distance.ave" to open this script.

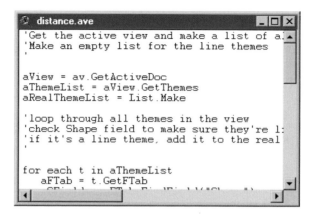

The script works on the last active document, so you need to make the view active before you can run it.

12 From the Window menu, choose "Using distance as a travel cost" to make the view active. Again from the Window menu, choose "distance.ave" to make the Script document active again.

13 Click the Run button to run the script. The script displays a list of all line themes in the view and asks you to choose the network theme. Select "Lat - Long," then click the OK button.

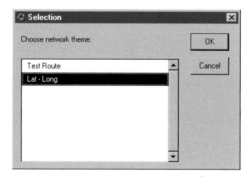

The script has finished running when the Script document becomes active again.

14 Close the Script document. Make the *Lat - Long* theme active and click the Open Theme Table button. Scroll all the way to the right so you can see the last field in the table.

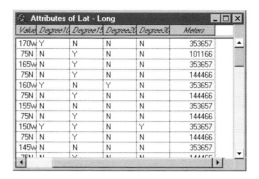

The unprojected line lengths, stored as decimal degrees in the theme's Shape field, have been converted to their equivalents in meters.

Now you'll create a new route based on the values in the Meters field.

15 Close the table. In the Problem Definition dialog, click the Properties button.

The Properties dialog lets you change the travel cost used by Network Analyst. By default, as you know, the travel cost is the length of the network theme's lines as measured in source data units. This value is displayed in the cost field of the Properties dialog as <Line Length>. The cost units field shows that the source data for this theme is in decimal degrees. The working units (the units that are used to report results) are displayed as miles because miles are the current setting in the View properties distance units.

16   In the *Cost field* drop-down list, choose "Meters."

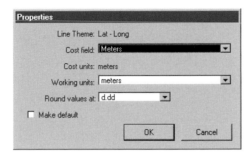

Now Network Analyst knows to solve any new problems using the length values in the Meters field you just created. The cost units and the working units both change automatically to meters.

17   In the *Working units* drop-down list, choose "miles."

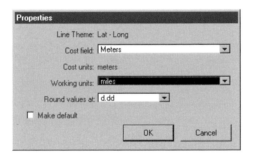

18   Click OK to close the Properties dialog. In the Problem Definition dialog, click the "Find best order" check box to turn it on. Click the Solve button.

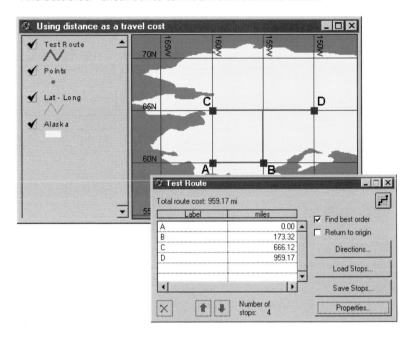

Network Analyst finds (correctly) that the shortest route is from A to B to C to D, and reports the length of this route as 959.17 miles. This route also traverses 25 degrees (five line segments). The order of stops is the same as in the first problem you solved, although the route itself is different.

19   From the File menu, choose Close All. Again from the File menu, choose Close Project. Click No when you're prompted to save your changes.

If you want to go on to the next exercise, leave ArcView GIS running. Otherwise, choose Exit from the File menu.

Using time as a travel cost

The routes you've created up to now have been based on distance values. The "best" route has been the one with the shortest accumulated line length between the origin and the destination. But using distance as a travel cost doesn't take into account that you can drive faster on some roads than on others.

Network Analyst includes a sample extension called the Speed Limit Calculator that applies speed limit information to an existing distance cost field (like the Meters field you created in the previous exercise). This gives Network Analyst a more sophisticated approach to solving problems: it can choose routes according to how long it actually takes to go from one place to another (a measurement known as drivetime), rather than how far apart those places are.

Speed limit information is only one of many factors that can be used to model drivetime. In chapters 6 and 7, you'll look at some others.

◆ *E x e r c i s e   3 b*

1   If necessary, start ArcView GIS. Navigate to the \extend\network\ch03 directory and open the project "ex03b.apr." When the project opens, you see a view that contains a network theme of Washington, D.C.

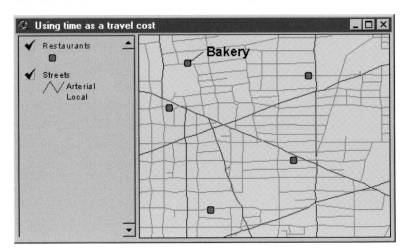

The *Restaurants* theme contains the locations of several restaurants awaiting deliveries from a bakery. You'll find the best delivery route, but the "best" route in this case will be the fastest, not the shortest one. You can't find the fastest route until you have a field of drivetime values in your network theme table, and to create this field you need to load and use the Speed Limit Calculator extension.

2   Using your operating system's file manager, copy the file slc.avx from the $AVHOME\samples\ext directory to the $AVHOME\Ext32 directory. ($AVHOME is the location where ArcView GIS is installed on your system, typically \esri\av_gis30\arcview.)

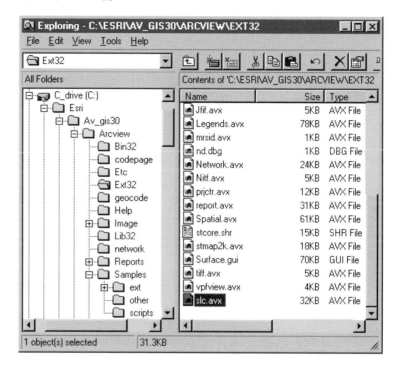

Extensions only appear in the Extensions dialog of your project when they've been copied to the Ext32 folder.

3   Make ArcView GIS the active application. From the File menu, choose Extensions. In the Extensions dialog, click on the Speed Limit Calculator check box to turn it on. Click OK.

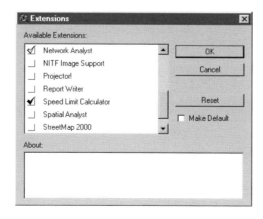

The Speed Limit Calculator extension is loaded into the current project.

Understanding the Speed Limit Calculator. The Speed Limit Calculator is a tool for multiplying street lengths by appropriate speed limits to create drivetime values. The Speed Limit Calculator doesn't know what speed limit is appropriate to a particular street segment; it has to be provided with this information, either directly (through a field of speed limit values in the network theme table) or indirectly (through a separate table that correlates network theme street segments to speed limit data). A great deal of geographic street data comes originally from the U.S. Census Bureau. One of the attributes of Census Bureau street data is a standard set of codes, called Census Feature Classification Codes (CFCC, or sometimes just FCC), that describe the characteristics of streets. For example, the CFCC code A11 is applied to primary or interstate highways, while the code A4 is applied to local roads. Network Analyst provides a database table, called cfcc.dbf, that contains speed limit values for every CFCC code. So as long as your network theme has a field of CFCC codes, you can use the Speed Limit Calculator to relate these codes to their corresponding speed limits and create drivetime values.

4   With the *Streets* theme active in the view, click the Open Theme Table button. Scroll through the table and note that it contains a field of CFCC codes. Scroll to the right to see that it also contains a field of distance units in meters.

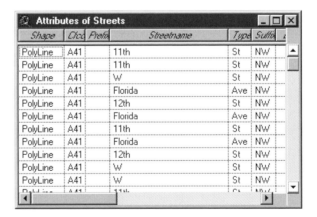

The CFCC codes are related to speed limit information in Network Analyst's cfcc.dbf table. You'll add this table to the project, then use the Speed Limit Calculator to create drivetimes. (Ordinarily, you wouldn't need to add the table to the project because the Speed Limit Calculator already knows where to find it on disk. But this extra step gives you a chance to see what the table looks like.)

5   In the Project window, click the Tables icon. Click the Add button and navigate to the $AVHOME\network directory. Select the table named cfcc.dbf and click OK.

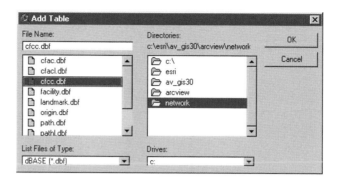

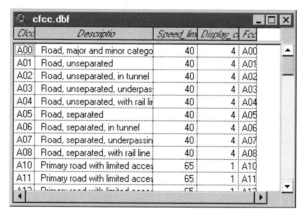

The table is added to the project. Note that every CFCC code has an associated speed limit. To create drivetimes, the Speed Limit Calculator will relate the network theme table to the cfcc.dbf table using CFCC codes. It will then look up the speed limit for each line segment and multiply it by the Meters value in the network theme table.

6   Close the Attributes of Streets table and the cfcc.dbf table. From the Network menu, choose Set Times From Speed to open the Speed Limit Calculator.

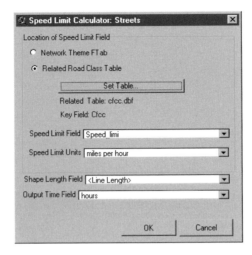

At the top of the dialog, there are two options for specifying the location of the speed limit field. If it's in your network theme table, use the Network Theme FTab button. If it's in a separate table, use the Related Road Class Table option. A related road class table must contain a field of CFCC or FCC codes for the Speed Limit Calculator to access it.

The Set Table button lets you specify the related table. By default, this is set correctly to cfcc.dbf.

The *Speed Limit Field* drop-down list is set to "Speed_limi," the name of the speed limit field in cfcc.dbf. The *Speed Limit Units* drop-down list is set to "miles per hour," the units in which the speed limit values are stored.

The Speed Limit Calculator uses a shape length field in conjunction with speed limits to create drivetime values. You'll set *Shape Length Field* to your existing distance cost field (Meters). If you leave it set to <Line Length>, your time cost values will be based on decimal degrees.

Output Time Field sets the units in which drivetime values are written to the network theme table.

7   Set *Shape Length Field* to "Meters" and *Output Time Field* to "minutes."

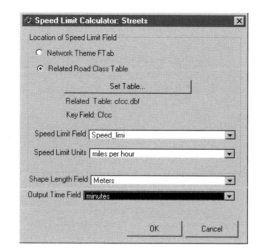

Although your distance units are in the metric system and your speed limit values are not, the Speed Limit Calculator will make the necessary conversions automatically.

8   Click OK. It may take a few minutes for the process to finish. When it does, the Speed Limit Calculator dialog will close. With the *Streets* theme active in the view, click the Open Theme Table button. Scroll to the last field in the table.

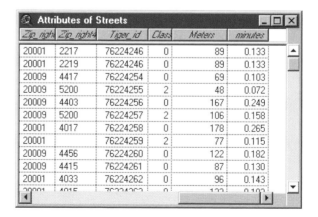

The minutes field contains the time it takes in minutes to traverse each line segment in the theme. Now you'll use this field in a network problem.

9   Close the table. Make sure the *Streets* theme is active. From the Network
     Menu, choose Find Best Route. When the *Route1* result theme is added
     to the view, open the Theme Properties dialog and change its name to
     Fastest Route. Click OK.

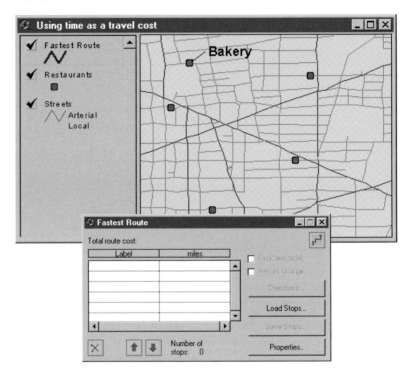

10   In the Problem Definition dialog, click the Load Stops button and choose the
      Restaurants theme. Click OK to load the stops. Click the "Find best order" and
      "Return to origin" check boxes to turn them on.

11   In the Problem Definition dialog, click the Properties button. In the *Cost
      field* drop-down list, choose "minutes." In the *Working units* drop-down list,
      choose "hh:mm:ss." Click OK.

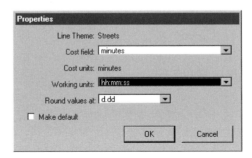

By setting the working units to hh:mm:ss you avoid reporting your
results in unwieldy fractions, such as 6.93 minutes, or 2.84 hours.

12   Click the Solve button.

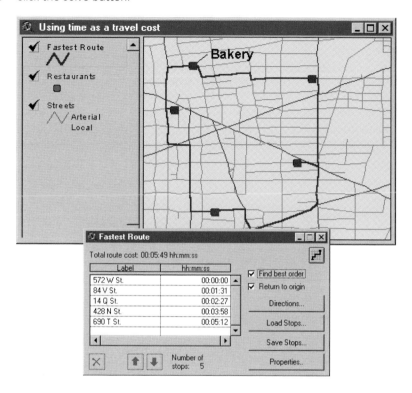

When time rather than distance is your travel cost, Network Analyst is far more likely to find routes that use major roads than routes that use local streets. If you like, you can test this by creating a new problem that uses the Meters field to find a route for the same stops. You'll see that the Meters route relies much more on side streets.

13   From the File menu, choose Close All. Again from the File menu, choose Close Project. Click No when you're prompted to save your changes.

If you're going on to the next chapter, leave ArcView GIS running. Otherwise, choose Exit from the File menu.

4

Finding the closest facility

Finding the closest facility

Finding several facilities

Creating directions

SO FAR,

you've used Network Analyst to find the best route among a series of stops. But this is only one kind of network problem. Suppose a traffic accident has occurred, and a motorist is injured. If you drove the victim from one hospital to another all over the city it wouldn't do much good, even if you were following the most efficient possible route. It would no doubt be better that you find the closest hospital and get to it straightaway.

This kind of problem, called a Closest Facility problem, involves finding the closest point or points to a given location. The points are called "facilities" and the location is called an "event." Network Analyst can calculate the best route either from events to facilities or from facilities to events.

Finding the closest facility

In this exercise, you'll use Network Analyst to find the closest fire station to a house that's burning. (It's not really burning, of course. So you can take your time on the exercise.)

This exercise uses fictional data and does not represent the actual state of city services.

◆ *E x e r c i s e   4 a*

1   If necessary, start ArcView GIS. Navigate to the \extend\network\ch04 directory and open the project "ex04a.apr." When the project opens, you see a view containing a network theme of the city of Santa Barbara, California.

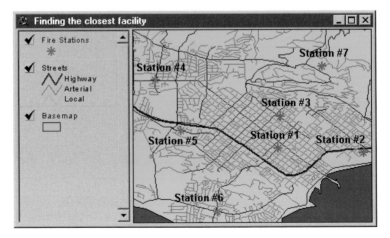

The *Fire Stations* theme contains the locations of seven firehouses.

2   With the *Streets* theme active, click the Open Theme Table button and scroll all the way to the right.

Zip_righ	Zip_right4	Tiger_id	Class	Meters	Seconds
93110	1218	108603083	0	42	3.753
93110	1264	108603083	0	5	0.417
93110	1264	108603083	0	112	10.008
93110	1261	108603085	0	133	11.918
93110	1235	108603086	0	127	11.321
93110	1237	108603086	0	127	11.321
93105	1924	108603089	0	66	5.901
93105	1926	108603089	0	66	5.901
93105	1928	108603089	0	66	5.901
93105	1930	108603089	0	66	5.901
93105	1958	108603089	0	66	5.901

Attributes of Streets

A drivetime field called "Seconds," created by the same method you learned about in the previous chapter, has already been added to the table. You'll use the values in this field to find the closest fire station and determine the quickest way to get to a fire that has been reported at 2703 Puesta del Sol Road. You don't yet know where that is, but you'll pinpoint the address in a moment.

3   Close the table. From the Network menu, choose Find Closest Facility to create a new result theme and display the Problem Definition dialog.

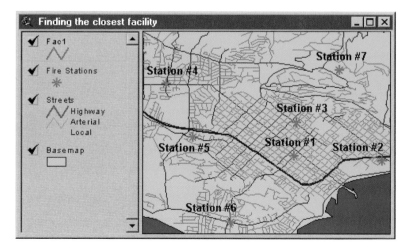

A new theme, named *Fac1* (Facilities theme 1), appears in the Table of Contents. *Fac1* will contain the solution to the Find Closest Facility problem you define, just as the result theme named *Route1* contained solutions to the Find Best Route problems you worked on previously.

In the Problem Definition dialog, the *Facilities* drop-down list contains all the point themes in the view. In this case, there's only one, the *Fire Stations* theme.

Because you'll be routing trucks from the closest station only, the number of facilities you need to find is one. If the fire were large enough, you might want to dispatch trucks from the two or three closest facilities. (Any number of facilities can be specified.)

The "Travel to event" option is selected by default. This means that Network Analyst will find the best route from the facility (the fire station) to the event (the fire).

Like stops, events can be specified in one of three ways: by loading a theme, by clicking on the view, or by entering an address. Since you've got the address of the fire, you'll use it to specify the event.

4   On the ArcView GIS button bar, click the Add Location by Address button. In the Locate Address dialog, type **2703 Puesta del Sol Road**. Click OK.

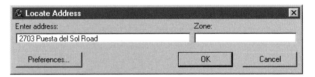

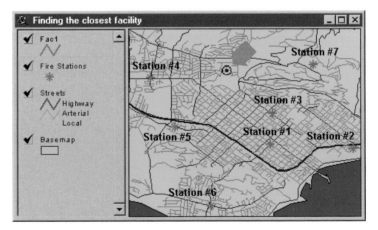

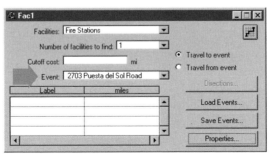

The address is marked in the view with a green bull's-eye. It also displays in the Event field of the Problem Definition dialog.

> **Understanding events and facilities.** The terms "event" and "facility" don't have their natural English meaning to Network Analyst. An event may be an actual event (like a fire) and a facility may be an actual facility (like a fire station), but from Network Analyst's point of view this is just a coincidence. In a closest facility problem, point features can be thought of as events or facilities based on how they're used. If several fires were burning, you could define fires as "facilities" and fire stations as "events" to find the closest fire to a given fire station.

You want to find which fire truck can get to the fire the quickest, so you'll change the travel cost units from miles to minutes.

5   In the Problem Definition dialog, click the Properties button. In the *Cost field* drop-down list, choose "Seconds." In the *Working units* drop-down list, choose "hh:mm:ss." Click OK.

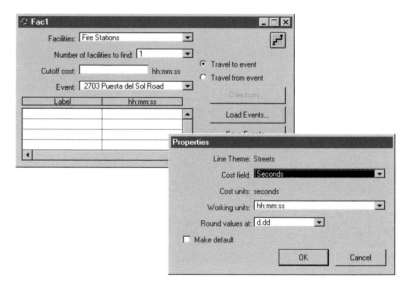

In the Problem Definition dialog, the name of the field where the travel costs will be reported changes from *miles* to *hh:mm:ss*.

6   In the Problem Definition dialog, click the Solve button.

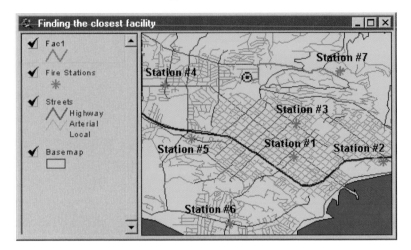

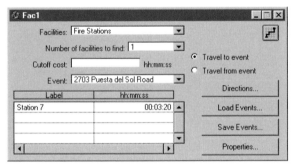

Network Analyst finds the station with the shortest drivetime to the fire. Station 7 is three minutes and twenty seconds away.

To display descriptive labels in the Problem Definition dialog, add a field called LABEL to your facilities theme's attribute table and populate the field with a description of each facility.

7   From the File menu, choose Close All. Again from the File menu, choose Close Project. Click No when you're prompted to save your changes.

If you want to go on to the next exercise, leave ArcView GIS running. Otherwise, choose Exit from the File menu.

Finding several facilities

You've seen how to find a closest facility. Now you'll see how to find all the facilities within a certain travel time or distance from an event. Instead of using an address, you'll use a point theme to specify the events.

◆ *E x e r c i s e   4 b*

1   If necessary, start ArcView GIS. Navigate to the \extend\network\ch04 directory and open the project "ex04b.apr." When the project opens, you see a view containing the streets of Santa Barbara.

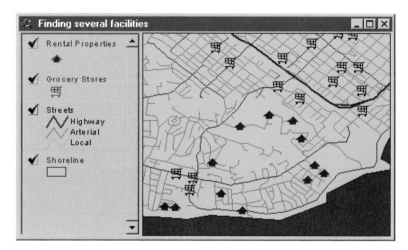

A local property management company wants to promote vacations in Santa Barbara. They've found that renters like to have grocery stores close by. Currently, the property at 825 Miramonte Avenue is unoccupied. You'll find the five closest grocery stores to this rental.

2   From the Network menu, choose Find Closest Facility. When the *Fac1* result theme is added to the view, open the Theme Properties dialog and change its name to **Closest Stores**.

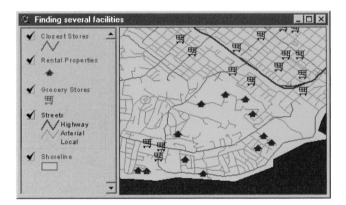

The *Rental Properties* theme contains the location of the vacation house you want to use as the event. You'll use the Load Events button to load the points, in the same way you loaded a stops theme in the Find Best Route problems you did earlier.

3   Click the Load Events button. In the Load Events dialog, choose the *Rental Properties* theme and click OK.

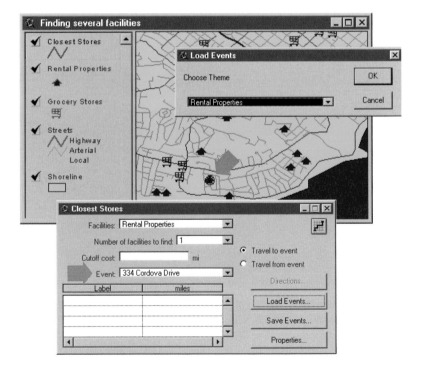

When you load the *Rental Properties* theme, points are loaded into the *Event* drop-down list in the order in which they appear in the theme table. Because Network Analyst finds the closest grocery stores for one rental property at a time, only one event can be selected in the list. Right now, the event is 334 Cordova Drive, so you'll need to change it to 825 Miramonte Drive.

To display descriptive labels in the *Event* drop-down list, add a field called LABEL to the point theme's attribute table and populate it with a description of each event.

---

4   In the *Event* drop-down list, choose "825 Miramonte Drive."

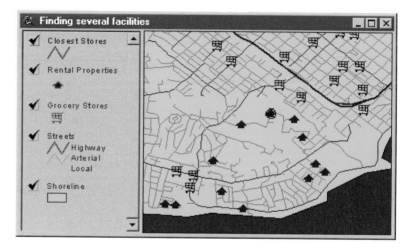

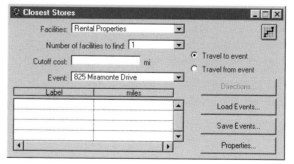

In the view, the green bull's-eye moves to mark the point feature for 825 Miramonte Drive.

5 In the *Facilities* drop-down list in the Problem Definition dialog, choose "Grocery Stores."

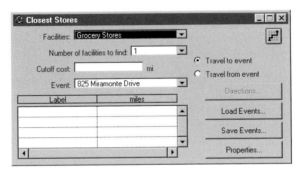

6 In the *Number of facilities to find* drop-down list, choose "5."

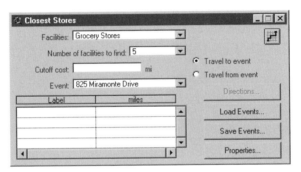

You can restrict Network Analyst's solution by specifying a cutoff cost. Network Analyst won't consider any grocery stores that fall beyond the distance or time specified as the cutoff. You've decided not to include any grocery stores that are more than fifteen minutes from the rental property.

The *Cutoff cost* units depend on the *Cost units* setting in the Properties dialog. You'll change the cost units from the default <Line Length> to a field called Seconds that's already been added to the *Streets* theme.

7   Click the Properties button to display the Properties dialog. In the *Cost field* drop-down list, choose "Seconds." In the *Working units* drop-down list, choose "hh:mm:ss." Click OK.

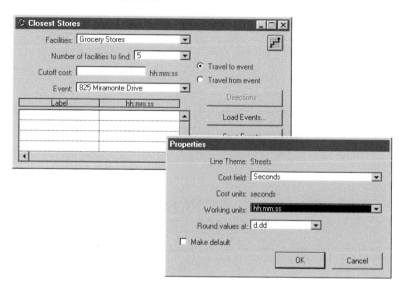

In the Problem Definition dialog, the cutoff cost units change to hh:mm:ss.

8   In the *Cutoff cost* field, type **00:15:00**.

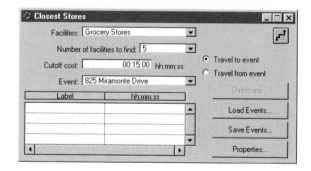

Selecting facilities.   Using a cutoff cost is one way to limit the number of facilities Network Analyst considers when finding more than a few nearby facilities. Another method is to select the facilities in the view before solving the problem. If you have a facilities theme with lots of points, selecting only those you know to be contenders will save time. In the online help, use the Find tab to locate the topic *Maximizing performance*.

Network Analyst lets you find the closest facility based on travel either from the facility to the event or from the event to the facility. Guests will go from the vacation property to the grocery store, so you'll change the default travel direction.

9   Click the "Travel from event" option.

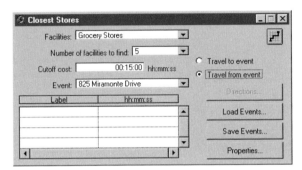

You've finished setting up the problem. When you click the Solve button, Network Analyst will find the five closest grocery stores within a fifteen-minute drivetime of 825 Miramonte Drive.

    10   In the Problem Definition dialog, click the Solve button.

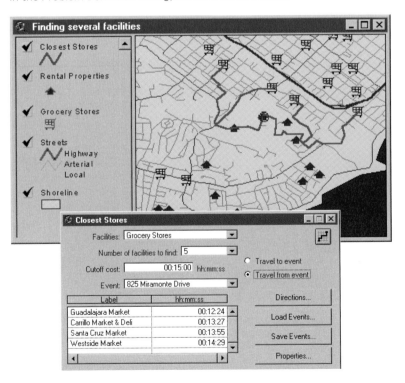

Network Analyst finds four grocery stores within a fifteen-minute drivetime of the rental property. The closest store is about twelve and a half minutes from the property.

11 From the File menu, choose Close All. Again from the File menu, choose Close Project. Click No when you're prompted to save your changes.

If you want to go on to the next exercise, leave ArcView GIS running. Otherwise, choose Exit from the File menu.

Creating directions

You know what directions are. Those things some people hate to ask for when they're lost. Network Analyst can help you navigate an unfamiliar route by providing detailed instructions on which way to turn onto what street, how far to travel along the street, and what landmarks to watch out for. The following graphic shows you an example.

Starting from **825 Miramonte Drive** ———————— *origin*
Turn left onto Miramonte Dr
  Travel on Miramonte Dr for **0.84 km** ———————— *how far to travel*
Turn right onto **W Carrillo St** ———————————— *street to travel along*
  Travel on W Carrillo St for 1.05 km passing
    Elementary School on right (0.69 km) ——— *landmark*
Turn right into **Carrillo Market & Deli** ———— *destination*

Total distance traveled is 1.89 km

Network Analyst gets the origin, destination, and street information from fields in the network theme table. It calculates how far to travel along each street using travel cost information. You can include landmarks in your directions if you have them stored in a point theme.

In this exercise, you'll create a set of directions for the closest facility problem you solved in the previous exercise. After all, a grocery store isn't fifteen minutes away if you don't know how to get there.

◆ *E x e r c i s e   4 c*

1 If necessary, start ArcView GIS. Navigate to the \extend\network\ch04 directory and open the project "ex04c.apr." When the project opens, you see a
   view containing the Find Closest Facility problem you solved in the previous
   exercise. The stars are points belonging to a theme of local landmarks.

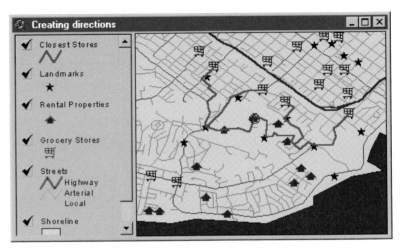

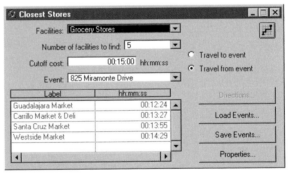

When you open a project that contains a result theme, the results
in the Problem Definition dialog will be gray, indicating that the
results are not up to date. If the network theme has been edited
(which might have happened while the project was closed or if the
network theme was referenced in another project), the results in
the dialog will be invalid. The gray values remind you to click the
Solve button and update the results.

2 Click the Solve button.

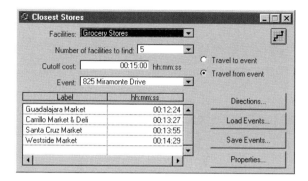

The values in the Problem Definition dialog are updated.

Now you'll make sure the network theme table contains the information needed to create the directions.

3 In the view, make the *Streets* theme active, then click the Open Theme Table button.

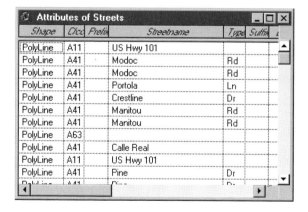

The network theme table stores information about each street in separate fields. The street names are stored in the Streetname field and the street types are stored in the Type field. Additional information (such as that which distinguishes E. Victoria St. from W. Victoria St.) is stored in the Prefix and Suffix fields.

By default, the street name is the only information Network Analyst includes in the directions. The proper field will be identified automatically if you give it one of the following names: STREET_NAME, STREETNAME, STREET_NAM, ST_NAME, STR_NAME, ROAD_NAME, ROADNAME, EDGENAME, FNAME, NAME.

4   Close the table. In the Problem Definition dialog, click the Directions button.

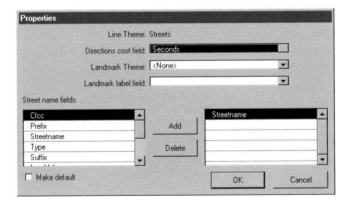

Network Analyst generates four sets of directions. Each one starts at 825 Miramonte Drive and ends at one of the grocery stores. You still need to add the street type, prefix, and suffix information.

5   In the Directions dialog, click the Properties button.

The Directions Properties dialog lets you customize your directions. The scrolling list on the left contains fields from the network theme's attribute table. Adding a field to the list on the right tells Network Analyst to include its information in the directions.

By default, the street name field is already added.

6   In the scrolling list on the left, select "Prefix" and click the Add button. The Prefix field is added to the list of fields on the right. Add the Type and Suffix fields, too.

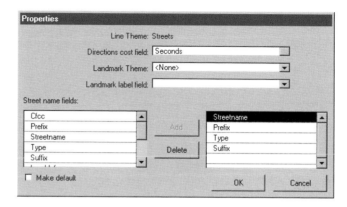

To make the prefix information come before the street name, you'll move it to the top of the list.

7   In the list on the right, click on the Prefix field to highlight it, then drag the field to the top of the list. Click OK to include the new information in the directions.

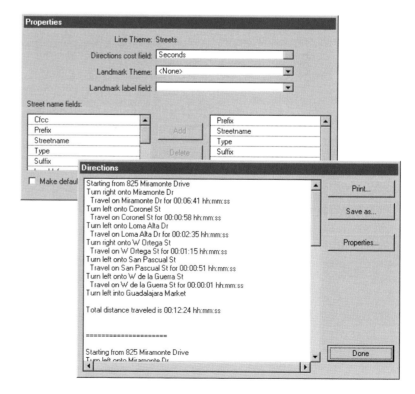

In the directions, "Miramonte" is replaced by "Miramonte Dr"; "Ortega" is replaced by "W Ortega St"; and so on.

The original closest facility problem was solved using seconds as the cost units and hh:mm:ss as the working units. By default, the directions display these working units. It can be difficult, however, to drive and monitor your wristwatch at the same time.

8   Click the Properties button again. In the *Directions cost field* drop-down list, choose "Miles." Click OK.

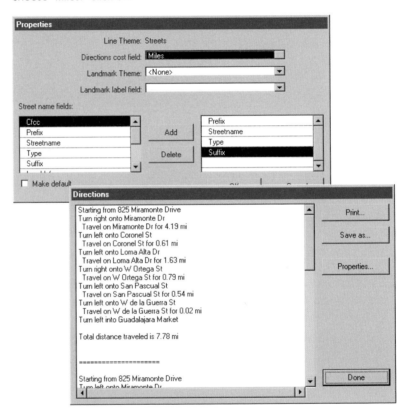

Network Analyst converts the directions to miles.

There's one more piece of information you can add to the directions: landmarks. In the view, the *Landmarks* theme contains information about well-known or easily recognized places. You'll use the information from this theme to make your directions easier to follow.

9   Click the Properties button again. In the *Landmark Theme* drop-down list, choose "Landmarks." Click OK.

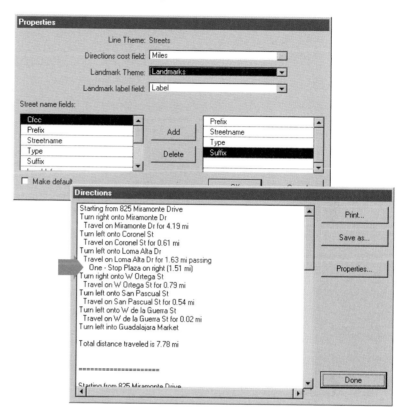

The directions now include information from the *Landmarks* theme, such as the One-Stop Plaza on Loma Alta Drive. When Network Analyst uses landmark information, it tells you on which side of the road and how far along it the landmark appears. Before using a landmark theme, make sure that its point features are precisely located. If a landmark falls on the wrong side of the line that represents the road, the directions will have you looking out the wrong window.

Of the grocery stores you analyzed, Guadalajara Market is the closest, and the most popular. It's located at a tricky intersection, and you'd like the directions to include information about an extra parking lot across the street. You'll create a new set of directions to the Guadalajara Market that includes landmarks. Then you'll add the information about parking.

10   In the Directions dialog, click the Done button. In the Problem Definition
      dialog, select Guadalajara Market.

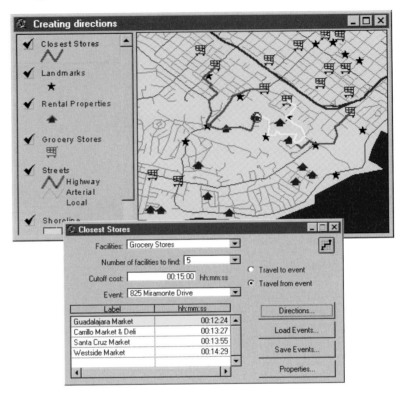

The corresponding route is selected in the view.

11   Click the Directions button.

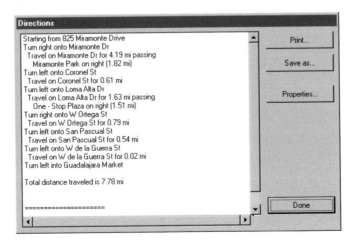

Because Guadalajara Market is selected, Network Analyst creates directions for that facility only.

12   In the window containing the directions, click above the last line (the one that gives the total distance traveled). Type **Extra parking across the street**.

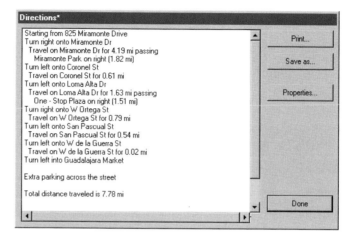

You can change the directions in any way that you like. When you make changes, Network Analyst places an asterisk in the title bar.

13   In the Directions dialog, click the Done button. The prompt tells you the directions have changed. Click No.

You can save directions as a .txt file for printing or distributing.

14   From the File menu, choose Close All. Again from the File menu, choose Close Project. Click No when you're prompted to save your changes.

If you're going on to the next chapter, leave ArcView GIS running. Otherwise, choose Exit from the File menu.

5

Finding service areas

Creating service areas

Using service areas in network analysis

UP UNTIL NOW,

you've been working with problems that involve finding distinct paths through a network. Another kind of problem that Network Analyst solves creates service areas and service networks.

A service network is a set of all the line segments in a network that lie within a specific distance or drivetime of a chosen point on the network. The distance or drivetime is determined along network paths.

A service area is a polygon drawn around the service network. Because it's easier to look at a bounding polygon than a dense network of lines, service areas make it easier to see what's within the given drivetime or distance of the chosen location.

Although Network Analyst always creates service areas and service networks together, for convenience the phrase "Service area" is often used to refer to both.

Creating service areas

In this exercise, you'll create ten-minute drivetime service areas for ambulance dispatch stations in San Bernardino, California. By finding all the streets that can be reached by an ambulance in ten minutes or less, you'll also identify the areas that can't be reached, which may require a new station.

This exercise uses fictional data and does not represent the actual state of city services.

◆ *E x e r c i s e   5 a*

1   If necessary, start ArcView GIS. Navigate to the \extend\network\ch05 directory and open the project "ex05a.apr." When the project opens, you see a view containing two themes, one of ambulance stations and one of the streets of south-central San Bernardino.

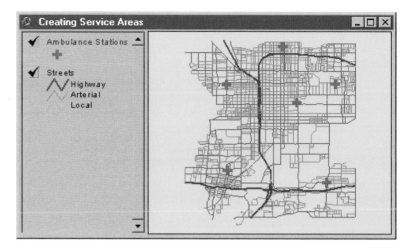

2   From the Network menu, choose Find Service Area.

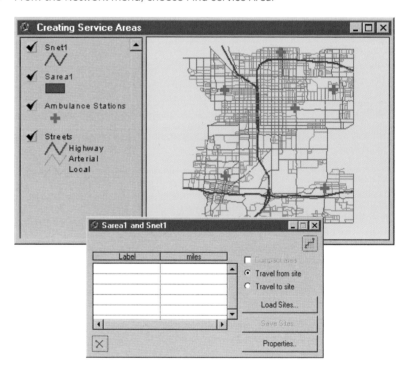

When the Problem Definition dialog opens, two result themes are created in the view. When you solve the problem, the service network is saved to the line theme *Snet1,* and the service area is saved to the polygon theme *Sarea1.* The themes are shapefiles stored as snet1.shp and sarea1.shp in your temporary directory until you close the project.

3   Make *Sarea1* the only active theme. Open the Theme Properties dialog and change its name to **Areas within range**. Click OK. Make the *Snet1* theme active, then open the Theme Properties dialog again and change its name to **Streets within range**. Click OK.

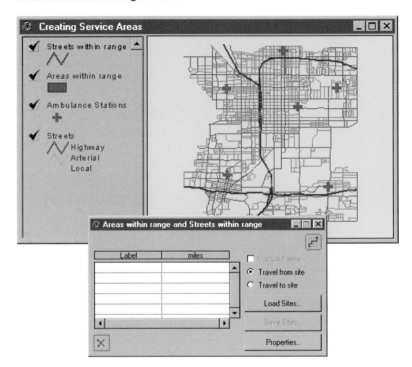

4   In the Problem Definition dialog, click the Load Sites button. In the Load Sites dialog, choose "Ambulance Stations" from the drop-down list and click OK. Resize the Problem Definition dialog so you can see all the stations.

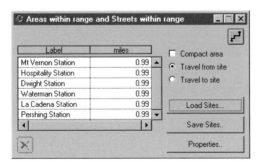

Network Analyst doesn't know in advance that you want to find a ten-minute service area. It provides you with a default value you have to override. The default is based on the spatial extent of the network theme. Since you want to find the areas of the network within a ten-minute drivetime of each station, you'll change the travel cost to units of time.

5   Click the Properties button. In the Properties dialog, in the *Cost field* drop-down list, choose "Minutes" and click OK.

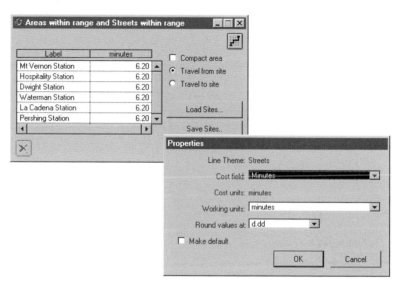

Network Analyst sets a default travel time of 6.20 minutes for each station. You'll change this value to 10.

6   Double-click in the minutes field of the first record and type **10**. Press Enter on the keyboard to move the cursor to the next record and type **10** again. Continue until all stations have a value of 10.

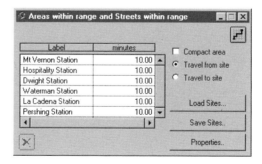

Because values are entered manually, you can set different values for each site if you like. This will create service areas of different dimensions.

7   Click the Solve button.

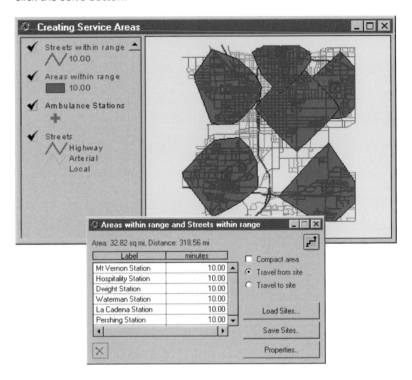

Network Analyst finds the service areas and service networks within a ten-minute drivetime of each site. By identifying all areas that can be reached by ambulance within ten minutes, Network Analyst also shows you the areas that can't be reached—these are areas that may need to be considered for a new station.

The Problem Definition dialog tells you that the total area covered by all six service areas is 32.82 square miles, and the total driving distance on all the service networks is 318.56 miles.

The service area polygons cover up the features in the *Ambulance Stations* and *Streets* themes. There are a couple of ways you can remedy this situation. One is to move the *Areas within range* theme to the bottom of the Table of Contents. The other is to change this theme's symbology to an outline.

8 Turn off the *Streets within range* theme. Make the *Areas within range* theme active and double-click on it to open the Legend Editor. Double-click on the polygon symbol in the Legend Editor to display the Fill Palette. Click on the upper-left symbol (outline) and, in the *Outline* drop-down list, choose "2." In the Legend Editor, click Apply. Close the Legend Editor and the Fill Palette.

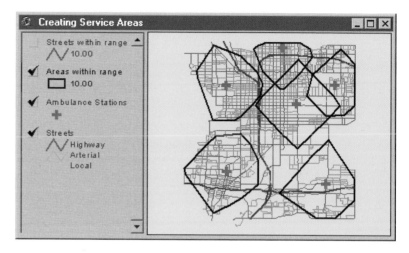

You can now see the theme features that lie within the service area polygons. You can also see that the service areas overlap in places.

The service areas you've just created are called generalized service areas. They're relatively smooth and simple shapes, making them useful for display, but they don't conform exactly to the service networks. You'll zoom in on the southeast service area to confirm this.

9 Turn on the *Streets within range* theme, then select the Zoom In tool. Draw a box around the southeast corner of the view to zoom in on it.

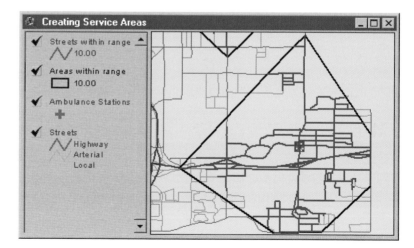

A few small street segments that aren't on the service network are nonetheless included in the generalized service area polygon. In the next exercise, you'll create compact service areas that conform precisely to the service network.

10 From the File menu, choose Close All. Again from the File menu, choose Close Project. Click No when you're prompted to save your changes.

If you want to go on to the next exercise, leave ArcView GIS running. Otherwise, choose Exit from the File menu.

Using service areas in network analysis

In this exercise, you'll use service areas to help choose between two proposed sites for a new child care center. You'll create service areas that lie within five-, ten-, and fifteen-minute drivetimes of each of the sites. Then you'll use the service areas to determine how many potential customers live nearby.

◆ *E x e r c i s e   5 b*

1 If necessary, start ArcView GIS. Navigate to the \extend\network\ch05 directory and open the project "ex05b.apr." When the project opens, you see a view that contains the streets of Boston, Massachusetts.

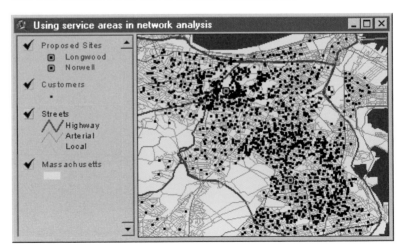

Market research has suggested two potential sites for a child care center. Through surveys, the research has identified a high number of potential customers who live within a reasonable driving distance of each site. The research has also shown that there aren't many competitors in the area. The two proposed sites are just about equal in terms of cost and building suitability, and all that remains is to choose between them.

The Norwell site is known to have more potential customers within a fifteen-minute drivetime. However, by examining the data, you've noticed that the Longwood site appears to have more customers within a closer vicinity. Your research has shown that parents are more likely to choose a child care center that's close to home. You'll see how many customers are within a five-minute drivetime of each site.

2 Turn off the *Customers* theme. From the Network menu, choose Find Service Area. Make the *Sarea1* theme the only active theme. Open the Theme Properties dialog and change the theme name to **Service Area**. Click OK. Make the *Snet1* theme active, then open the Theme Properties dialog and change its name to **Service Network**. Click OK.

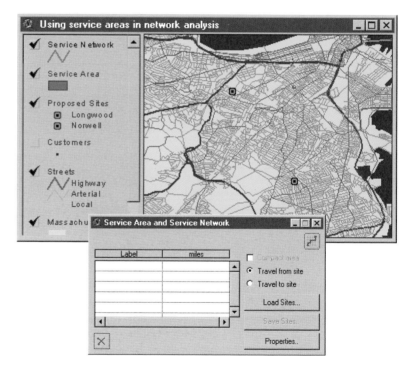

In this case, you'll create a compact service area to make sure you find only the customers within the extent of the service area. Since customers will travel from the surrounding area to the child care center, you'll use the "Travel to site" option.

3   Click the Load Sites button. In the Load Sites dialog, choose the *Proposed Sites* theme and click OK. Click the "Compact area" check box to turn it on and choose the "Travel to site" option.

4   Click the Properties button. In the Properties dialog, in the *Cost field* drop-down list, choose "Minutes." In the *Round values at* drop-down list, choose "d." Click OK.

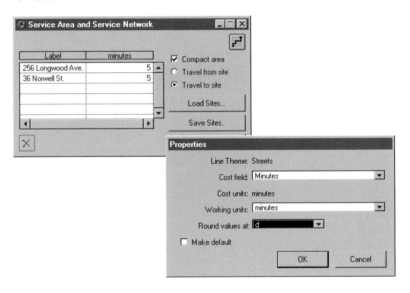

You've decided to analyze five-, ten-, and fifteen-minute drivetimes around each site. This involves the creation of what are known as "nested" service areas.

5   Double-click in the minutes field next to 256 Longwood Ave. Type **5,10,15** and press Enter on the keyboard. Do the same for 36 Norwell St.

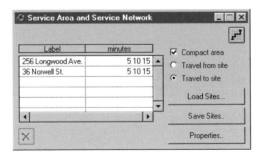

If you specify more than one travel time or distance for a site, separate them with a blank space or a comma. You can specify as many cost values as you like, so long as you don't exceed 254 characters.

6   Click the Solve button.

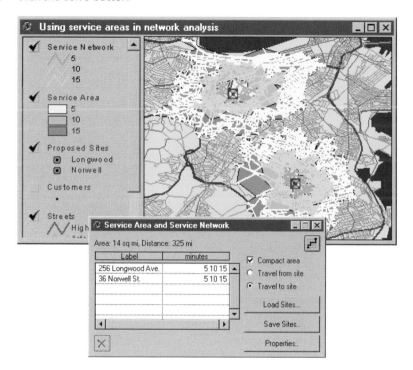

The nested service areas are arranged concentrically around each site and don't overlap. The five-, ten-, and fifteen-minute service areas are symbolized in different colors.

Now you'll make it easier to see the themes in relation to the service areas.

7   Turn off the *Service Network* theme. Drag the *Customers* theme to the top of the Table of Contents, then drag the *Proposed Sites* theme to the position directly beneath it. Turn on the *Customers* theme.

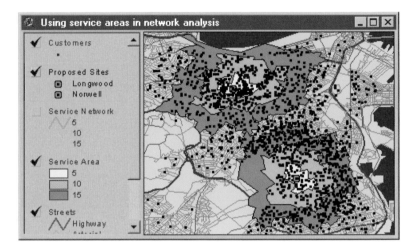

Note that the compact service areas are quite jagged compared to the generalized areas you created in the previous exercise. At some aesthetic cost, they represent the edges of the service network more precisely. You'll need this accuracy to find the number of prospective customers within a five-minute drivetime of each site.

8   Make the *Service Area* theme active and click the Select Feature tool. In the view, click on the five-minute drivetime polygon for the Norwell site to select it.

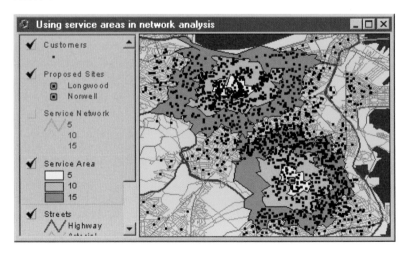

You'll use Select By Theme to count the customers within a five-minute drive of the Norwell site.

9   Make the *Customers* theme active. From the Theme menu, choose Select By Theme. In the Select By Theme dialog, choose "Service Area" from the lower drop-down list. From the upper drop-down list, choose "Are Completely Within." Your selections form the sentence: "Select features of active themes that are completely within the selected features of Service Area." Click the New Set button.

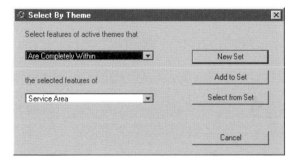

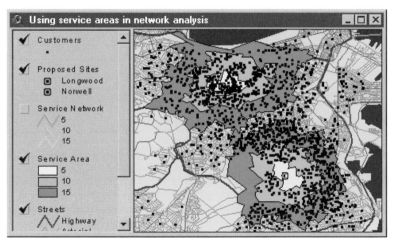

Prospective customers within zero to five minutes of the Norwell site are selected. To find out how many there are, you'll open the Customers theme table.

10   Click the Open Theme Table button, then click the Promote button.

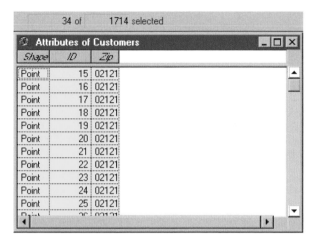

There are thirty-four prospective customers within five minutes of the Norwell site.

11   Close the table. Click the Clear Selected Features button, then click the Select Feature tool. In the view, make the *Service Area* theme active. Click on the five-minute drivetime polygon for the Longwood site to select it.

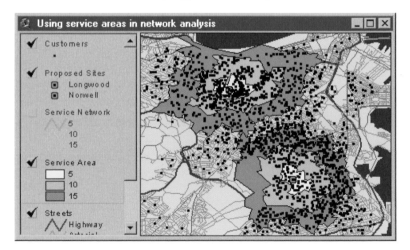

12   Make the *Customers* theme active. From the Theme menu, choose Select
      By Theme. In the Select By Theme dialog, choose "Service Area" from the
      lower drop-down list. From the upper drop-down list, choose "Are Com-
      pletely Within." Your selections form the sentence: "Select features of active
      themes that are completely within the selected features of Service Area."
      Click the New Set button.

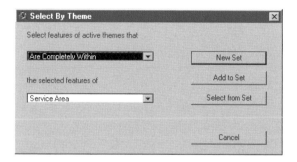

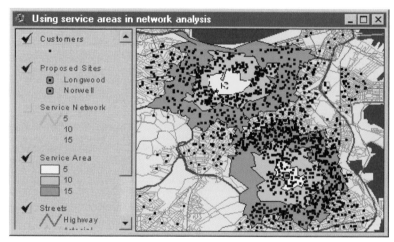

Prospective customers within zero to five minutes of the Longwood
site are selected.

13 Click the Open Theme Table button, then click the Promote button.

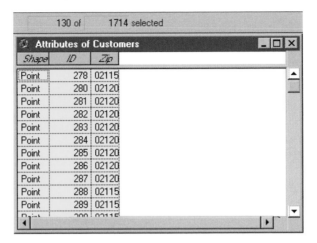

One hundred and thirty prospective customers can drive to the Longwood site in five minutes, as opposed to the thirty-four who can get to the Norwell site. Despite the fact that the Norwell site has more customers within a fifteen-minute drivetime, the Longwood site has more than three times as many customers only five minutes away.

You decide to go ahead with the Longwood site as the best location for the new child care center.

14 From the File menu, choose Close All. Again from the File menu, choose Close Project. Click No when you're prompted to save your changes.

If you're going on to the next chapter, leave ArcView GIS running. Otherwise, choose Exit from the File menu.

6

Modeling traffic flow

Modeling one-way streets

Creating travel costs for different directions

BY NOW,

you're familiar with the basic problem-solving capabilities of Network Analyst. In reality, street networks are complicated. For instance, travel along a street is rarely a matter of maintaining a constant speed. Construction, accidents, and the vagaries of everyday traffic all contribute to how fast you can travel along a street, or whether you can travel on it at all. Nor is getting from point to point simply a matter of driving straight along until you need to turn. Some streets can be traveled only in one direction, and some forbid left turns for much of their length or at certain times of day.

Network Analyst can't account for the car that pulls in front of you and proceeds at 30 miles per hour in a 45-MPH zone. But you can use it to model more predictable things, like whether you can travel in both directions or only one on a certain street, and whether one lane or one direction is faster or slower at a given time of day. Modeling real-world traffic problems involves getting into details. In this chapter and the next, get ready to shift gears as you explore how Network Analyst manages the complexities of street networks.

The exercises in this chapter use fictional data that does not represent the actual state of city services.

Modeling one-way streets

A street that's designated as one-way can obviously be traveled in just one direction. But two-way streets are similarly restricted—travel in a northbound lane can only be northerly, and so forth.

Note Stop #2 on the following bus route. It lies on the southbound side of a divided arterial. Unless you give instructions to the contrary, Network Analyst will go to that stop in the most direct way, even if it means traveling north on the southbound lanes, as it does here.

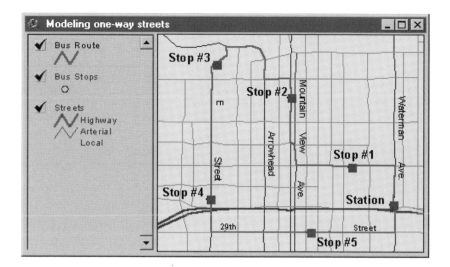

Defining one-way traffic is more than just identifying the northbound and southbound streets (or lanes) in a theme table using an attribute like "north" or "south." Network Analyst doesn't know about compass directions like north, south, east, and west. It knows what a line segment is and it knows where a line segment begins and ends, but it has no idea whether these lines run north–south, east–west, or any other direction.

Network Analyst has its own way of understanding line direction: the "from–to" way. It understands every line segment as beginning at a certain point and ending at a certain point and running in the direction of the beginning (from) point to the ending (to) point. Technically, these points are called "nodes." They're found wherever line segments intersect, and wherever line segments begin or end.

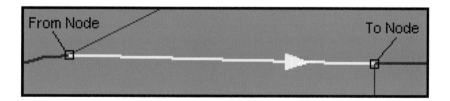

In the graphic above, Network Analyst doesn't think of the yellow line segment as running from west to east. It thinks of it simply as running from the From Node to the To Node. Any directional instructions you give it (such as "Don't travel west on this line segment") have to be translated into its terms.

Every line segment in every network theme has this from–to directional information built in. The direction is determined by how the line was digitized. When you create a new line theme in ArcView GIS and draw a single line segment, you've just digitized a line. The direction of that line runs from the first point you clicked to the last point you clicked. Every line theme you acquire, from whatever source, has the same inherent directional information. Bear in mind that Network Analyst doesn't care which way you want to travel on any given line segment. If you tell it to, it can just as easily go "to–from" as it can go "from–to" (by default, it already uses both directions). Finally, avoid confusing the concept of a node with that of a vertex. A line segment can have many vertices; it always has exactly two nodes.

In the following exercise, you'll set up Network Analyst to consider such nuances in making a route. You'll create a one-way field in the network theme table and populate it with directional information that tells Network Analyst which streets are one-way streets and in which direction travel along those streets is permitted.

◆ *E x e r c i s e   6 a*

1   If necessary, start ArcView GIS. Navigate to the \extend\network\ch06 directory and open the project "ex06a.apr." When the project opens, you see a view containing two themes.

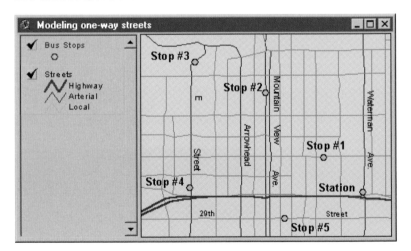

The *Bus Stops* theme contains the stops along a new bus route in San Bernardino. One of the streets on the route (the only one with divided lanes) is Mountain View Avenue. This is the street on which you want to restrict travel direction to the proper lanes. To do this, you first need to know in which direction the lines were digitized. There's a simple way to find this out, using the Symbol Palette.

2   Double-click on the *Streets* theme to open the Legend Editor. In the Legend Editor, double-click on the symbol for Arterial streets to display the Pen Palette. (Mountain View is classified as an arterial.) In the Pen Palette, scroll down and click on one of the arrow symbols to select it.

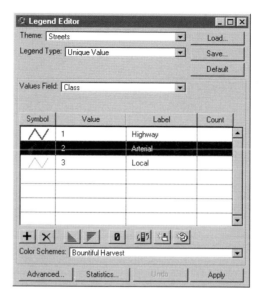
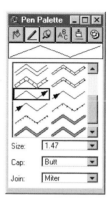

3   In the Legend Editor, click Apply. Close the Symbol Palette and the Legend Editor.

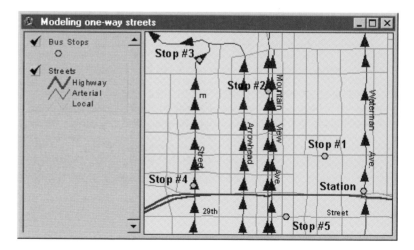

The arrows show you the direction in which the streets were digitized (bottom to top from your perspective, but "from–to" as far as Network Analyst is concerned). Now you'll add a "ONEWAY" field to the network theme table and use this line direction information to restrict traffic to the proper lanes.

4   With the *Streets* theme active, click the Open Theme Table button.

Shape	Fname	Suffix	Class	Spee
PolyLine	40th		2	4
PolyLine	40th		2	4
PolyLine	Electric		3	3
PolyLine	40th		2	4
PolyLine	40th		2	4
PolyLine	E		2	4
PolyLine	1st		3	3
PolyLine	40th		2	4
PolyLine	40 Th		2	4
PolyLine	Johnson		2	4
PolyLine	40 Th		2	4

Mountain View Avenue, like most streets in the network, is composed of many line segments. The line segments that represent the northbound lanes are designated by the suffix "N" and the line segments that represent the southbound lanes are designated by the suffix "S." Only the Mountain View Avenue line segments have "N" and "S" values in the Suffix field. You'll use these values to select the proper lanes for north and southbound travel.

5   From the Table menu, choose Start Editing. From the Edit menu, choose Add Field to open the Field Definition dialog. In the Field Definition dialog, name the new field ONEWAY. In the *Type* drop-down list, choose "String." Click OK to add the field to the table.

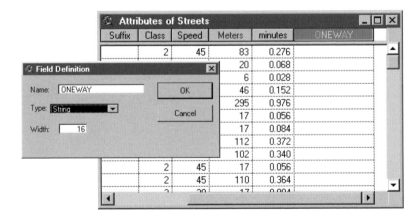

You don't want to make all the streets in the network one-way, just Mountain View Avenue. You'll select the northbound line segments first.

6 Click the Query Builder button. In the *Fields* scrolling list, double-click on [Suffix] to add it to the expression box. Click the "=" button. In the *Values* scrolling list, double-click on "N." Click the New Set button and close the Query Builder.

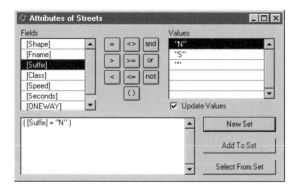

7 With the Attributes of Streets table active, click the Promote button. Scroll to the left so you can see the Fname and Suffix fields.

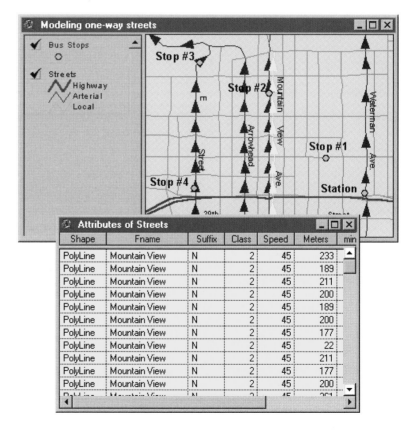

Northbound street segments of Mountain View Avenue are selected in the table and the view. Remember that the only line directions Network Analyst understands are "from–to" and "to–from." Putting the abbreviation "FT" in the ONEWAY field restricts travel to the direction in which the street was digitized. In this case, that corresponds to the appropriate travel direction (south to north) for the northbound lane of Mountain View Avenue.

8   Scroll to the right and make sure the ONEWAY field is highlighted in the table. With the Attributes of Streets table active, click the Calculate button to open the Field Calculator. In the expression box, type **"FT"** (including the quotation marks). Click OK.

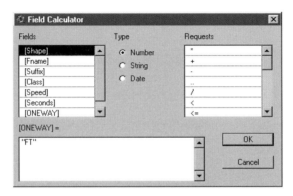

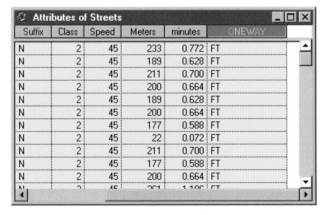

The selected records are updated. Travel in the northbound lanes will be in the from–to direction, the same direction in which the line segments were digitized.

Now you'll select and update the southbound lanes of Mountain View Avenue, which have a Suffix field value of "S."

9 Click the Query Builder button. In the *Fields* scrolling list, double-click on [Suffix] to add it to the expression box. Click the "=" button. In the *Values* scrolling list, double-click on "S." Click the New Set button and close the Query Builder.

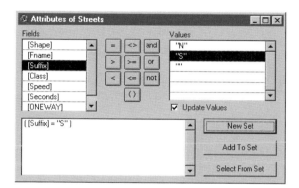

10 With the Attributes of Streets table active, click the Promote button. Scroll all the way to the left.

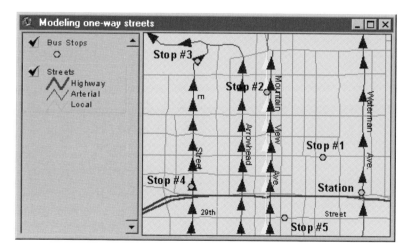

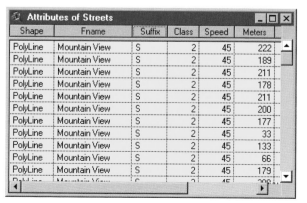

The southbound lanes of Mountain View Avenue are selected. This time, the appropriate travel direction (north to south) runs opposite to the from–to line direction. In other words, it corresponds to the to–from line direction. You therefore need to use the value of "TF" in the ONEWAY field.

11   Scroll to the right and make sure the ONEWAY field is still highlighted in the table. Click the Calculate button to open the Field Calculator. In the expression box, type **"TF"** (including the quotation marks). Click OK to update the table.

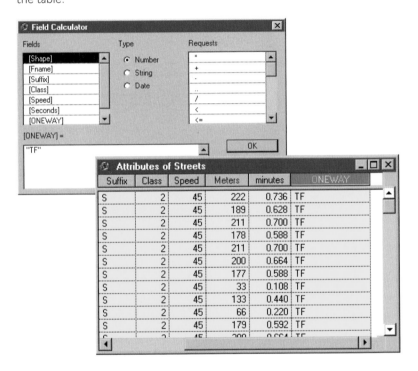

Travel in the southbound lanes will be in the to–from direction, opposite to the direction in which the lines were digitized.

Not all the records in the network theme need to be updated with a value in the ONEWAY field. If there's no value in the ONEWAY field, or if the value is something other than FT, TF, or N (which means the street is closed to travel), Network Analyst assumes that travel is permitted in both directions.

12 From the Table menu, choose Stop Editing. At the prompt, click Yes to save your edits. Click the Select None button to clear the selected records, then close the table.

Before you create a route that uses the information from the ONEWAY field, you'll change the arrow symbol back to a normal line.

13 In the view, double-click on the *Streets* theme to open the Legend Editor. Double-click on the symbol for Arterial streets to open the Symbol Palette. In the Pen Palette, click on the first line symbol to select it. In the Legend Editor, click Apply, then close both the Symbol Palette and the Legend Editor.

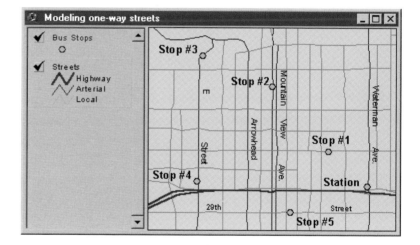

14   Make sure the *Streets* theme is active. From the Network menu, choose
      Find Best Route. When the *Route1* result theme is added to the view, open
      the Theme Properties dialog and change its name to **Bus Route**. Click OK.

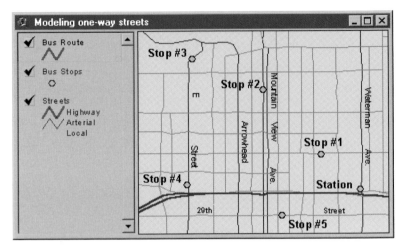

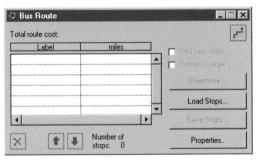

15   In the Problem Definition dialog, click the Load Stops button and choose
      the *Bus Stops* theme. Click OK to load the stops. Click the "Return to origin"
      check box so that it's turned on.

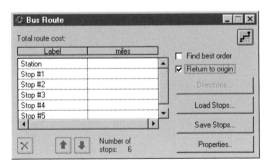

16 In the Problem Definition dialog, click the Properties button. In the *Cost field* drop-down list, choose "minutes." In the *Working units* drop-down list, choose "hh:mm:ss." Click OK.

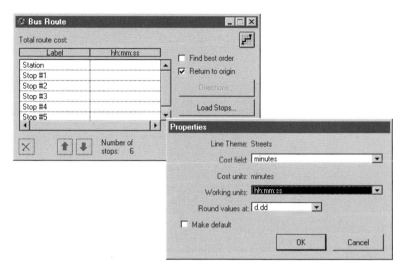

  17 Click the Solve button.

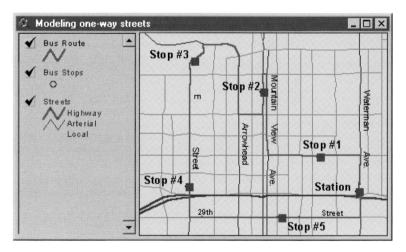

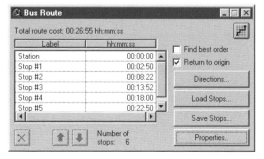

Network Analyst applies the directional information you added to the ONEWAY field. The bus route follows the northbound lanes of Mountain View Avenue to the street one block north of Stop #2, then turns around and follows the southbound lanes.

18 From the File menu, choose Close All. Again from the File menu, choose Close Project. Click No when you're prompted to save your changes.

If you want to go on to the next exercise, leave ArcView GIS running. Otherwise, choose Exit from the File menu.

Creating travel costs for different directions

The routes you've created so far have taken travel time to be the same no matter which direction you're going. This may be roughly true most of the time, but it will certainly not be true during rush hour. Southbound traffic on Mountain View Avenue, for instance, is slower in the morning than northbound traffic, and just the reverse in the afternoon.

The route that you created in the previous exercise is shown below. It treats the northbound and southbound lanes properly, thanks to the one-way field. However, it assumes that travel time is constant, regardless of the direction of travel or the time of day. Downtown San Bernardino is southwest of this area and during morning rush hour (from about 6 A.M. to 9 A.M.), southbound traffic is more congested than northbound traffic.

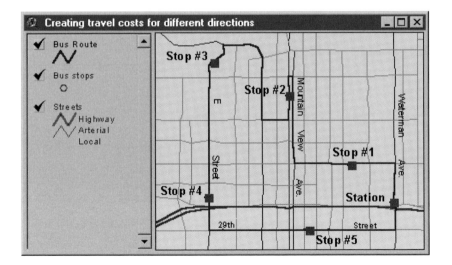

In this exercise, you'll assign different travel times to different directions along the arterial streets. Using these travel times, you can model rush hour congestion.

◆ *E x e r c i s e   6 b*

1   If necessary, start ArcView GIS. Navigate to the \extend\network\ch06 directory and open the project "ex06b.apr." When the project opens, you see a view that contains the stops on the bus route from the previous exercise.

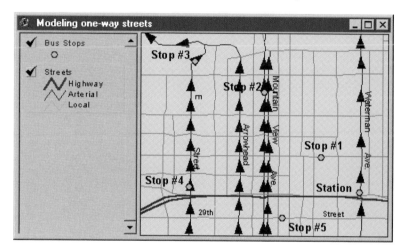

The arterial streets are symbolized with arrows that show you the direction in which the lines were digitized. You'll use this information to populate two travel cost fields. One field will contain time values for northbound arterial streets (corresponding to the from–to line direction). The other will contain time values for southbound arterials (corresponding to the to–from line direction). The basic idea is similar to that of the ONEWAY field you created in the previous exercise. The difference is that instead of telling Network Analyst, "You can only go south on this street," you're saying, "If you're going south on this street, use one travel cost, and if you're going north, use another."

2   With the *Streets* theme active, click the Open Theme Table button and scroll to the right.

Suffix	Class	Speed	Meters	Minutes	ONEWAY	FT_Minutes	TF_Minutes
	2	45	83	0.276		0.000	0.000
	2	45	20	0.068		0.000	0.000
	3	30	6	0.028		0.000	0.000
	2	45	46	0.152		0.000	0.000
	2	45	295	0.976		0.000	0.000
	2	45	17	0.056		0.000	0.000
	3	30	17	0.084		0.000	0.000
	2	45	112	0.372		0.000	0.000
	2	45	102	0.340		0.000	0.000
	2	45	17	0.056		0.000	0.000
	2	45	110	0.364		0.000	0.000

Attributes of Streets

The table contains a Class field and a Minutes field. The values in the Class field classify all streets into Highways (1), Arterials (2), and Local streets (3). Because the bus route traverses several arterial streets and these streets are heavily affected by rush-hour congestion, you'll select the arterials and update them with slower, rush-hour travel times.

The table also contains two fields populated with zeros: an FT_Minutes field and a TF_Minutes field. These fields will be used to store two different sets of rush-hour travel costs: one to be used for traffic moving in the from–to direction and the other for traffic moving in the to–from direction. (Ordinarily, you would have to add these fields yourself. To save time, they've been added for you.)

3   In the table, click on the FT_Minutes field name to highlight it. From the Table menu, choose Start Editing.

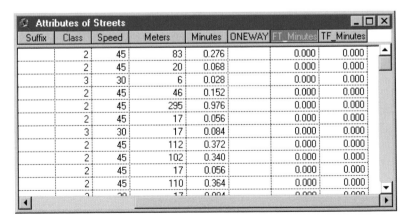

Suffix	Class	Speed	Meters	Minutes	ONEWAY	FT_Minutes	TF_Minutes
	2	45	83	0.276		0.000	0.000
	2	45	20	0.068		0.000	0.000
	3	30	6	0.028		0.000	0.000
	2	45	46	0.152		0.000	0.000
	2	45	295	0.976		0.000	0.000
	2	45	17	0.056		0.000	0.000
	3	30	17	0.084		0.000	0.000
	2	45	112	0.372		0.000	0.000
	2	45	102	0.340		0.000	0.000
	2	45	17	0.056		0.000	0.000
	2	45	110	0.364		0.000	0.000

Attributes of Streets

4   Make sure FT_Minutes is the active field. Click the Calculate button to open the Field Calculator. In the *Fields* scrolling list, double-click on the [Minutes] field. Click OK.

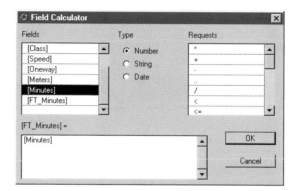

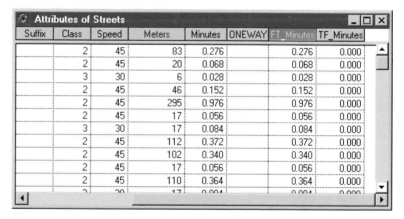

The FT_Minutes field is updated with the same cost values as the Minutes field. These values don't need to be changed. Now you'll create the travel costs for the southbound traffic. This involves a couple of steps.

5   In the table, click on the TF_Minutes field name to highlight it. Click the Calculate button to open the Field Calculator. In the *Fields* scrolling list, double-
click on the [Minutes] field. Click OK.

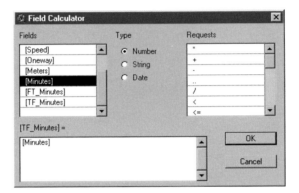

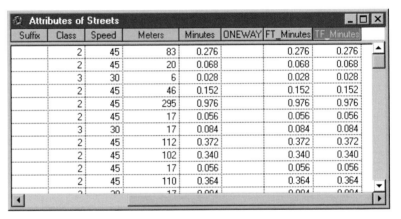

The TF_Minutes field is updated with the same cost values as the
Minutes field.

Now you'll select the arterial streets to replace their TF_Minutes values with values that apply to morning rush hour. Arterial streets
have a Class field value of 2.

6   Click the Query Builder button. In the *Fields* scrolling list, double-click on [Class] to add it to the expression box. Click the "=" button. In the *Values* scrolling list, double-click on "2." Click the New Set button and close the Query Builder.

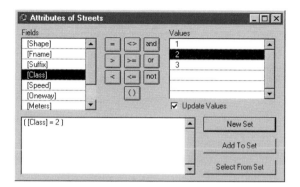

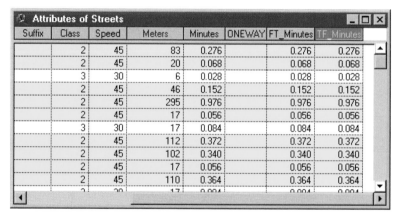

The arterial streets are selected.

Suppose that southbound rush-hour traffic takes twice as long as usual. This means that you need to double the current values in the TF_Minutes field.

7   Make sure the TF_Minutes field is highlighted in the table. Click the Calculate button to open the Field Calculator. In the *Fields* scrolling list, double-click on the [TF_Minutes] field. In the *Requests* list, double-click the "*" (multiplication) operator, then type **2**. Click OK.

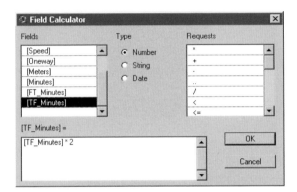

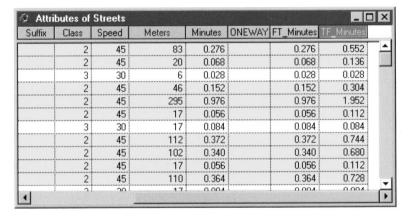

Suffix	Class	Speed	Meters	Minutes	ONEWAY	FT_Minutes	TF_Minutes
	2	45	83	0.276		0.276	0.552
	2	45	20	0.068		0.068	0.136
	3	30	6	0.028		0.028	0.028
	2	45	46	0.152		0.152	0.304
	2	45	295	0.976		0.976	1.952
	2	45	17	0.056		0.056	0.112
	3	30	17	0.084		0.084	0.084
	2	45	112	0.372		0.372	0.744
	2	45	102	0.340		0.340	0.680
	2	45	17	0.056		0.056	0.112
	2	45	110	0.364		0.364	0.728
	2	30	17	0.084		0.084	0.084

The TF_Minutes values for the selected arterials are doubled.

8   From the Table menu, choose Stop Editing. At the prompt, click Yes to save your edits. Click the Select None button to clear the selected records, then close the table.

9   In the view, double-click on the *Streets* theme to open the Legend Editor. Double-click on the symbol for Arterial streets to open the Symbol Palette. In the Pen Palette, click on the first line symbol to select it. In the Legend Editor, click Apply, then close both the Symbol Palette and the Legend Editor.

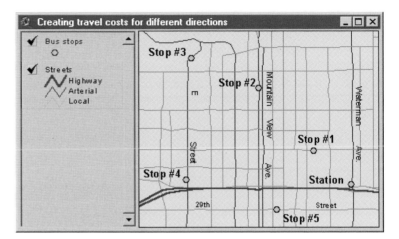

10 Make sure the *Streets* theme is active. From the Network menu, choose Find Best Route. When the *Route1* result theme is added to the view, open the Theme Properties dialog and change its name to **Bus route 6-9 am**. Click OK.

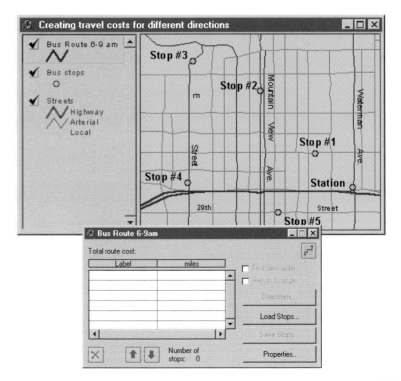

11   In the Problem Definition dialog, click the Load Stops button and choose the *Bus Stops* theme. Click OK to load the stops. Click the "Return to origin" check box so that it's turned on.

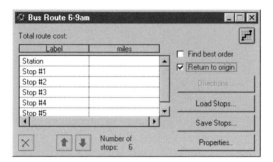

12   In the Problem Definition dialog, click the Properties button. In the *Cost field* drop-down list, choose "Minutes (directional)." In the *Working units* drop-down list, choose "hh:mm:ss." Click OK.

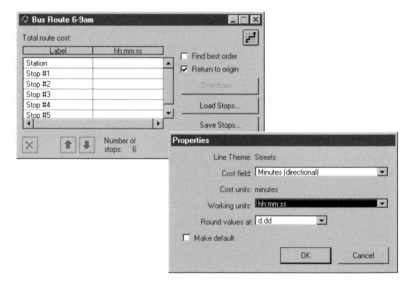

The cost field "Minutes (directional)" tells Network Analyst to use both the FT_Minutes and TF_Minutes values as the travel times when calculating the best route. (This special cost field name is used only when the network theme table contains both directional and nondirectional cost fields—like the ordinary Minutes field— so that Network Analyst can distinguish between them.)

13   Click the Solve button.

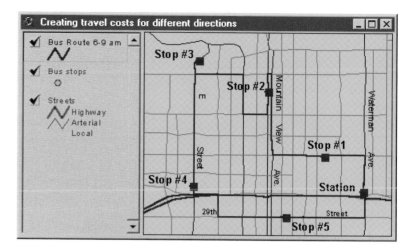

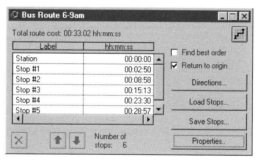

During morning rush hour, the bus route takes on average about 33 minutes to complete—somewhat longer than the usual 26 minutes and 55 seconds that you calculated in the previous exercise.

14   From the File menu, choose Close All. Again from the File menu, choose Close Project. Click No when you're prompted to save your changes.

If you're going on to the next chapter, leave ArcView GIS running. Otherwise, choose Exit from the File menu.

7

Modeling intersections

Modeling closed streets

Modeling overpasses

Modeling turns

Now that your network data

contains information about one-way streets and directional travel costs, you're ready to add even more traffic rules. Sometimes, streets are closed temporarily (because of accidents or construction) or permanently (so that only pedestrians may go there). Network Analyst needs to know that these streets are forbidden so that it can make valid routes.

Network Analyst also needs to know if some places where lines cross aren't intersections, but rather overpasses or underpasses, where turning is impossible or can be made only on ramps.

And that's not all. In the exercises you've done so far, intersections where turning is possible have failed to include a travel cost. A left turn against oncoming traffic can be like watching a parade. Except for those rare occasions when you go screaming through a yellow light, an intersection takes some time to negotiate.

In this chapter, you'll learn how to set up networks to include traffic rules for closed streets, overpasses, and intersections.

Modeling closed streets

In this exercise, you'll learn about the various methods for modeling closed streets and how to choose the method that best suits your situation. If streets are selected in the view, Network Analyst won't include them when it calculates the route. You can also confine a route to particular streets by defining an expression in the Theme Properties dialog for the network theme.

This exercise uses fictional data and does not represent the actual state of city services.

◆ *E x e r c i s e   7 a*

1   If necessary, start ArcView GIS. Navigate to the \extend\network\ch07 directory
    and open the project "ex07a.apr." When the project opens, you see a view that
    contains a network theme of Santa Barbara.

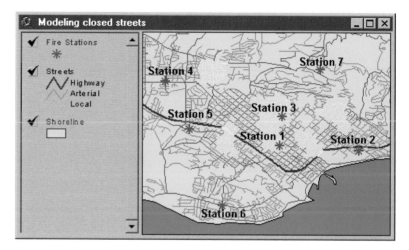

An earthquake has just shaken the area. Your office at City Hall is
inundated with information about fallen overpasses, streets flooded
by ruptured water lines, and roads blocked with debris or traffic.
You've been tracking the damage reports of which roads are closed.
Network Analyst doesn't include selected streets when it calculates
network problems, so you've been using the Query Builder to select
the closed streets. As you can see from the yellow patches in the
view, much of the city is inaccessible.

Setting closed streets. How you set closed streets depends on
how long they'll be closed. If they'll be closed only a short while, there
are two methods to prevent Network Analyst from considering them
part of the network. One is to select the streets using either the Select
Feature tool or the Query Builder and the other is to define a feature
selection for the network theme using the Theme Properties dialog.
The first method highlights closed streets in bright yellow, while the
second displays only the streets that are open to traffic. If the streets
will be closed for a longer period, you have more options. You can put
a value of "N" in the ONEWAY field or put negative values in the cost
field. In the online help, use the Find tab to locate the topic *Setting
closed streets and other streets to avoid.*

2   Make sure the *Streets* theme is active and click the Open Theme Table button. Scroll all the way to the right.

Zip_right	Zip_right4	Tiger_id	Class	Meters	Seconds
		108601941	1	356	35.394
		108601945	1	807	80.232
		108601953	0	329	58.876
		108601954	1	100	9.942
		108601956	1	145	14.416
		108601957	1	44	4.374
		108601958	1	1211	120.396
		108601960	1	187	18.592
93111	1348	108601961	0	89	15.926
93111	1334	108601962	0	20	3.580
93111	1350	108601962	0	222	39.728
93111	1314	108601962	0	241	43.120

The values in the Class field classify the streets into Highway (1), Arterial (2), and Local streets (0). The values in the Seconds field are the travel times that Network Analyst will use to solve the route.

There's a fire near the center of town, but the closest fire stations are boxed in by closed streets and can't respond. You'll use Network Analyst to determine which of the next closest stations can get to the fire.

Emergency crews have cleared the major arteries in the city, but the local streets are still jammed with traffic, debris, and people. The freeway has been damaged in several places and will be closed for a while. You'll define an expression in the Theme Properties dialog so that only arterial streets are included in the analysis.

3   Close the table. With the *Streets* theme active, from the Theme menu, choose Properties. Make sure the Definition icon is selected.

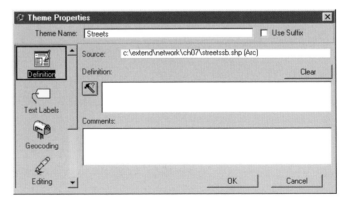

In the Definition box, you can create an expression that determines which theme features are displayed in the view. As far as Network Analyst is concerned, only displayed features represent possible paths.

4   In the dialog, click the Query Builder button. In the *Fields* scrolling list, scroll down and double-click on the [Class] field to add it to the expression box. Click the "=" button, then type **2**. Click OK.

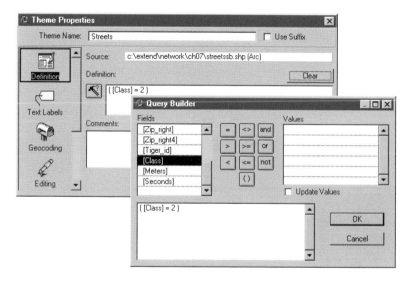

Clicking the Clear button in the Theme Properties dialog will remove the definition.

5   In the Theme Properties dialog, click OK.

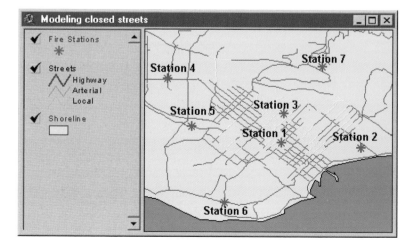

In the view, only arterial streets are now displayed.

6   Make sure the *Streets* theme is active. From the Network menu, choose Find Closest Facility. When the *Fac1* result theme is added to the view, open the Theme Properties dialog and change its name to **Available Stations**. Click OK.

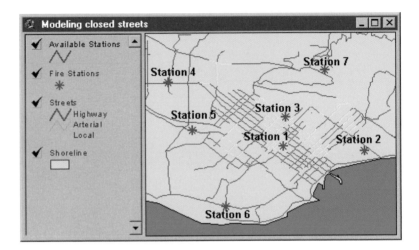

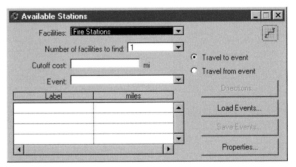

Now you'll enter the address of the fire.

7   With the *Available Stations* theme active, click the Add Location by Address button. In the Locate Address box, type **234 Carrillo St.** Click OK.

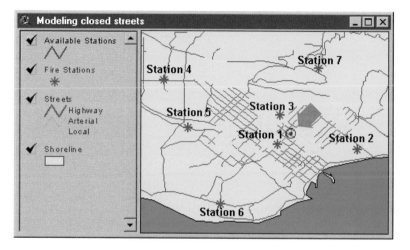

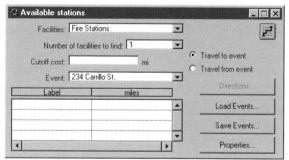

The location of the fire is marked by a green bull's-eye.

8   In the Problem Definition dialog, the *Fire Stations* theme is already selected. In the *Number of facilities to find* drop-down list, choose "2."

9   Click the Properties button to open the Properties dialog. In the *Cost field* drop-down list, choose "Seconds." In the *Working units* drop-down list, choose "hh:mm:ss." Click OK.

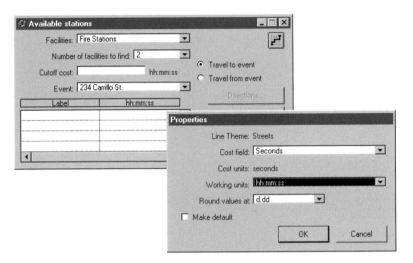

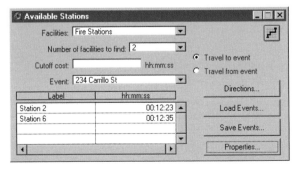

10 In the Problem Definition dialog, click the Solve button.

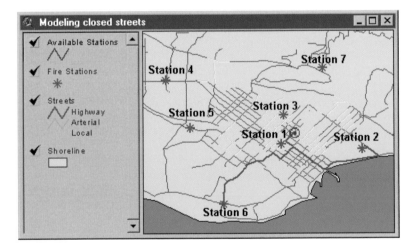

The Problem Definition dialog shows the two stations able to respond the most quickly under the given conditions. Both Station 2 and Station 6 are about twelve-and-a-half minutes away.

11 From the File menu, choose Close All. Again from the File menu, choose Close Project. Click No when you're prompted to save your changes.

If you want to go on to the next exercise, leave ArcView GIS running. Otherwise, choose Exit from the File menu.

Modeling overpasses

You already know that a network theme is made up of interconnected line features. But when lines in a network theme cross each other, it doesn't necessarily mean you can turn there, or even that the two streets meet. If one line segment represents an overpass and the other an underpass, for example, you wouldn't want Network Analyst making a turn where they cross, sending you off a bridge.

In the previous chapter, you learned that nodes exist wherever line segments intersect. This is true as long as the line segments are planar features. Planar features (features that lie on a common plane) represent streets that are actually connected.

It's also possible, however, for line segments to cross without a node at the crossing point. Line segments that cross without "intersecting," in the sense defined above, are called "nonplanar" features to indicate that the streets they represent aren't connected (like overpasses and underpasses).

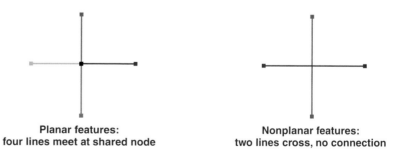

Planar features:
four lines meet at shared node

Nonplanar features:
two lines cross, no connection

Network Analyst only considers lines "connected" if they meet at a node. As it traces paths through a network searching for the best route, it stops at each node and compares all the line segments that intersect there. If there's no node where two lines cross, Network Analyst won't stop there.

Whether features are planar or nonplanar depends on how the data was digitized. Often, data sets will contain both planar and nonplanar features. If a real-world street intersection (where it really is possible to turn) is represented in the network by nonplanar features, you can create a node where the lines cross using the Line Split tool. If, on the other hand, your network shows an intersection (planar features meeting at a node) where the real-world location has an overpass or underpass, you'll need to model the bridge using two fields in the network theme table. These fields, called elevation fields, contain values that tell Network Analyst which of the line segments that meet at the intersection are truly connected, and which are not. The elevation fields don't contain actual elevation values, but rather symbolic values that identify connected line segments.

◆ *E x e r c i s e   7 b*

1   If necessary, start ArcView GIS. Navigate to the \extend\network\ch07 directory and open the project "ex07b.apr." When the project opens, you see a view of the intersection of Highway 60 and Highway 91.

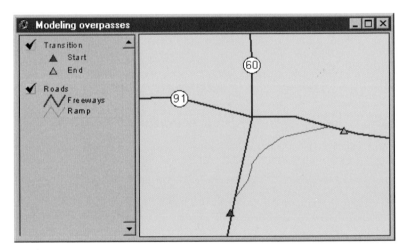

The *Transition* theme contains two stops (though you wouldn't really be stopped there) that you'll use to model travel from State Highway 60 to State Highway 91.

2   Make sure the *Roads* theme is active. From the Network menu, choose Find Best Route. When the *Route1* result theme is added to the view, open the Theme Properties dialog and change its name to **Transition Route**. Click OK.

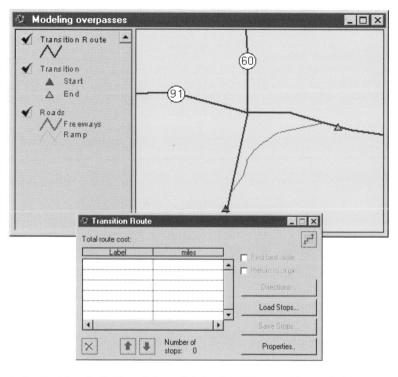

3   In the Problem Definition dialog, click the Load Stops button and choose the *Transition* theme. Click OK to load the stops.

4   In the Problem Definition dialog, click the Properties button. In the *Cost field* drop-down list, choose "Seconds." In the *Working units* drop-down list, choose "hh:mm:ss." Click OK.

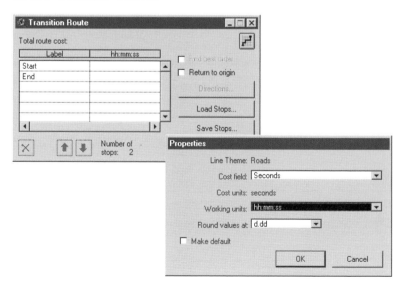

5   Click the Solve button.

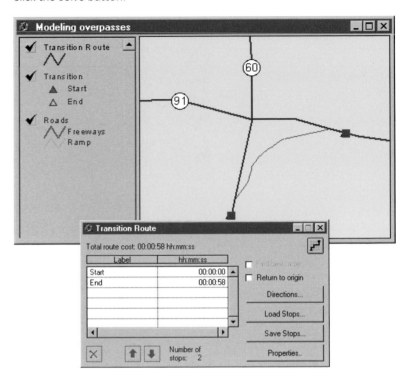

The intersection of the 60 and the 91 is modeled with planar features, so Network Analyst finds the route by turning from the 60 directly onto the 91. This is understandable, because you can drive faster on the highways than you can on the ramp. The problem, of course, is that there isn't actually an intersection where the freeways cross; rather, the 60 passes over the 91. Network Analyst has you making a sharp right turn over the guard rail.

Now you'll tell Network Analyst not to make this turn and to use the ramp instead.

6 Turn off the *Transition Route* theme. Make the *Roads* theme active, then click the Select Feature tool. Draw a box around the intersection to select the four street segments that converge there.

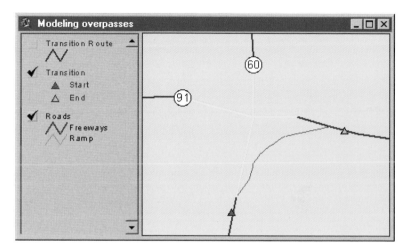

7 With the *Roads* theme active, click the Open Theme Table button. From the Table menu, choose Start Editing. Click the Promote button and make the table wide enough to display all the fields.

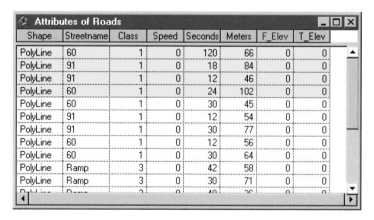

The freeway crossing is represented by four line segments that converge at the freeway overpass. Two belong to the 60 and two to the 91. To make Network Analyst recognize the freeway crossing as an overpass, you need to add two new fields to the network theme table. To save time, these two fields, called F_Elev and T_Elev, have been added for you.

If your line theme contains overpasses and underpasses represented by planar lines, you can prevent Network Analyst from making invalid turns by assigning different elevation values to the line segments. The values needn't represent actual elevation.

Elevation values correspond to line direction. The "From" elevation value is associated with the "From" end of the line, and the "To" elevation value is associated with the "To" end of the line. When lines meet at a node, Network Analyst checks whether they have the same value in the elevation field. Those that do are connected; those that don't are not.

Understanding elevation values

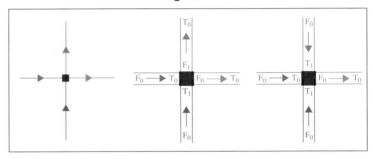

No elevation values—Network Analyst doesn't recognize an overpass or underpass and will turn anywhere.

Elevation values tell Network Analyst that travel is permitted N to S or S to N, and E to W or W to E. The overpass is recognized and no turn is permitted.

The actual line direction and elevation values for Highway 60 and Highway 91.

In this case, you'll give the Highway 60 records a T_Elev value of 1. Because the line segments representing Highway 91 already have a value of 0, Network Analyst will know that it can't make a turn where these lines cross.

8   Select the Edit tool and click in the T_Elev field of the first selected record. (It has a Streetname value of 60.) Type **1** and press the Enter key. In the T_Elev field, do the same for the other selected Highway 60 record.

Shape	Streetname	Class	Speed	Seconds	Meters	F_Elev	T_Elev
PolyLine	60	1	0	120	66	0	1
PolyLine	91	1	0	18	84	0	0
PolyLine	91	1	0	12	46	0	0
PolyLine	60	1	0	24	102	0	1
PolyLine	60	1	0	30	45	0	0
PolyLine	91	1	0	12	54	0	0
PolyLine	91	1	0	30	77	0	0
PolyLine	60	1	0	12	56	0	0
PolyLine	60	1	0	30	64	0	0
PolyLine	Ramp	3	0	42	58	0	0
PolyLine	Ramp	3	0	30	71	0	0

Attributes of Roads

9   From the Table menu, choose Stop Editing. At the prompt, click Yes to save your edits. Click the Select None button to clear the selected records, then close the table.

You have told Network Analyst that the two selected Highway 60 line segments, which meet at their "To" ends and have the same T_Elev value of 1, aren't really connected to the Highway 91 line segments, which share a value of 0. The line segments that are connected have the same value. A node still exists where the four line segments intersect, but now Network Analyst will ignore it.

10   In the view, turn on the *Transition Route* theme. In the Problem Definition
     dialog, click the Solve button.

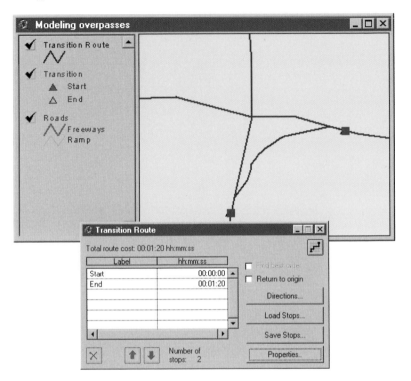

Network Analyst reads the values in the F_Elev and the T_Elev
fields and sees that it can't turn from Highway 60 directly onto
Highway 91. This time, it takes you safely down the ramp.

11   From the File menu, choose Close All. Again from the File menu, choose
     Close Project. Click No when you're prompted to save your changes.

If you want to go on to the next exercise, leave ArcView GIS running. Otherwise, choose Exit from the File menu.

Modeling turns

In the real world, when you arrive at an intersection, you know what to do. If there's a red light, you wait until traffic clears to make a right (at least in most places), or you wait for the green light to make a left, hang a U-turn, or go straight on through.

But in the network world, a turn is more complicated. To Network Analyst, turns are defined in terms of line segments and nodes. Wherever a node exists, a turn can be made from one line segment to another. And continuing in the same direction at a node is also defined as a turn. A "straight" turn, for Network Analyst, is no different from a right or a left.

In this exercise, you'll assign cost values to turns to model the fact that in the real world, traffic flow is impeded by intersections.

It's possible to do this because every line segment and every node in a network theme is identified by a unique number. Every possible turn, therefore, can be identified as a particular combination of these numbers. Once a turn is identified, it can be assigned a cost.

The graphic below shows a left turn. To Network Analyst, the turn begins at line segment 1 (called the "From line" or "From edge"), moves through node 3, and ends at line segment 3 (called the "To line" or "To edge").

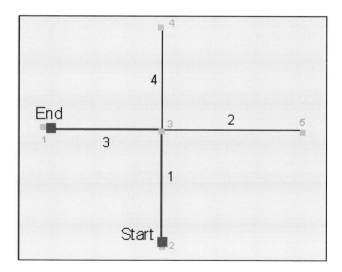

The line segment numbers, node numbers, and cost values for turns are added to a .dbf table, called a turntable, which you create. Each record in the table represents a single turn.

The process of creating a turntable involves several steps that are outlined below. You may not understand these steps now, but you'll work through them in the exercise. Then you can refer back to them when creating turntables on your own.

1   Solve a network problem to create a nodes.dbf table in the network index directory.

2   Use a script to copy the node information to the network theme table. The script copies record numbers for each of the line segments in the network theme.

3   In the view, select the line segments that meet at the intersection where you want to create the turn.

4   In the network theme table, identify the node number that the selected records share.

5   Create an empty .dbf table in the project.

6   Add four fields to the table called Node_, F_Edge, T_Edge, and Seconds. (The cost field must have the same units and field name as the cost field in the network theme table).

7   Add the node number to the turntable.

8   Enter the record number of the line segment where the turn begins in the F_Edge field of the turntable.

9   Enter the record number of the line segment where the turn ends in the T_Edge field of the turntable.

10 Enter the cost of the turn in the Seconds field of the turntable.

11 Continuing adding turns to the turntable until all the turns you want modeled are represented.

12 Save the edits to the turntable.

13 Run a script to declare the turntable so that Network Analyst knows to use it when solving network problems.

14 Solve your network problems.

◆ *E x e r c i s e   7 c*

1　If necessary, start ArcView GIS. Navigate to the \extend\network\ch07 directory and open the project "ex07c.apr." When the project opens, you see a view that contains a network of streets.

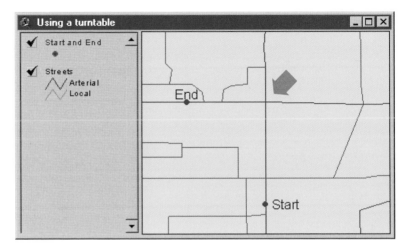

The *Start and End* theme will be used to create a route that makes a left turn at the intersection marked by the arrow.

If you want to create a cost for a turn, the first thing you need to know is the node number of the intersection. However, node numbers aren't readily available. Node information is written to a table called nodes.dbf created in the network index directory when you solve a network problem.

Understanding the network index directory.　The network index directory, created when you open a Problem Definition dialog, contains indexes of travel cost and node information for the network theme. It's created in the same location as your network source data and is given the same name as the network data, with the suffix .nws for shapefiles, .nwc for ArcInfo coverages, and .nwo for CAD drawings. Any project that uses the network data will use the same index directory. For more information, see appendix C, "Data file structures." In the online help, use the Find tab to locate the topic *Network index directory*.

You'll begin by solving a route in order to create a network index directory that contains the nodes.dbf table.

2   With the *Streets* theme active, from the Network menu, choose Find Best Route. When the *Route1* theme is added to the view, open the Theme Properties dialog and change its name to **Left Turn**.

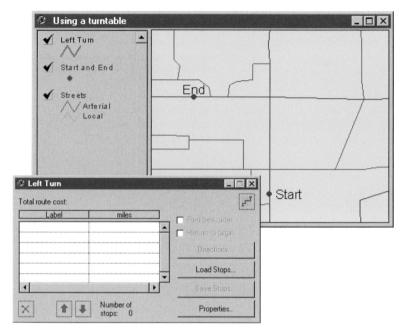

3   In the Problem Definition dialog, click the Load Stops button and choose the *Start and End* theme. Click OK to load the stops.

4   In the Problem Definition dialog, click the Properties button. In the *Cost field* drop-down list, choose "seconds." In the *Round values at* drop-down list, choose "d." Click OK.

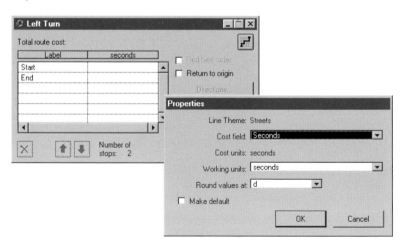

5   Click the Solve button.

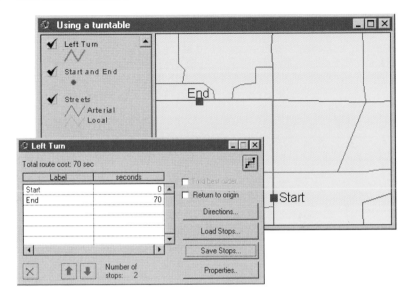

The total route cost of seventy seconds doesn't include the cost of the turn. You'll compare this cost with the cost of the route after you create and apply the turntable.

The next step is to use the nodenum.ave script to copy the node information to the network theme table so you'll be able to tell which nodes are connected to which lines. The script also copies the record number of each line segment to the network theme table. You'll use this information to figure out which From line, To line, and node to place in the turntable for a given turn. The script is available in the online help under the topic *Copying Over Node Numbers*. For convenience, it has already been added to the project for you.

6   In the Project window, click the Scripts icon. Double-click on "nodenum.ave" to open it.

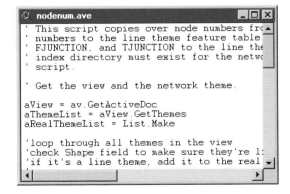

The script operates on the last active document. You need to make sure this was the view.

7 From the Window menu, choose "Using a turntable." Again from the Window menu, choose "nodenum.ave." With the Script document active, click the Run button. In the message box, choose "Streets" as the network theme and click OK. The script is finished running when the Script document becomes active again.

8 Close the Script document. Make the *Streets* theme active in the view and click the Open Theme Table button. Scroll all the way to the right so you can see the last three fields in the table.

Speed	Seconds	Record#	Fjunction	Tjunction
30	8	1	312	311
30	8	2	549	554
45	5	3	216	215
45	3	4	425	431
30	18	5	554	533
45	3	6	534	533
30	18	7	568	554
45	6	8	161	160
30	6	9	160	164
30	7	10	164	177
45	2	11	431	424

Attributes of Streets

Three new fields have been added to the table: Record#, Fjunction, and Tjunction. The Record# field contains an identifier for each line feature in the network. You'll use these values to tell Network Analyst which line feature the turn starts on and which line feature it ends on. The Fjunction and Tjunction fields contain the From node and To node numbers associated with each line segment. For example, the From node for line segment 1 is 312, and the To node for this segment is 311.

When many line segments intersect at a node, the node is shared by all those lines—it's a To node for some and a From node for others. For example, in the Attributes of Streets table, you can see that the line segment with a record number of 5 has a From node of 554, which is also the To node of the line segment with a record number of 7.

By selecting the four line segments that meet at the intersection, then examining their Fjunction and Tjunction values, you can figure out which node they have in common. This intersection node will become a record in the turntable.

9   Make the view active and turn off the *Left Turn* theme. Use the Select Feature tool to drag a small box around the intersection to select the four line segments that meet there.

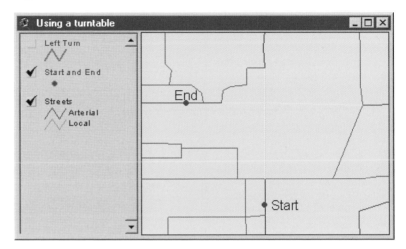

The process will be easier to follow if you label the line segments.

10   With the *Streets* theme active, from the Theme menu, choose Properties. Click on the Text Labels icon. In the *Label Field* drop-down list, choose "Record#" and click OK.

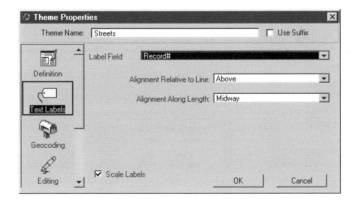

11   Select the Label tool and click on each of the selected line segments to label them in the view. When you're finished, use the Pointer tool to deselect the last selected label.

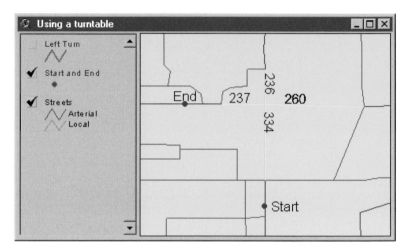

 12   Make the Attributes of Streets table active and click the Promote button.

Speed	Seconds	Record	Fjunction	Tjunction
45	50	236	263	264
45	12	237	263	210
45	60	260	328	263
45	20	334	262	263
30	8	1	312	311
30	8	2	549	554
45	5	3	216	215
45	3	4	425	431
30	18	5	554	533
45	3	6	534	533
30	18	7	568	554
45	6	8	161	169

The node number of the intersection is the one that's shared (either as an Fjunction or a Tjunction node) by all four selected line segments. It just takes a moment to see that this is node number 263. This is the node you want to add to the turntable.

Ordinarily, you would need to create a new .dbf table and add the fields. To save time, this has been done for you.

13   Close the Attributes of Streets table. In the Project window, click the Tables icon and open turntable.dbf.

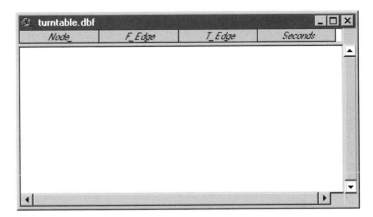

The turntable must contain four fields: the Node field (called Node_, Node#, or Junction), the From and To line segment fields (called F_Edge and T_Edge, F-Edge and T-Edge, Arc1_ and Arc2_, or Arc1# and Arc2#), and finally the cost field. The turntable itself, however, can be called anything you like.

14   From the Table menu, choose Start Editing. From the Edit menu, choose Add Record. Select the Edit tool and click in the empty cell in the Node_ field. Type **263** and press Enter.

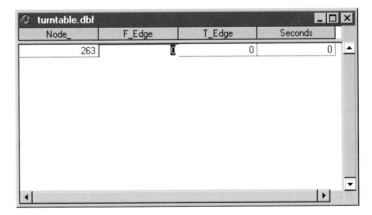

You want to model a left turn, from the line labeled 334 in the view to the line labeled 237. You'll enter these values in the F_Edge (From line) and T_Edge (To line) fields.

15 With the cursor in the F_Edge field, type **334**, then press Enter. In the T_Edge field, type **237**, then press Enter.

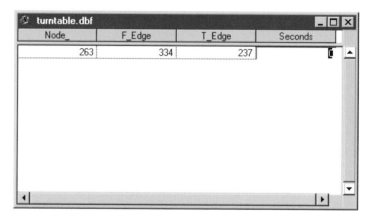

The Seconds field will contain the cost of making the turn. It's a left turn, so it probably takes longer, on average, than turning right or going straight. You'll use a value of 45 seconds to model this turn.

16 In the Seconds field, type **45**, then press Enter.

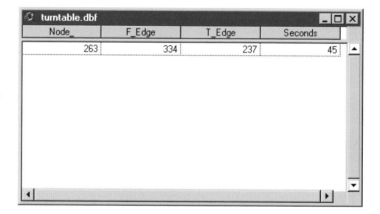

If you wanted to model additional turns, you'd continue adding records to the turntable—one for each turn—and update them with the intersection node number, the From and To line numbers, and the cost value of the turn.

You don't have to represent all turns in the network in the turntable. If the turn doesn't have a record in the turntable, Network Analyst assumes it has no cost. A negative cost value in the turntable indicates that the turn is prohibited.

17 From the Table menu, choose Stop Editing. At the prompt, click Yes to save your changes.

Network Analyst doesn't know to use the information in the turntable until you tell it to by running a script called declare.ave. Once a turntable has been applied to a network theme, the turntable information will be used in all subsequent routes in the view that use the network theme. The declare.ave script can be found in the online help under the topic *Declaring a Turntable*. A modified version of the script has already been loaded into the project for you.

18 Close the turntable.dbf table. In the Project window, click on the Scripts icon and open the script declare.ave. From the Window menu, choose "Using a turntable." Again from the Window menu, choose "declare.ave." Click the Run button.

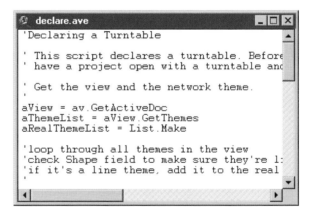

```
'Declaring a Turntable

' This script declares a turntable. Before
' have a project open with a turntable and

' Get the view and the network theme.
'
aView = av.GetActiveDoc
aThemeList = aView.GetThemes
aRealThemeList = List.Make

'loop through all themes in the view
'check Shape field to make sure they're l:
'if it's a line theme, add it to the real
'
```

19   The script displays a list of all the line themes in the view. Choose *Streets* and click OK.

The script displays a list of all the tables in the project. Choose "turntable.dbf" and click OK. Click OK in the message box that tells you that the turntable has been declared.

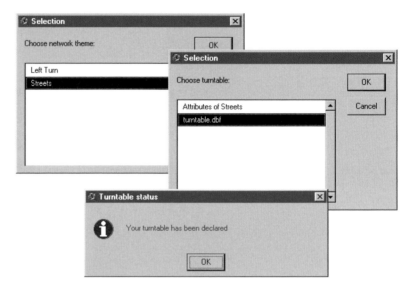

Now you'll solve the route with the turntable information applied.

20   Close the Script document. With the *Streets* theme active in the view, click the Clear Selected Features button. Turn on the *Left Turn* theme.

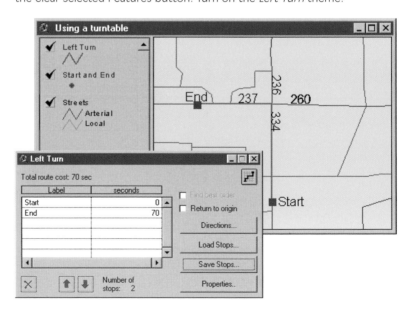

21 In the Problem Definition dialog, click the Solve button.

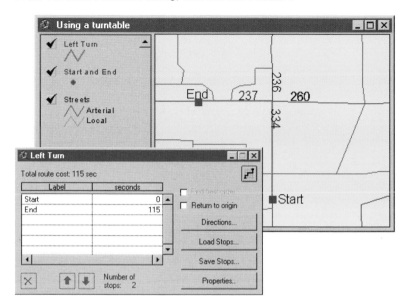

The new route cost is 115 seconds, compared to the 70 seconds when you solved it without the turntable. The difference of 45 seconds is equal to the travel cost you assigned to the turn.

When you solve the problem for the first time after declaring the turntable, the travel cost units may be set back to miles. If this happens, click the Properties button and set the Cost field to Seconds. Click OK, then click the Solve button again. The results should now be properly reported in seconds.

22 From the File menu, choose Close All. Again from the File menu, choose Close Project. Click No when you're prompted to save your changes.

If you're continuing on to the next section of the book, leave ArcView GIS running. Otherwise, choose Exit from the File menu.

8

Introducing ArcView Spatial Analyst

Introducing ArcView Spatial Analyst

Exploring ArcView Spatial Analyst

POINTS, LINES, AND POLYGONS

are good at representing geographic objects with distinct shapes. They're less good with geographic objects that are distributed continuously across a surface. Think of temperature. You can't go someplace where there isn't one. It's cold in some spots and hot in others, but temperature itself is continuous. So is elevation. So are land cover, noise levels, and chemical concentrations. None of these things has a shape to speak of (although the surfaces they're found on do). What they have instead are measurable values for any given location.

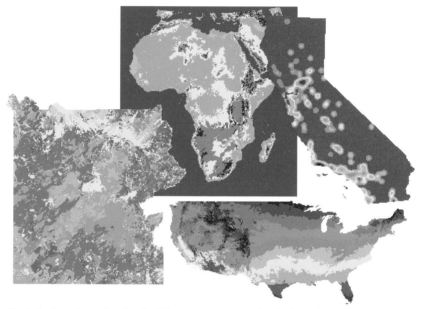

Clockwise from top: elevation in Africa; average ozone density in California for 1998; U.S. average annual temperatures for a thirty-year period; varieties of land cover in Yellowstone National Park.

Introducing ArcView Spatial Analyst

ArcView Spatial Analyst provides a way to represent and analyze geographic objects of this kind. (It sounds odd to call them objects, but it's a convenient term.) Instead of drawing them as shapes, it divides the surface on which they're distributed into a matrix of identically sized square cells. Each cell is filled in with a number that stores the object's value at that location. So if you were representing average daily temperature in degrees Centigrade, the cells would hold numbers like 13, 20, 26, and so on.

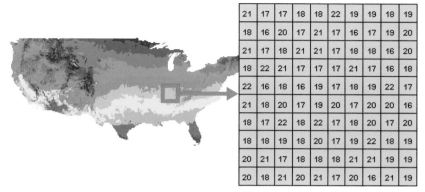

21	17	17	18	18	22	19	19	18	19
18	16	20	17	21	17	16	17	19	20
21	17	18	21	21	17	18	18	16	20
18	22	21	17	17	17	21	17	16	18
22	16	18	16	19	17	18	19	22	17
21	18	20	17	19	20	17	20	20	16
18	17	22	18	22	17	18	20	17	20
18	18	19	18	20	17	19	22	18	19
20	21	17	18	18	18	21	21	19	19
20	18	21	20	21	17	20	16	21	19

The area bordered by the red box would be divided into many more cells than are shown here, but the principle is the same.

When you represent geographic objects as numbers in cells, you're working with the raster data model. (Points, lines, and polygons belong to the vector data model.) In ArcView Spatial Analyst, the raster data sets themselves are called grids.

There are a lot of things that ArcView Spatial Analyst can do with grids. It can derive new information from information that already exists.

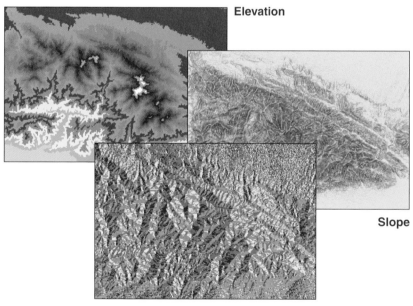

Elevation

Slope

Aspect (direction of slope)

From a grid of elevation, ArcView Spatial Analyst can make grids of slope and aspect, helping you decide where it's too steep to build or where you'll get maximum sun exposure. It can also figure out which way water will flow, and where it will drain, allowing you to model stream networks and watersheds.

ArcView Spatial Analyst can estimate values for an entire surface from a limited number of sample points. This process, called interpolation, lets you build a landscape from a small amount of data, or predict where resources are likely to be found.

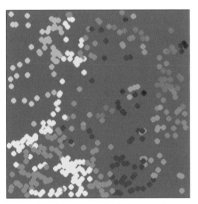 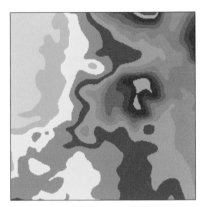

The point theme on the left contains 414 measured elevation points. The grid theme interpolated from it has over 50,000 estimated elevation values.

ArcView Spatial Analyst can measure how far away things are from one another and how densely they're concentrated.

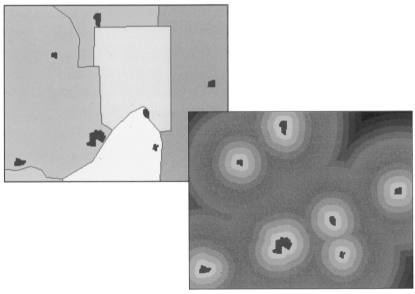

On the left are airports (green polygon features). On the right is a distance grid calculated from them. Each cell in the grid stores the distance to the nearest airport as its value.

Different grids can be overlaid and queried.

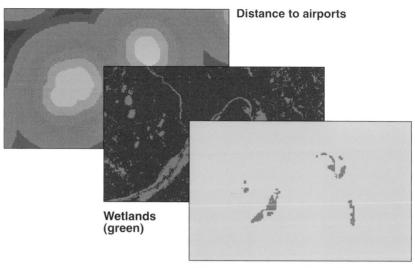

Distance to airports

Wetlands (green)

Wetlands near airports (red)

A distance grid is overlaid with a grid of wetlands to find wetlands within 2 kilometers of an airport. These areas need protection.

ArcView Spatial Analyst does what it does thanks to map algebra. Map algebra is math applied to grids, and it's possible because grids are geographically referenced arrays of numbers. If you stack them on top of each other like a mathematical sandwich, you can do anything from simple arithmetic to the most sophisticated algorithms.

Grid A ≤ 2   **AND**   **Grid B = 3**

2	1	1	1	3			2	3	4	2	1
3	1	5	2	0	1	0	0	0	3	3	3	3
2	5	3	3	0	1	0	1	1	4	2	3	5
3	2	2	2	0	0	0	0	0	5	1	3	2
4	1	1	4	0	0	0	1	0	5	2	3	3
				0	0	0	0	1				

Grid C

1 = True
0 = False

A logical query on two overlaid grids (A and B). In grid A, ArcView Spatial Analyst checks for cells with values less than or equal to 2. In grid B, it checks for cells with values equal to 3. The results of the query are stored in grid C. Spatially corresponding cells that meet both conditions are assigned the value 1. All other cells are assigned 0.

With ArcView Spatial Analyst, you can model the environment in ever-increasing layers of complexity. Elevation, slope, land use, zoning, plant and animal habitat, sensitive areas, soil, geology—all these can be combined with vector data like roads, rivers, administrative boundaries, and land parcels as a basis for planning and action.

The following example is a simple model for assessing wildfire risk. Three factors are considered: slope, vegetation type, and the amount of rainfall received in the preceding year. Each is assumed to be an equally important risk factor.

From a grid of elevation, a grid of slope is derived.

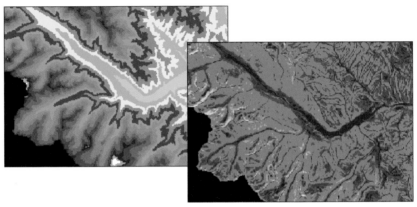

The grid on the left shows elevation. Blue and green areas are low; oranges and browns are high. On the right is a grid of slope. The values are symbolized with blue (flattest), green, and yellow (steepest).

The other two grids are of vegetation and precipitation.

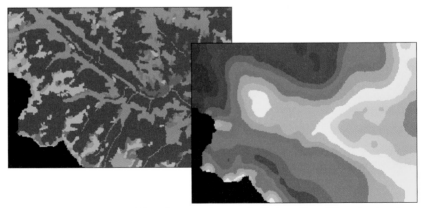

On the left is a land cover grid. Each vegetation type is displayed in a different color. On the right is a rainfall grid. The values range from browns (driest) to yellows, greens, and blues (wettest).

The first step is to assign risk to each grid individually. Slopes of 35 degrees or more are considered a risk factor. So are areas of brushy chaparral. And so are areas that received 25 inches of rain or less during the previous year. From these grids, three new grids are created identifying the risk areas. Each new grid has just two cell values: 1, for areas of risk, and 0, for areas of no risk.

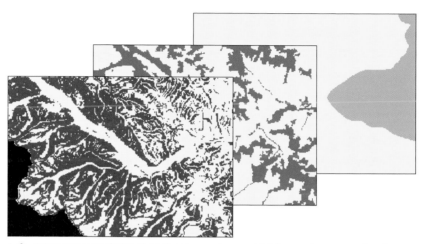

Left: green areas are slopes of 35 degrees or steeper. Middle: purple areas are brushy chaparral. Right: orange areas received no more than 25 inches of rain.

The next step is to make an overall evaluation of risk. Areas that are neither steep, nor brushy, nor dry have a negligible fire risk. Areas meeting just one of the three conditions are low risk. Areas meeting two conditions have a moderate risk. High-risk areas satisfy all three conditions.

ArcView Spatial Analyst takes the three grids and adds the values of their spatially corresponding cells. The final fire risk grid looks like this:

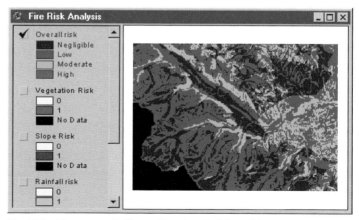

The high-risk areas are in the southeast part of the grid.

Many factors were left out of this analysis. What about prevailing wind conditions? What about the locations of roads or campsites? And each of the three input grids had only two values (risk or no risk) assigned to it instead of a range. Furthermore, each factor was considered equally important, rather than weighted.

The point, however, was not to make a realistic model, but to show that the value of ArcView Spatial Analyst is not in abstract queries or calculations, but in helping you use information to solve problems. ArcView Spatial Analyst can't tell you what factors are important in determining wildfire risk, or in choosing a site for a dam, or in balancing growth with environmental protection, or anything else. What it can do is analyze all the factors you supply in any combination you choose and give you a firm basis for making decisions.

Exploring ArcView Spatial Analyst

In this exercise, you'll add an elevation grid theme of the San Gabriel Mountains to a view and symbolize it. You'll create a distance grid to find distances to the nearest roads in these mountains. And you'll derive a hillshade grid that lets you display the elevation surface in relief.

◆ *E x e r c i s e   8 a*

1   If necessary, start ArcView GIS. In the Welcome to ArcView GIS dialog, select "Open an existing project" and click OK. (If ArcView GIS is running and you've already dismissed the Welcome dialog, choose Open Project from the File menu.)

2   In the Open Project dialog, navigate to the extend\spatial\ch08 directory and open the project "ex08a.apr."

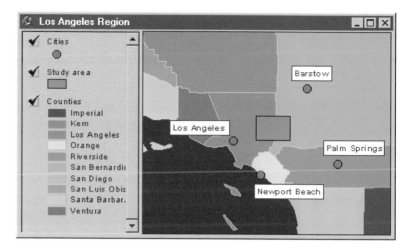

When the project opens, you see a view of the area around Los Angeles. The *Study area* theme, symbolized by a green rectangle, covers part of the San Gabriel Mountains range.

3   Close the view and open the San Gabriel Mountains view.

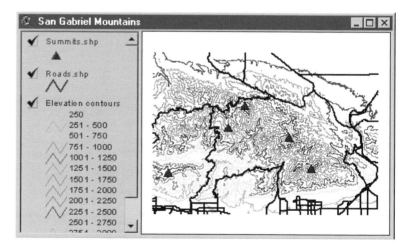

The view contains three vector themes: a point theme of summits, a line theme of roads, and a line theme of elevation contours. (Contour lines connect points of equal elevation.)

First, you'll load the ArcView Spatial Analyst extension.

4 From the File menu, choose Extensions to open the Extensions dialog. Scroll through the list of available extensions and make sure none of them is turned on. Click on the Spatial Analyst check box to turn it on. Click OK.

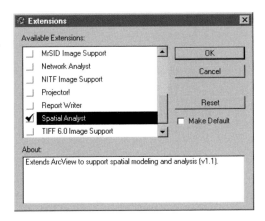

In the remaining exercises in this section, the ArcView Spatial Analyst extension will already be loaded when you open a project.

When the extension is loaded, the ArcView GIS interface changes. There are two new menus, the Analysis menu and the Surface menu. There's also a new button (the Histogram button) and a new tool (the Contour tool). Both are disabled because there's no active grid theme in the view.

5   Click the Add Theme button. In the Add Theme dialog, set the *Data Source Types* drop-down list to "Grid Data Source." Navigate to the extend\spatial\ch08 directory and add the *Sgm_elev* theme to the view. In the view Table of Contents, make the theme active and turn it on.

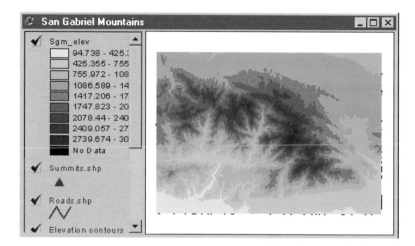

The grid theme displays elevation as a continuous surface (every location on the theme has an elevation value). You'll rename the theme and change its randomly selected color scheme.

6   From the Theme menu, choose Properties to open the Theme Properties dialog. Rename the theme **Elevation in meters** and click OK.

Make the *Elevation contours* theme active. From the Theme menu, choose Hide/Show Legend to hide its legend, then turn it off. Make the *Elevation in meters* theme active and drag it to the bottom of the Table of Contents.

7　Double-click on "Elevation in meters" to open the Legend Editor. Click the Classify button and set the number of classes to 13. (This number makes best use of the color gradations in preset color ramps.) Click OK. From the *Color Ramps* drop-down list, select "Elevation #1." Click Apply, then close the Legend Editor.

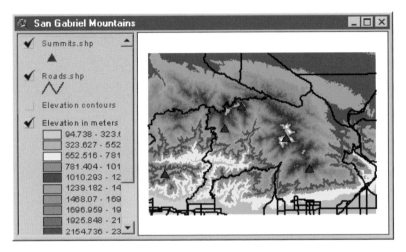

The grid is displayed in a predefined elevation color scheme. The vector themes are drawn on top of it.

8　From the View menu, choose Properties to open the View Properties dialog.

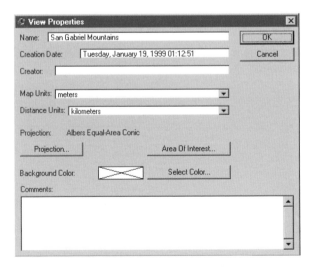

The map units are meters and the distance units are kilometers. The view projection is Albers Equal-Area Conic.

Grid themes and map projections.   Projecting a view has no effect on a grid theme. Unlike feature themes, you can't project grid themes "on the fly" in ArcView GIS by setting a projection in the View properties. This is seldom a problem, as most grid data sets that you acquire will already be in projected coordinates. Setting a projection in a view simply allows you to align unprojected feature data with your projected grid. It's important that your grid data be projected, because many analytical operations aren't valid on unprojected grids. For more information, see appendix B, "Aligning your data."

9   Close the View Properties dialog and select the Identify tool. With the *Elevation in meters* theme active, click on a few different locations on the elevation surface. Wherever you click, an elevation value is reported.

Make the *Summits.shp* theme active and identify a couple of summits. The *Summits.shp* theme contains a name attribute, but no elevation values. Close the Identify Results window.

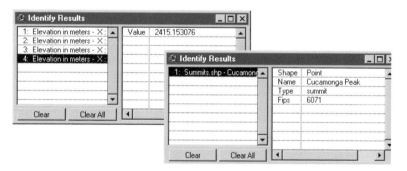

10   With the *Summits.shp* theme active, hold down the Shift key and click on the *Elevation in meters* theme to make it active as well.

Select the Zoom In tool and zoom in on any summit. Select the Identify tool and identify the summit. The Identify Results window displays information for both active themes, letting you find the elevation of any summit. Close the Identify Results window.

Suppose that each summit is being considered as the site of a new lookout station. One factor in the decision could be the site's accessibility, as measured by its distance to the nearest road. You'll create a distance grid to make this analysis.

11   Click the Zoom to Full Extent button, then click on the roads theme to make it the only active theme.

12   From the Analysis menu, choose Find Distance. In the Output Grid Specifica-
     tion dialog, set the *Output Grid Extent* drop-down list to "Same as Elevation
     in meters." (This will make your new grid the same size as the existing eleva-
     tion grid.)

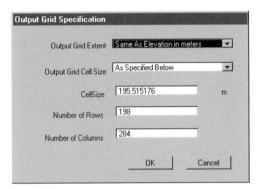

13   Leave the other settings as they are and click OK. When the *Distance to
     Roads.shp* grid theme is added to the view, make it active and turn it on.
     In the Table of Contents, drag it below the summits and roads themes.

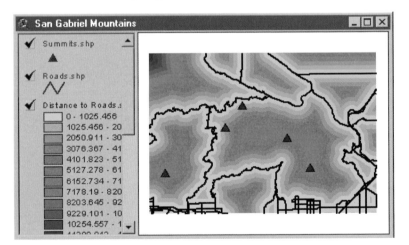

The distance grid makes straight-line measurements from cell center to cell center. When you use it to find the summit closest to a road, the effects of slope won't be considered.

14 Make sure the distance grid theme is active. Hold down the Shift key and click on the summits theme to make it active as well. Zoom in on each summit and identify it to find its distance to the nearest road.

You should find that the closest summit to a road is Mount Baden–Powell, about 1,564 meters away. The next closest is South Mount Hawkins, about 2,150 meters away. (There are better ways to get this information than by zooming and identifying. You'll learn how to create grid statistics in chapter 14.)

Now you'll create another grid, one that can be derived from elevation. Hillshade grids show the effects of illumination on an elevation surface.

15 Click the Zoom to Full Extent button. Click on the *Distance to Roads.shp* theme to make it the only active theme. From the Theme menu, choose Hide/Show Legend to hide its legend, then turn it off.

16 Click on the *Elevation in meters* theme to make it active. From the Surface menu, choose Compute Hillshade.

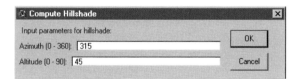

In the Compute Hillshade dialog, the default values position the sun in the northwest (azimuth values run clockwise from 0, which is due north). Its altitude is 45 degrees above the horizon (90 is directly overhead).

17 Click OK to accept the defaults. When the *Hillshade of Elevation in meters* grid theme is added to the view, turn it on.

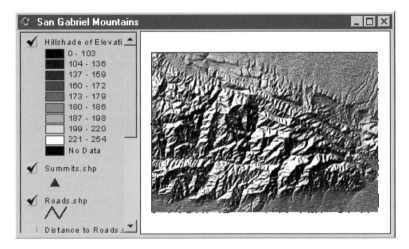

Each cell in the hillshade grid is assigned a number between 0 and 255, corresponding to a shade of gray. The effect simulates light and shadow, giving a relief perspective.

18 Make the hillshade theme active. From the Theme menu, choose Properties to open the Theme Properties dialog.

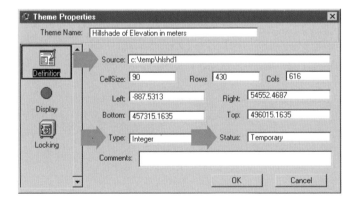

The grid data set has a directory path (to your c:\temp or working directory) and a name, "hlshd1," for "Hillshade1." Note that its status is "Temporary." By default, ArcView Spatial Analyst doesn't save to disk the grids you create. The reason is that you frequently make intermediary grids that you don't intend to keep, as well as grids that turn out not to be exactly what you wanted. The grid's type is "Integer."

Integer and floating-point grids. There are two kinds of grid themes. Integer grids (like the hillshade grid) store integers as cell values and have theme tables. Floating-point grids (like the elevation and distance grids) store numbers with decimal places. Floating-point grids don't have theme tables because the number of possible unique cell values is too large. Generally speaking, floating-point grids represent continuous data, that is, data that lacks sharp boundaries and varies by magnitude (elevation, for instance, or chemical concentrations). Integer grids represent discrete data. Discrete data has well-defined boundaries, and its grid cell values are numeric codes standing for descriptions or categories rather than measurements. Zoning is a typical example, where cell values like 100, 200, and 300 might stand for categories like "residential," "commercial," and "industrial." There is, however, no perfectly clear division between continuous and discrete data. Phenomena represented by integer grids, like hillshade, soil type, and land cover, have continuous properties. Conversely, measured phenomena (like elevation) are often represented by integer grids. In the online help, use the Find tab to locate the topic *Frequently asked questions about grid themes.*

19   Close the Theme Properties dialog. Make sure the hillshade theme is active. From the Theme menu, choose Save Data Set. In the Save Data Set dialog, accept the default grid name and path. Click OK.

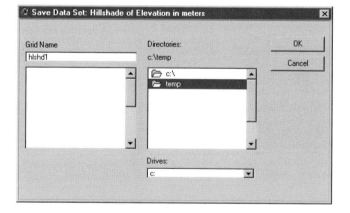

The grid data set is saved to your c:\temp directory. (You can also save a temporary grid simply by saving the project.) Don't try to delete this grid on your own. You'll do that in the next chapter.

Finally, you'll apply the hillshade grid's relief effect to the *Elevation in meters* theme.

20   Turn off the hillshade, summits, and roads themes. Double-click on the *Elevation in meters* theme to open the Legend Editor.

At the bottom of the Legend Editor, click the Advanced button. In the Advanced Options dialog, set the *Brightness Theme* drop-down list to "Hillshade of Elevation in meters." Click OK.

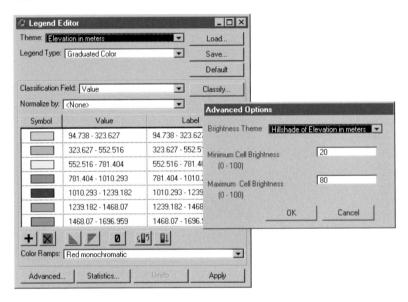

21   Click Apply in the Legend Editor and close the Legend Editor.

The hillshade grid's cell values vary the brightness of the *Elevation in meters* theme. The result is a realistic surface.

22   From the File menu, choose Close All. Again from the File menu, choose Close Project. Click No when you're prompted to save your changes.

If you're going on to the next chapter, leave ArcView GIS running. Otherwise, choose Exit from the File menu.

9

Investigating grids

Identifying and displaying grids

Querying and managing grids

WITH FEATURE DATA
in standard ArcView GIS, you know how to do the basics: identify features, edit a legend, select records with the Query Builder, make a chart, and so on. Most of these operations are the same when you use grid data, but there are variations.

You saw one, for instance, in the last exercise, when you applied a brightness theme in the Legend Editor to make an elevation surface stand out in relief.

The way you get information on grid themes is different. You can use the Identify tool on particular grid cells to get their values, but grids are arrays of cells and you're usually interested in the big picture. You get this aggregate information with histograms—charts that show you the distribution of cell values in a grid.

Grid queries are similar to feature theme queries, but more powerful because you can use multiple themes. (For example, a query might use both a land cover grid and a city general plan grid to find forested areas slated for housing development.) Whereas the result of a query on a feature theme is a record selection, a grid theme query creates a new grid.

Grid data sets are stored on disk in two separate directories. This means they can't be copied or deleted in the usual way with your operating system's file manager. The ArcView GIS Source Manager is a tool for safely managing grid data on disk.

Identifying and displaying grids

In this exercise, you'll identify individual grid cell values, create histograms to see the overall value distribution, and modify a grid legend. You'll work with a grid of average rainfall for the state of Oregon and an elevation grid of Curry County in the southwest corner of the state.

◆ *Exercise 9a*

1   If necessary, start ArcView GIS. Navigate to the extend\spatial\ch09 directory and open the project "ex09a.apr." When the project opens, you see a view with Oregon rainfall data.

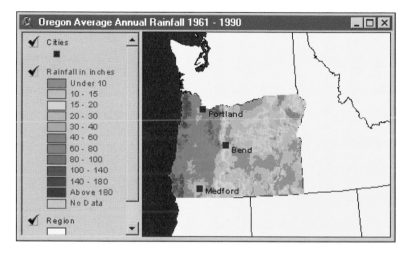

The rainfall theme is a grid theme with a custom precipitation legend. (The cities and region themes are feature themes.) You'll zoom in and identify some grid cells.

2   Make sure the *Rainfall in inches* theme is active. Click the Zoom to Active Theme(s) button.

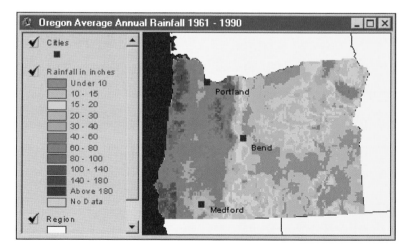

This won't be close enough. At this scale (about 1:9,000,000), you could click on a cell and identify it, but you wouldn't know which cell it was.

3 Select the Zoom In tool and zoom in on the southwest corner of the state. Your map scale should be about 1:750,000. Select the Identify tool and identify a few cells.

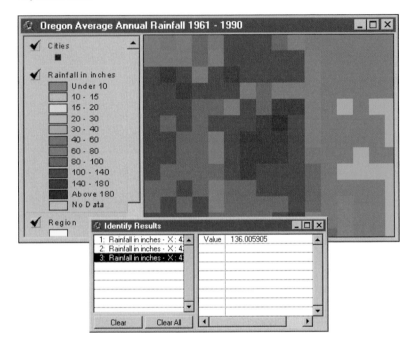

At this scale, the cellular structure of the grid is apparent and you can see the cells you identify.

Identifying cells is fine when you're interested in the values of a few specific locations, but it doesn't tell you anything about the overall distribution of values. Your map display and theme legend do give you a sense of this (that's what maps are for), but a histogram breaks the information down as a bar chart.

4   Close the Identify Results window. Click the Zoom to Active Theme(s) button. Click the Histogram button to create a histogram of the rainfall theme. Resize the histogram to make the entire legend visible.

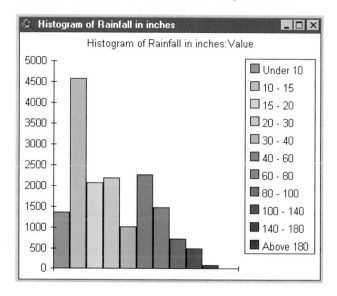

The histogram legend matches the theme legend in the Table of Contents. The y-axis shows the number of grid cells in each rainfall class. There are about 1,400 cells with values under 10 inches, about 4,500 cells with values between 10 and 15 inches, and so on. (You can use the Identify tool on each column to get an exact count.) The predominant rainfall value in Oregon is between 10 and 15 inches per year.

By redefining classes in the Legend Editor, you change the way your histogram values are reported.

Histograms can also be used to get information about specific areas of a grid theme. You'll find out about the rainfall patterns around the city of Bend.

5 Close the histogram. In the view, make the *Cities* theme active. Use the Select Feature tool to select the city of Bend. From the Theme menu, choose Create Buffers to start the Create Buffers wizard.

In the first panel, click the radio button to buffer "the features of a theme." Make sure that the theme is *Cities* and that the check box to "use only the selected features" is checked. Click the Next button.

In the second panel, click to buffer features "at a specified distance." Type **50** in the input box. Make sure that the distance units are set to miles, then click the Next button.

In the third panel, save the buffer "as graphics in the view." Click the Finish button.

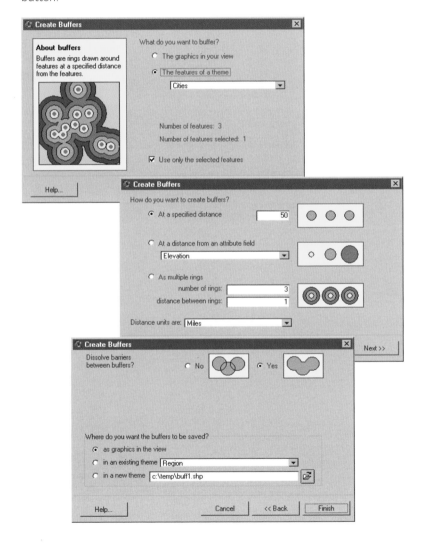

A circle with a 50-mile radius is drawn around Bend.

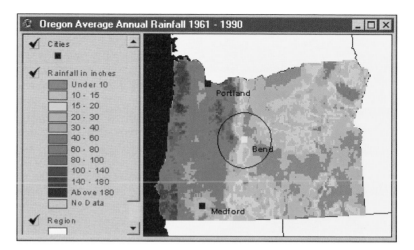

6   Make the *Rainfall in inches* theme active. Select the buffer graphic with the Pointer tool, then click the Histogram button. Resize the histogram to make the entire legend visible.

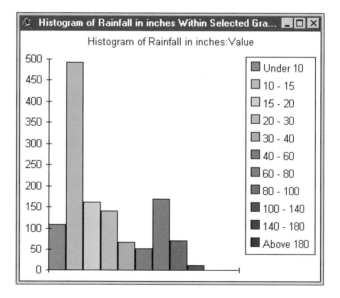

Values are displayed for only those grid cells within a 50-mile radius of Bend (as indicated in the title bar). The most prevalent values are still between 10 and 15 inches a year, but higher amounts aren't uncommon.

7   Close the histogram and the view. Open the Curry County, Oregon, view.

The view contains an elevation theme symbolized by a red mono-chromatic color ramp. You'll apply an elevation color ramp to the legend. You'll also change the symbol for No Data values (cells that have no elevation values because they lie outside the Curry County boundary) from black to transparent.

8   With the *Elevation in meters* theme active, click the Zoom to Active Theme(s) button.

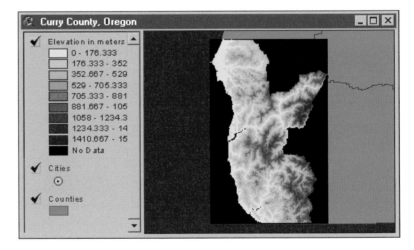

Because grids are composed of rows and columns of square cells, their spatial extents are always rectangular. This wasn't obvious with the Oregon rainfall theme because the No Data area was sym-bolized as transparent. In this elevation theme, the No Data area is black.

9   Double-click on the *Elevation in meters* theme to open the Legend Editor.
    From the *Color Ramps* drop-down list, select "Elevation #1."

    Scroll to the bottom of the list of symbols and double-click on the black
    symbol representing No Data. In the Color Palette, select the transparent
    symbol. Click Apply in the Legend Editor, then close the Legend Editor and
    the Symbol Palette.

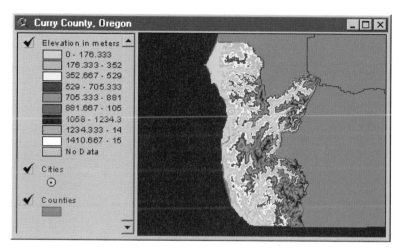

You could go on to make further refinements to the legend, such as
manually defining a class that had only values of zero. This would
let you distinguish areas of water at sea level from low-lying land.

The only available legend type for floating-point grids is Graduated Color
and the only classification types are Equal Interval and Standard Deviation. Integer grids can have either a Graduated Color or Unique Value
legend type and can use all standard ArcView GIS classification types.

---

10 From the File menu, choose Close All. Again from the File menu, choose
    Close Project. Click No when you're prompted to save your changes.

    If you want to go on to the next exercise, leave ArcView GIS run-
    ning. Otherwise, choose Exit from the File menu.

Querying and managing grids

In this exercise, you'll symbolize an integer grid theme of vegetation in Curry County. You'll see how cell values are represented in a grid theme table and you'll create a map query involving two grid themes. Finally, you'll learn how to manage grid data sets on disk.

◆ *E x e r c i s e   9 b*

1   If necessary, start ArcView GIS. Navigate to the extend\spatial\ch09 directory and open the project "ex09b.apr."

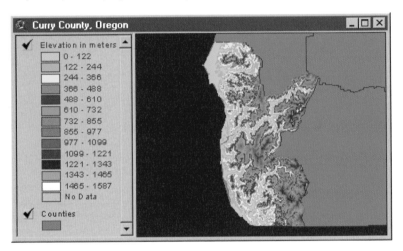

When the project opens, you see a view of Curry County, symbolized as it was at the end of the previous exercise. You'll add a grid theme of vegetation to the project.

2   Click the Add Theme button and navigate to the extend\spatial\ch09 directory. Make sure the *Data Source Types* drop-down list is set to "Grid Data
Source." Select "veggrd" and click OK. In the view Table of Contents, make
the *Veggrd* theme active and turn it on.

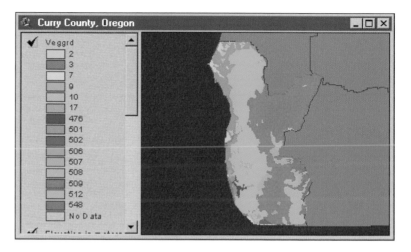

The theme is displayed with a Unique Value legend type in randomly chosen colors.

Integer grids having fewer than thirty-two unique values are displayed
by default with a Unique Value legend. Integer grids having thirty-two or
more unique values are displayed with a Graduated Color legend. The
legend type can be changed in the Legend Editor.

The *Veggrd* theme maps the different types of vegetation in Curry
County. Because each type is labeled with a numeric code, you
can't interpret the map.

3   From the Theme menu, choose Properties to open the Theme Properties
dialog. Change the theme name from *Veggrd* to **Vegetation**. The grid type
is integer. Click OK.

4   Click the Open Theme Table button. Integer grids have theme tables and can therefore store attributes. The Vegetation theme table has four fields, including a Name field describing each vegetation type. Widen the table to see all the fields.

Value	Count	Class	Name
2	5256	Grasses and meadows	agricultural cropland and imp
3	755	Grasses and meadows	urban and industrial areas
7	991	Grasses and meadows	American and European bea
9	110	Grasses and meadows	open water
10	7581	Grasses and meadows	clearings
17	66	Grasses and meadows	Idaho fescue-junegrass cany
476	2682	Woodlands & shrublands	Oregon oak-California oak/D
501	38747	Conifers & mixed forest	Sitka spruce-western hemloc
502	1605	Conifers & mixed forest	redwood forest
506	3118	Conifers & mixed forest	oak-Pacific madrone forests
507	10683	Conifers & mixed forest	Siskiyou mixed evergreen for

Attributes Of Vegetation

5   With the Select tool, click on the record with the value 509 to highlight it.

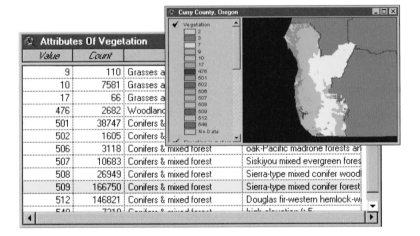

Attributes Of Vegetation

Value	Count		
9	110	Grasses a	
10	7581	Grasses a	
17	66	Grasses a	
476	2682	Woodland	
501	38747	Conifers &	
502	1605	Conifers &	
506	3118	Conifers & mixed forest	oak-Pacific madrone forests ar
507	10683	Conifers & mixed forest	Siskiyou mixed evergreen fores
508	26949	Conifers & mixed forest	Sierra-type mixed conifer wood
509	166750	Conifers & mixed forest	Sierra-type mixed conifer forest
512	146821	Conifers & mixed forest	Douglas fir-western hemlock-wi

Grid cells with the value 509 are highlighted in the view. Selecting a record in a grid theme table is like selecting a record in a feature theme table. As with feature theme operations, many grid operations work on selected sets.

Grid theme tables. Every integer grid has a theme table containing at least two fields: the Value field, representing each unique cell value found in the grid, and the Count field, giving the number of cells that have each value. Grid theme tables can be edited, joined, and queried just like feature theme tables. Do not, however, edit the Value or Count fields, as this may corrupt your data set. In the online help, use the Find tab to locate the topics *Frequently asked questions about grid themes* and *What is a grid theme?*

You'll resymbolize the vegetation theme so that its legend shows descriptions. You'll also apply a color ramp.

6   With the theme table active, click the Select None button. Close the table. In the view, double-click on the *Vegetation* theme to open the Legend Editor.

From the *Values Field* drop-down list, choose "Name." From the *Color Schemes* drop-down list, choose "Warm Tones." Click Apply and close the Legend Editor.

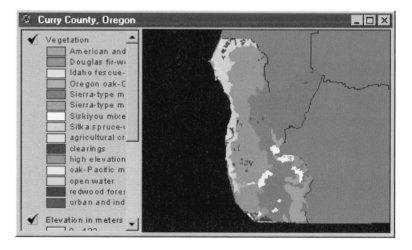

The No Data symbol is no longer displayed. It was turned off when you changed the values field to "Name." You can control the display of the No Data class by clicking the Null Values button in the Legend Editor and turning the No Data check box on or off. No Data values are displayed in the view whether or not the symbol is shown in the theme legend. (In the vegetation theme, No Data values are transparent.)

Now you'll query the *Vegetation* theme to find all areas of a particular vegetation type.

7   From the Analysis menu, choose Map Query to open the Map Query 1 dia-
    log. The *Layers* scrolling box contains five grid layers.

    Double-click on the [Vegetation . Name] layer to add it to the expression
    box. Click the "=" button. Double-click on "Sierra-type mixed conifer forest"
    in the *Unique Values* scrolling box. Your expression should match the one in
    the following graphic.

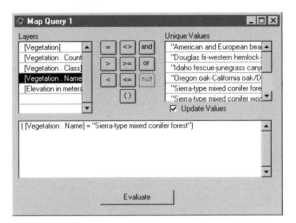

Each field in the *Vegetation* theme's theme table is one layer. The
Elevation in meters theme, which has no theme table, is a single
layer—only its cell values can be queried.

8   Click the Evaluate button. When the query is completed, a new grid theme
    is added to the view. Close the dialog. Turn off the vegetation and elevation
    grid themes. Make the *Map Query 1* theme active and turn it on.

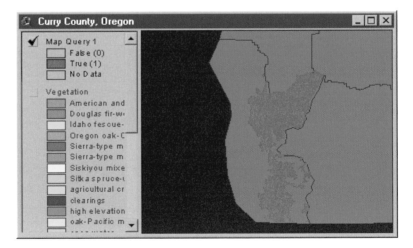

By default, map query themes are symbolized in red for cells that satisfy the query and transparent for those that don't. Map query themes are temporary integer grids that always contain just two values: 0 and 1.

9   Double-click on the *Map Query 1* grid theme to open the Legend Editor. Change the color symbol for the False (0) value to white. Click Apply and close the Legend Editor and Symbol Palette.

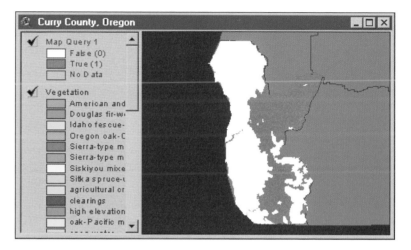

Now you'll create a query for Sierra-type mixed conifer forests that are found at high elevations. You could start over with a new map query, but it's easier to edit your existing one.

10   Make sure the *Map Query 1* theme is active. From the Theme menu, choose Edit Theme Expression to open the dialog containing your previous query.

Delete the closing parenthesis and click the "and" button. In the *Layers* box, double-click on [Elevation in meters]. Click the ">" button and type **1000**, then add a closing parenthesis.Your expression should be:

([Vegetation . Name] = "Sierra-type mixed conifer forest") and ([Elevation in meters] > 1000)

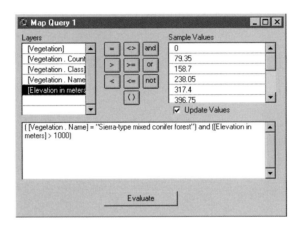

11   Click Evaluate. (If you get a Syntax Error message, edit the expression or delete it and start over.) When the new query is completed, close the dialog.

The *Map Query 1* theme shows the results of the new query. The symbology reverts to the default.

Forming expressions. Many operations in ArcView Spatial Analyst are carried out with expressions entered in the Map Query dialog or the Map Calculator dialog, which you'll see in the next chapter. You can build expressions by clicking on items in the dialog or by typing directly into the expression box (or by combining the two methods). In any case, making sure that your expressions are well formed requires care. To avoid misspellings and syntax problems, you should add grid names to an expression by double-clicking on them in the *Layers* list. Keep track of your open and closed parentheses. You can make your expressions easier to read by putting spaces or carriage returns (as many as you like) between grid names, operators, and the other components of an expression. Don't become frustrated by syntax error messages—everyone gets them. If you have particular trouble with an expression, it may help to copy it to a text editor, edit it there, and paste it back into the Map Query or Map Calculator dialog.

12   Double-click on the *Map Query 1* theme to open the Legend Editor. Change the color symbol for the False (0) value back to white. Click Apply and close the Legend Editor and the Symbol Palette.

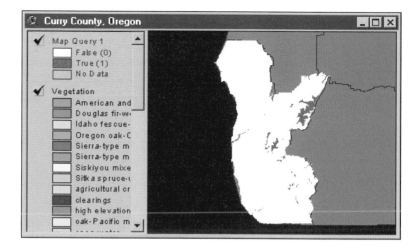

Rather than create a second Map Query grid theme, ArcView Spatial Analyst has recalculated the existing one. The red areas on the grid identify areas of Sierra-type mixed conifer forests above 1,000 meters.

When you close the project without saving changes, the map query theme won't be saved to disk. Of the three grids you've created so far in the last exercise and this one (a distance grid, a hillshade grid, and a map query grid), only the hillshade grid was saved.

You'll see what this grid looks like on disk, then how to delete it using the Source Manager.

13   Open your operating system's file manager and navigate to your c:\temp directory (or wherever you saved the hillshade grid).

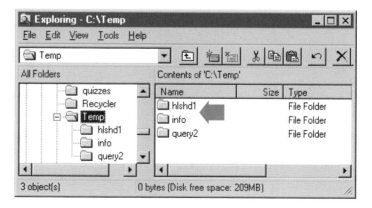

Among the other files and folders that may be there are a folder called "hlshd1" and one called "info." (The query2 folder is the data set for your edited map query theme. It will disappear when you close the project.)

Both folders contain files that are part of the hillshade grid data set. And a single info folder may contain files belonging to several grid data sets. If you try to move, copy, or delete grids with operating system tools, you leave bits and pieces behind, corrupting your data.

For more information on the grid data structure, see appendix C, "Data file structures."

14 Close the file manager and return to ArcView GIS. From the File menu, choose Manage Data Sources to open the Source Manager dialog. In the dialog, navigate to your c:\temp directory. Make sure the *Source Types* drop-down list is set to "Grid." Click on "hlshd1" in the scrolling box.

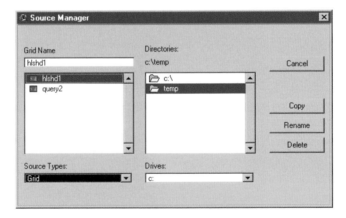

15 Click the Delete button. At the prompt, click Yes to delete the grid theme, then click Cancel to close the Source Manager.

The Source Manager can also be used to copy, rename, and delete shapefiles (and TIN themes in ArcView 3D Analyst).

16 From the File menu, choose Close All. Again from the File menu, choose Close Project. Click No when you're prompted to save your changes.

If you're going on to the next chapter, leave ArcView GIS running. Otherwise, choose Exit from the File menu.

10

Creating surfaces

Interpolating point data

Comparing interpolated surfaces

Deriving new surfaces from elevation

you'll learn how to model continuous elevation surfaces by interpolating values from sample point data. You'll compare different models to each other. You'll also see how an elevation model can be used to derive other surface properties like slope and aspect.

Interpolating point data

ArcView Spatial Analyst can make grid themes of continuous surfaces from feature point themes through a process called interpolation. The points represent known values at specific locations for geographic phenomena that are distributed throughout a surface. The interpolation process fills in the blanks.

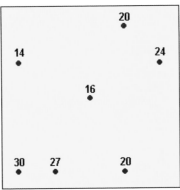

On the left is a point theme of known elevation values. On the right is a grid interpolated from these points. Unknown values are estimated with a mathematical formula that uses the values of nearby known points.

Just about any kind of point data that represents a continuous surface phenomenon can be interpolated. Elevation, temperature, soil chemistry, water pollution, seismic motion, and aircraft noise levels are a few examples.

The nice thing about interpolation is that it works. Accurate weather maps, for instance, can be created from the data gathered at a limited number of weather stations. Correct predictions can be made about where mineral deposits will be found. Fertilizers can be applied to maximize crop growth and minimize environmental damage.

There are various interpolation methods, but they all share one key assumption: that unknown values can be estimated from their spatial proximity to known values. The mathematics are complex, but the basic idea is not. If you're standing in the rain, it's more likely to be raining 10 meters away from you than a hundred kilometers away. Of course, it's possible that it's raining a hundred kilometers away and perhaps even not raining across the street. The formulas used in interpolation can't account for the full complexity of reality; they do provide a useful approximation. The better your input data (the more sample points you have, the more accurate their measurements, the more appropriately distributed they are), the better your surface model will be.

In this exercise, you'll create two different elevation models of an area in Kansas.

◆ *E x e r c i s e   1 0 a*

1   If necessary, start ArcView GIS. Navigate to the extend\spatial\ch10 directory and open the project "ex10a.apr." When the project opens, you see a view of eastern Kansas.

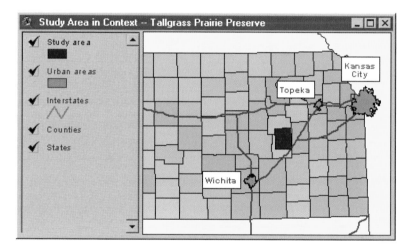

The study area encompasses the Tallgrass Prairie Preserve in the Flint Hills region of Kansas.

2   Close the view and open the Elevation Model view. The view is zoomed to the extent of the study area. Turn on the *Elevation points* theme.

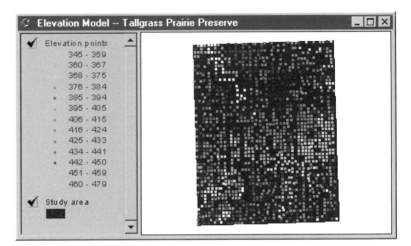

Each point represents a measured elevation value within the study area. The points are classified in an Equal Interval classification. The map units are in meters, as are the elevation, or *z*, values.

The values for a surface that represent a measurement other than planar (x,y) position are known as z values (z units, z coordinates). In an elevation or terrain surface, z values are elevation values; in other surface models they may represent the density or quantity of an attribute.

3   With the *Elevation points* theme active, click the Open Theme Table button. There are 1,258 records, each of which stores the elevation value of an x,y location. Close the theme table.

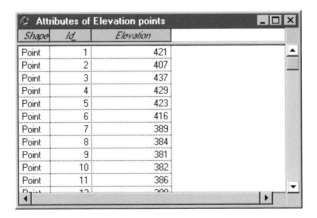

The extent of the study area is about 1,360 square kilometers. This means there's roughly one known elevation value per square kilometer. You'll use these known values to interpolate a continuous elevation surface.

To interpolate a grid, you first specify its spatial extent and cell size. Then you choose an interpolation method and set its parameters.

4   Make sure the *Elevation points* theme is active. From the Surface menu, choose Interpolate Grid. In the Output Grid Specification dialog, set the *Output Grid Extent* drop-down list to "Same As Study Area." (You can set the extent to match that of the view, the display, or any theme in the view.)

In the Output Grid Cell Size field, change the default value to 100. This sets the size of each cell to 100 meters by 100 meters. Press the Enter key on your keyboard to see how many rows and columns the grid will have. Click OK.

In the Interpolate Surface dialog, set the *Method* to "Spline" and the *Z Value Field* to "Elevation." (This is the Elevation field from the *Elevation points* theme table.) Leave the other settings as they are. Click OK.

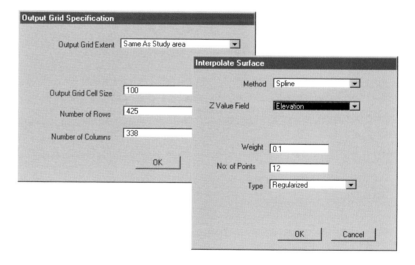

It takes some time to interpolate a surface. How much time depends on the number of sample data points you have, the grid cell size you choose, the parameters you set in the Interpolate Surface dialog, and the capabilities of your computer.

When the process is finished, a new grid theme is added to the view.

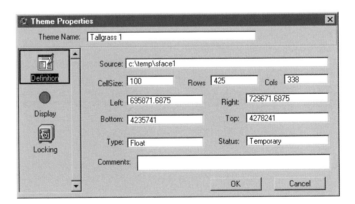

5   Make the grid theme active. From the Theme menu, choose Properties to
    open the Theme Properties dialog. Change the theme name from *Surface
    from Elevation points* to **Tallgrass 1**.

Note the other theme properties. The source data directory is called
"sface1" (the default naming convention for interpolated surfaces).
The cell size is 100. There are 425 rows and 338 columns, which
means the grid has 143,650 cells. Its type is floating point and its
status is temporary.

6   Click OK to apply the new theme name and close the dialog.

7　Double-click on the *Tallgrass 1* theme to open the Legend Editor. Click the Classify button. In the Classification dialog, change the number of classes to 13 and round the values to d. Click OK. Change the color ramp to "Elevation #1." Click Apply and close the Legend Editor, then turn on the *Tallgrass 1* theme.

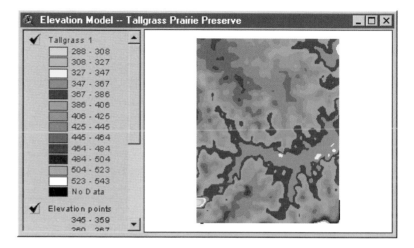

The continuous surface is a detailed model of the landscape. From 1,258 known values, 143,650 have been estimated.

8　In the Table of Contents, compare the high and low values for the *Tallgrass 1* theme with the high and low values for the *Elevation points* theme.

Some of the estimated values are well above and below the extremes of the sample data. This effect doesn't occur with all interpolation methods, but is characteristic of the regularized Spline method that you used.

9　Move the *Elevation points* theme to the top of the Table of Contents and make both it and the *Tallgrass 1* theme active. Select the Zoom In tool and zoom in on any part of the view until your map scale is about 1:50,000. Select the Identify tool and identify some points from the *Elevation points* theme.

Elevation values for both active themes are displayed in the Identify Results window. Spline interpolations preserve the values of all sample data points, so the values for corresponding locations should be nearly identical.

10　Close the Identify Results window and click the Zoom to Full Extent button. Turn off the *Elevation points* theme and drag it below the *Tallgrass 1* theme.

Now you'll interpolate another surface from the same points using slightly different parameters.

11   Make sure the *Elevation points* theme is active. From the Surface menu, choose Interpolate Grid. Set the *Output Grid Extent* drop-down list to "Same As Study area." Set the *Output Grid Cell Size* to "Same As Tallgrass 1." (This is equivalent to typing a value of 100 in the CellSize field.) Click OK.

In the Interpolate Surface dialog, set the *Method,* if necessary, to "Spline" and the *Z Value Field* to "Elevation." In the *Type* drop-down list, change the type from "Regularized" to "Tension." Click OK.

The grid is interpolated and, after a few moments, added as a theme to the view.

12   Make the new grid theme active. Open the Theme Properties dialog and change its name to **Tallgrass 2**. Click OK.

13   Double-click on the *Tallgrass 2* theme to open the Legend Editor. Change the number of classes to 13 and round the values to d. Set the color ramp to "Elevation #1." Click Apply and close the Legend Editor, then turn on the *Tallgrass 2* theme.

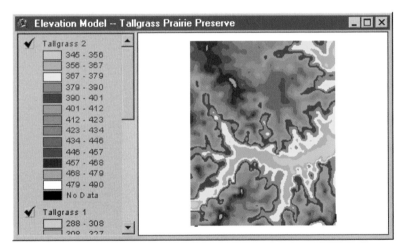

14   In the view Table of Contents, compare the range of values in *Tallgrass 2* to the value range of *Elevation points*.

The tension spline interpolation conforms more closely to the sample data value range than does the regularized one.

15   Compare *Tallgrass 2* and *Tallgrass 1* by turning *Tallgrass 2* off and on a
      few times.

      The differences are less pronounced than they seem. Because the
      two themes have different value ranges, their symbology doesn't
      match. You'll get a better idea of the resemblance by applying the
      Tallgrass 1 legend to the *Tallgrass 2* theme.

16   Double-click on the *Tallgrass 2* theme to open the Legend Editor. Click the
      Load button and navigate to the extend\spatial\ch10 directory.

      In the Load Legend dialog, click on the "tall_1.avl" legend file to select it and
      click OK. In the next Load Legend dialog, make sure the *Field* drop-down list
      is set to "Value" and click OK. Click Apply in the Legend Editor and close it.

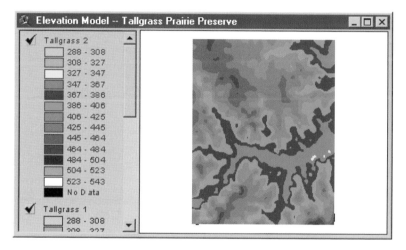

17   Compare the two themes again.

      They look much more alike than they did. In the next exercise,
      you'll quantify the differences.

      For information on the different interpolation methods available in
      ArcView Spatial Analyst, open the Script document "Interpolation notes"
      in this project.

      ---

18   From the File menu, choose Close All. Again from the File menu, choose
      Close Project. Click No when you're prompted to save your changes.

      If you want to go on to the next exercise, leave ArcView GIS run-
      ning. Otherwise, choose Exit from the File menu.

Comparing interpolated surfaces

In this exercise, you'll look at different ways to measure your surfaces against each other. You'll also try to evaluate how well your models conform to the real world.

◆ *Exercise 10b*

1 If necessary, start ArcView GIS. Navigate to the extend\spatial\ch10 directory and open the project "ex10b.apr." When the project opens, you see a view containing the two grid themes you interpolated in the last exercise.

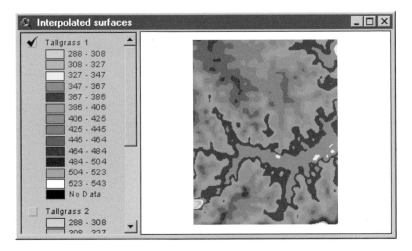

Tallgrass 1 is a regularized spline interpolation and *Tallgrass 2* is a tension spline interpolation. You can read about the technical differences between the two methods in the ArcView GIS online help, but for now, you'll analyze the differences between the two grids by subtracting the cell values of one from the other and seeing what remains.

To do this, you'll create a map algebra expression in the Map Calculator.

2   From the Analysis menu, choose Map Calculator to open the Map Calcula-
    tion 1 dialog.

    In the *Layers* scrolling box, double-click on [Tallgrass 1] to add it to the
    expression box. (All grid themes in the view appear as layers. It doesn't
    matter whether or not they're active or turned on.)

    Click the "–" button, then double-click on [Tallgrass 2]. Your completed
    expression should match the one in the graphic.

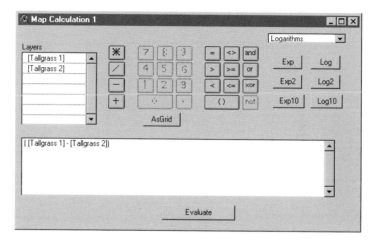

You're about to subtract one grid from another. More precisely, the
value of each cell in *Tallgrass 2* will be subtracted from the value of
the corresponding cell in *Tallgrass 1*. The results will be stored in a
new grid theme.

3   Click the Evaluate button at the bottom of the dialog. When the *Map Calcu-
    lation 1* theme is added to the view, close the Map Calculator.

4   Make the *Map Calculation 1* theme active and open the Theme Properties
    dialog. Change the theme name to **T1 minus T2**. The grid is a temporary
    floating-point grid with the same cell size as the two input grids. Its source
    file name is calc1.

    Click OK to apply the new theme name and close the dialog.

5   Double-click on the *T1 minus T2* theme to open the Legend Editor. In the Classification dialog, change the classification type to "Standard Deviation." Set the class breaks, if necessary, to one standard deviation and round the values to d. Click OK in the Classification dialog and leave the Legend Editor open.

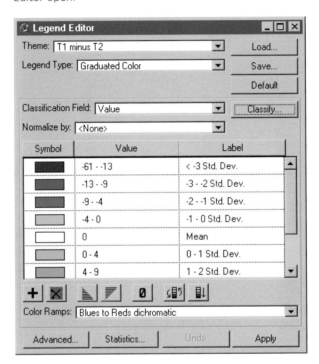

The color ramp defaults to "Blues to Reds dichromatic." The mean value for the *T1 minus T2* grid is 0 and the standard deviation is 4. Where values are light blue or light red, the Tallgrass 1 and Tallgrass 2 values are within 4 meters of each other. Where they're one shade darker, the values are between 4 and 9 meters of each other. The lighter the colors, the closer the corresponding cell values in the two grid themes.

6   Click Apply and close the Legend Editor. Turn on the *T1 minus T2* theme.

Most of the cells fall within one standard deviation of the mean. Most of the extreme variation occurs along the borders of the grid. This is because the regularized spline interpolator tends to underestimate and overestimate values at the edges of a spatial extent.

You've just compared *Tallgrass 1* and *Tallgrass 2* mathematically (or map algebraically) and displayed the differences between the two surfaces as another surface—not of elevation, but of change in value. This shows you how the two surfaces differ from each another, but not which one might better approximate reality. Since you don't have the luxury of going to Kansas to make additional field measurements, you'll use a simpler technique to accomplish the same end.

7   Close the Interpolated Surfaces view and open the Subset Analysis view.

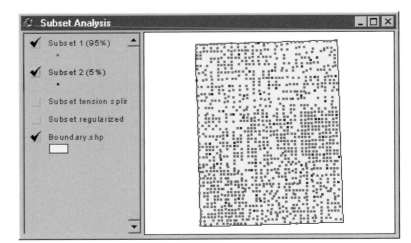

The view contains two point themes, *Subset 1* and *Subset 2*. Together, they include all the elevation points you worked with in the previous exercise. *Subset 2* contains 5 percent of the original points (62 in all), selected at random. *Subset 1* contains the remaining 95 percent (1,196).

For information on how the subset selections were made, open the Script document "Selecting a random subset of elevation points" in this project.

The idea is to make new regularized and tension spline interpolations from the *Subset 1* point theme. These interpolations should be very similar to *Tallgrass 1* and *Tallgrass 2*. You can then check the values in the new interpolations at locations corresponding to the known values in the *Subset 2* point theme. If one of the interpolation methods consistently comes closer to the known values, you have some reason to consider it a better method for your data set.

To save time, these interpolations have been done for you.

8   Turn off the *Subset 1* theme. Turn on the *Subset regularized spline* and *Subset tension spline* grid themes. Make *Subset 2*, *Subset tension spline*, and *Subset regularized spline* active.

9 Select the Zoom In tool and zoom in close (the closer the better) on any of the points in the *Subset 2* theme. Select the Identify tool and identify the point. The Identify Results window lets you compare the interpolated elevation values of the two interpolated themes with the known value of the point theme.

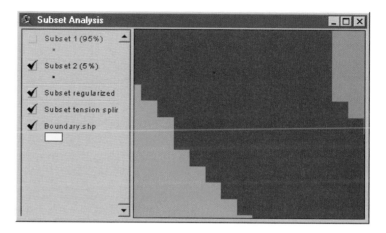

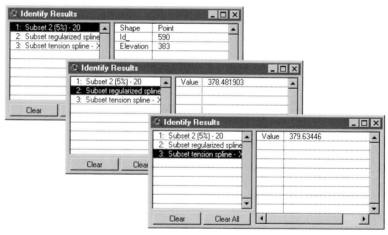

10 Zoom to other parts of the surface and identify some more points. When you're finished, close the Identify Results window.

You probably found that in some cases both interpolated values were quite close to the known value and in other cases neither was especially close. You may have found, too, that sometimes one and sometimes the other interpolator was nearer the real value.

To make a more systematic comparison of your results, refer to the Script document "Comparing Known and Interpolated Values" in this project.

So far, you've interpolated two elevation grids from the same set of sample data. You've compared these grids using the Map Calculator and a statistical technique to see how and where they differ. As a final comparison, you'll add another set of data to the view. It won't tell you which elevation model is better, but it will give you some idea of how well your models accommodate other geographic data.

11 Close the Subset Analysis view and open the Interpolated surfaces view. Make the *T1 minus T2* theme active. From the Edit menu, choose Delete Themes. Click Yes at the prompt.

12 Click the Add Theme button and navigate to the extend\spatial\ch10 directory. Make sure the *Data Source Types* drop-down list is set to "Feature Data Source." Select "rivers.shp" and click OK.

13 In the view Table of Contents, turn on the *Rivers.shp* theme.

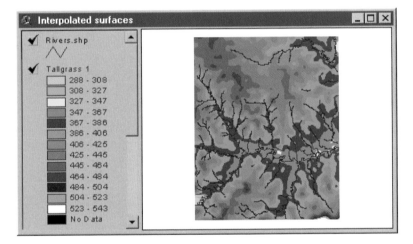

Both elevation surfaces (at this map scale they look about the same) seem to follow the streams fairly well as they flow from higher elevations into the valley.

14 From the File menu, choose Close All. Again from the File menu, choose Close Project. Click No when you're prompted to save your changes.

If you want to go on to the next exercise, leave ArcView GIS running. Otherwise, choose Exit from the File menu.

Deriving new surfaces from elevation

Once you've interpolated an elevation model, you can derive additional information from it. From an elevation grid, ArcView Spatial Analyst can calculate slope (the steepness of changes in elevation), aspect (the compass direction of slope), and hillshade (the surface illumination when the sun is at a specified position in the sky). Hydrological features like stream networks can also be derived.

◆ *E x e r c i s e   1 0 c*

1   If necessary, start ArcView GIS. Navigate to the extend\spatial\ch10 directory and open the project "ex10c.apr." When the project opens, you see a view containing the *Tallgrass 2* elevation grid theme.

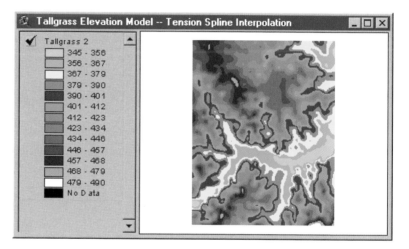

2   From the Surface menu, choose Derive Slope.

You don't need to set parameters to derive slope and aspect grids. The cell size and extent of the output grid is the same as that of the input grid. When the process is finished, a new grid theme called *Slope of Tallgrass 2* is added to the view. The cell values express slope in degrees from 0 to 90 for the Tallgrass 2 elevation surface.

3   Make the *Slope of Tallgrass 2* theme active and open the Legend Editor. In the Legend Editor, click the Load button and navigate to the extend\ spatial\ch10 directory. Select the legend file "slope.avl" and click OK.

In the next Load Legend dialog, make sure the Field is set to "Value" and click OK. Click Apply in the Legend Editor and close it. Turn on the *Slope of Tallgrass 2* theme.

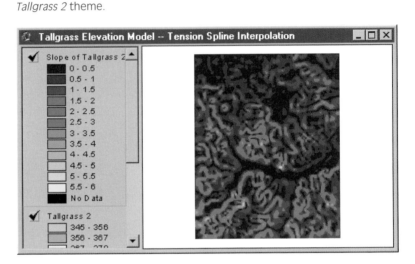

The slope values range from 0 to 6 degrees. (Remember, it's Kansas.) The steepest slopes are symbolized in yellow.

4   Make the *Tallgrass 2* theme active. From the Surface menu, choose Derive Aspect. When the *Aspect of Tallgrass 2* theme is added to the view, turn it on.

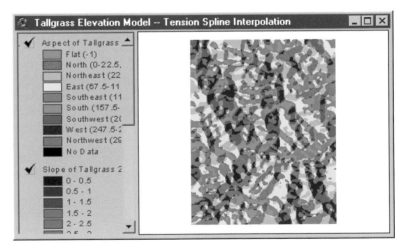

The default legend uses a Full Spectrum color scheme and labels each aspect classification with its compass orientation and value in degrees. Because the aspect changes so much across the surface, it's hard to know which values predominate.

5   Make the *Aspect of Tallgrass 2* theme active. Click the Histogram button. Resize the window so that all values appear in the histogram legend.

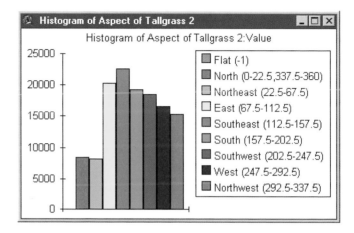

The histogram shows you that slopes facing north and northeast are the least common.

The process of delineating streams and drainage areas involves too many steps to undertake here. You'll simply look at the results of such a process.

Deriving surfaces.   For more information on how slope, aspect, and hydrological features are derived in ArcView Spatial Analyst, refer to the Script documents "Slope and aspect notes" and "Hydrology notes" in this project. Both documents include references to online help topics.

6 Close the histogram and the view. Open the Tallgrass Hydrology Model view.

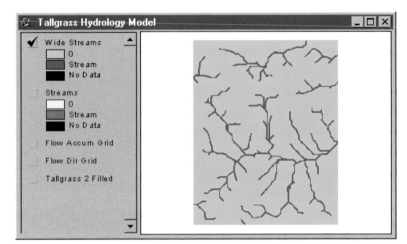

The *Wide Streams* grid theme is turned on. It shows a stream network derived from the *Tallgrass 2* elevation theme. The other grid themes in the view are intermediate steps in the process.

On your own, you might want to add the *Rivers.shp* theme from the previous exercise to this view. That will give you an idea of how the stream network created from the Tallgrass 2 elevation model compares to stream data from an independent source. The correspondence between the two themes turns out to be fairly close, although there are a number of qualifications to keep in mind. For one thing, the stream network created from Tallgrass 2 is the result of a process that involved decisions at various stages—in other words, it could have come out differently than it did (as could the elevation model itself). For another thing, it's dangerous to draw conclusions when you know so little about how the data was created or the kinds of operations that have been performed on it.

7 From the File menu, choose Close All. Again from the File menu, choose Close Project. Click No when you're prompted to save your changes.

If you're going on to the next chapter, leave ArcView GIS running. Otherwise, choose Exit from the File menu.

11

Analyzing density and distance

Calculating density

Finding distance and assigning proximity

IN THE PRECEDING CHAPTER,
you saw how to interpolate values where actual values are unknown. ArcView Spatial Analyst can also create surfaces in which grid cell values are based on measurements rather than interpolation. Density, distance, and proximity grids are three examples of this sort of surface.

Density grids measure the distribution of a quantity per unit of space: population per square mile, for example, or lightning strikes per square kilometer.

Distance grids measure the distance from each location on a surface to the nearest specified feature. You created one in chapter 8, when you measured distances to the nearest roads in the San Gabriel Mountains.

Proximity (or allocation) grids assign each cell a value on the basis of the vector theme feature nearest to it. Another way to put this is to say that every cell is allocated to a feature.

Calculating density

In this exercise, you'll create density grids of cultural sites and population in the area around Minneapolis–St. Paul, Minnesota.

◆ *Exercise 11a*

1   If necessary, start ArcView GIS. Navigate to the extend\spatial\ch11 directory and open the project "ex11a.apr." When the project opens, you see a view of the state of Minnesota.

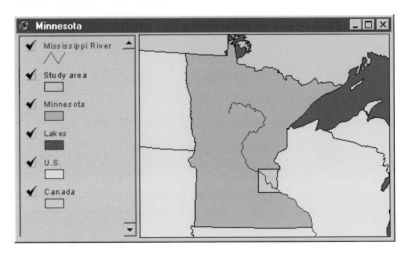

The study area includes the twin cities of Minneapolis and St. Paul, as well as the Mississippi National River and Recreation Area, a 72-mile corridor of the Mississippi River and its adjacent land.

2   Close the view and open the *River area* view. Turn on the *Cultural sites* theme.

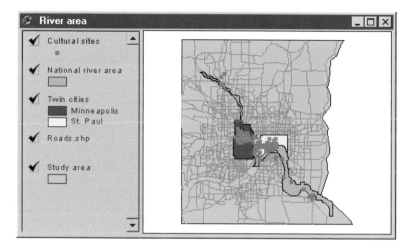

The view shows the Mississippi National River and Recreation Area and the boundaries of the Twin Cities against a background theme of roads. Cultural sites are red points.

3   With the *Cultural sites* theme active, click the Open Theme Table button. The table lists 151 sites of cultural importance.

Shape	Id	Name	Code_1	Code Description
Point	1	Ford Hydroelectric Facilities	DOE	Determination of Eligibility
Point	2	Woodbury Fisk House	NRL	National Register - Local
Point	3	New Main, Augsburg Seminary	NRL	National Register - Local
Point	4	New Century Mill	NRL	National Register - Local
Point	5	Fire Station No. 19	NRL	National Register - Local
Point	6	Triune Masonic Temple	NRL	National Register - Local
Point	7	Vienna and Earl Apartment Buil	NRL	National Register - Local
Point	8	Pilgrim Baptist Church	NRL	National Register - Local
Point	9	University Hall (Old Main), Ham	NRS	National Register - State
Point	10	United Church Seminary	NRL	National Register - Local
Point	11	William G. Le Duc House	NRS	National Register - State
Point	12	Eckberder Clinic	NRS	National Register - State

Most of the sites are clustered within the Twin Cities boundaries. A density grid will show you the distribution in a way that's easier to interpret.

4   Close the table. From the Analysis menu, choose Calculate Density. In the Output Grid Specification dialog, set the output grid extent to "Same As Study area." Set the output grid cell size to 100 meters. Press the Enter key to update the number of rows and columns, then click OK.

In the Calculate Density dialog, replace the default search radius with **1.5** (kilometers). Leave the other settings as they are and click OK.

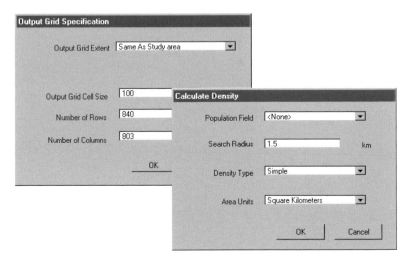

The density grid is calculated and added as a theme to the view.

5   Make the new grid theme active. Open the Theme Properties dialog and change the theme name to **Simple density**. Click OK. Turn the theme on.

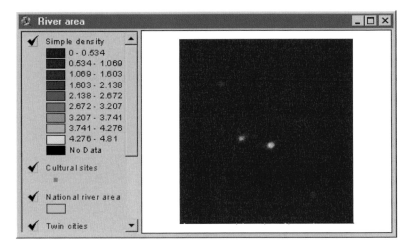

The values range from 0 to 4.81 (sites per square kilometer). With the default classification and color scheme, the grid isn't easy to interpret. You'll apply a custom legend.

6   Double-click on the *Simple density* theme to open the Legend Editor. Click the Load button and navigate to the extend\spatial\ch11 directory. Double-click on the "site1.avl" legend file. In the Load Legend dialog, click OK. Click Apply in the Legend Editor and close the Legend Editor.

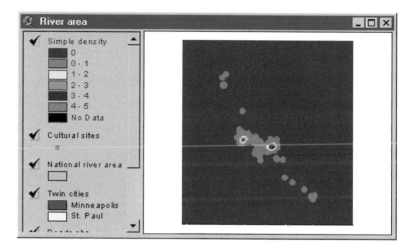

The density map is now easier to interpret. Red areas have a density of 0 to 1 cultural sites per square kilometer. Yellow areas have between 1 and 2, and so on.

7   Select the Zoom In tool and zoom in on the high-density areas. Select the Identify tool and identify some grid cells. When you're finished, close the Identify Results window.

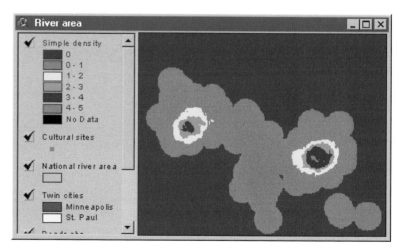

A density grid gives you a feel for the distribution of values and areas of concentration. As the Identify operation shows, it can also give you specific values.

Be aware of what these values mean. They don't tell you that there are, for instance, 4.2 cultural sites within the area of a particular grid cell (that would be like your having 4.2 children). Rather, they tell you that there are 4.2 sites per square kilometer in the area around the grid cell—in this case, an area with a radius of 1.5 kilometers.

The density values form ring-like patterns, but the borders of these rings are ragged. By changing a setting in the Calculate Density dialog, you can get a smoother distribution of values. While you're at it, you'll experiment with a larger search radius.

8   Click the Zoom to Full Extent button. Turn off the *Simple density* grid. From the Theme menu, choose Hide/Show Legend to hide its legend. Make the *Cultural sites* theme active. From the Analysis menu, choose Calculate Density.

In the Output Grid Specification dialog, set the output grid extent to "Same As Study area." Set the output grid cell size to "As Specified Below" and the cell size to 100 meters. Click OK.

In the Calculate Density dialog, change the search radius to 2.5 kilometers and the density type to "Kernel." Leave the other settings as they are and click OK.

The new density grid is calculated and added as a theme to the view.

9   Make the new grid theme active. Open the Theme Properties dialog and change the theme name to **Kernel density**. Click OK, then turn the theme on.

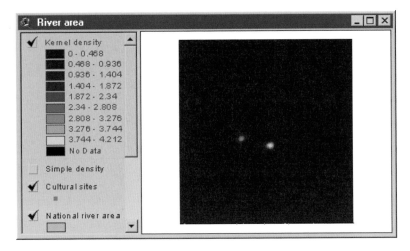

Superficially, the kernel density grid looks like the simple density grid. The value range, however, is a bit different. (It stops at 4.2 in this grid and went to 4.8 in the simple density grid.) Changing parameters, such as the density type and the search radius, changes the distribution of grid values. This doesn't mean that one grid is more accurate than the other. It just means that different assumptions yield different results.

10   Double-click on the *Kernel density* theme to open the Legend Editor. In the Legend Editor, click the Load button. Navigate to the extend\spatial\ch11 directory and load the "site2.avl" legend file. Click Apply in the Legend Editor and close the Legend Editor.

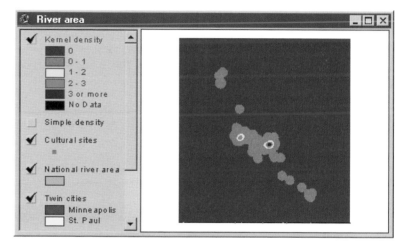

   11   As before, select the Zoom In tool and zoom in on the high-density areas.

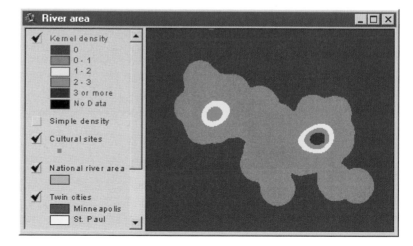

The output of a kernel density grid is smooth, which makes it visually appealing.

In the density grids you've created so far, each cultural site was counted once in the density calculation. Now you'll create a density grid in which each point in the input point theme may have a different value.

Calculating density. Density grids are created from point themes. Each cell in the grid has a circular search area applied to it. In a simple density calculation, points that fall within the search area are totaled and divided by the search area size to get each grid cell's density value. The points may be counted as individual units (for instance, each point may represent a building) or as variable values (for instance, one population point might represent a thousand people while another represents fifty). A kernel density calculation weights the points lying near the center of a grid cell's search area more heavily than those near the periphery. The result is a smoother distribution of values. For more information and a graphic example, see the Script document "Calculating density" in this project. In the online help, use the Find tab to locate the topics *Calculate Density Dialog* and *Calculating density from point estimates of a population*.

12 Close the view and open the Minneapolis view. Turn on the *Population points* theme.

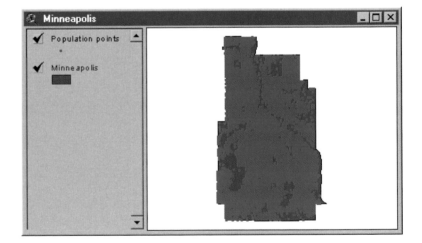

13   With the *Population points* theme active, click the Open Theme Table button.

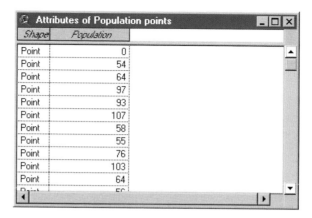

Each point represents the people living in a particular census block. Your density grid will use the values in the Population field.

14   Close the theme table. From the Analysis menu, choose Calculate Density. In the Output Grid Specification dialog, set the output grid extent to "Same As Minneapolis." Change the output grid cell size to 100 meters. Click OK.

In the Calculate Density dialog, set the *Population Field* drop-down list, if necessary, to "Population." Change the search radius to 1 kilometer. Change the density type to "Kernel" and click OK.

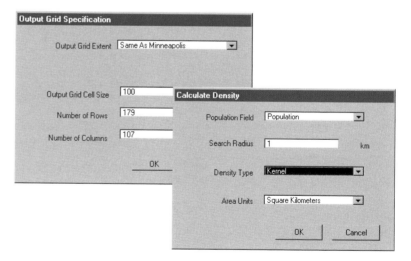

The density grid is added to the view.

15 Turn off the *Population points* theme. Make the density grid theme active and turn it on.

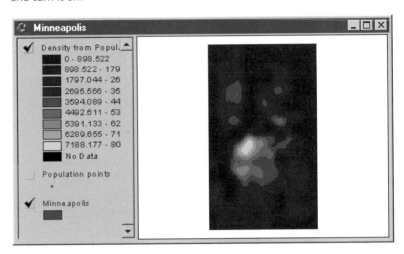

16 Double-click on the *Density from Population points* theme to open the Legend Editor. Click the Load button and navigate to the extend\spatial\ch11 directory. Load the "pop.avl" legend file. Click Apply in the Legend Editor and close the Legend Editor.

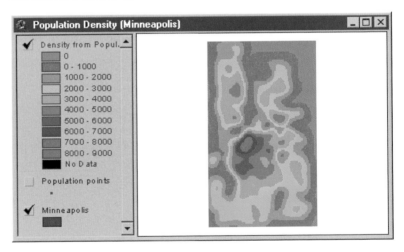

The density grid shows you how population is distributed throughout Minneapolis.

17 From the File menu, choose Close All. Again from the File menu, choose Close Project. Click No when you're prompted to save your changes.

If you want to go on to the next exercise, leave ArcView GIS running. Otherwise, choose Exit from the File menu.

Finding distance and assigning proximity

In this exercise, you'll create a grid that measures distances to local parks within the study area. You'll use a population density grid in conjunction with this distance grid to find areas that are both close to parks and have a high population density. These are areas in which "breathing room"—relief from urban overcrowding in an open, green space—is a critical need that's being met. Finally, you'll create a proximity grid to determine which parks provide this breathing room and how effectively they do so.

◆ *E x e r c i s e   1 1 b*

1   If necessary, start ArcView GIS. Navigate to the extend\spatial\ch11 directory and open the project "ex11b.apr."

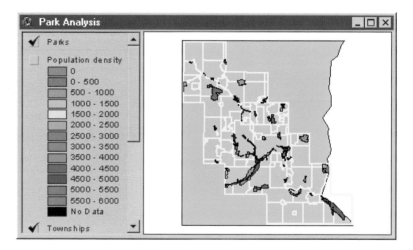

When the project opens, you see a view called Park Analysis that shows parks and township boundaries in the study area. There's also a theme of population density that's not turned on.

2   With the *Parks* theme active, click the Open Theme Table button. There are
    102 records in the table. Each park has a unique ID number and a name.
    (The names aren't unique because there are six parks called "unnamed
    park.") Close the theme table.

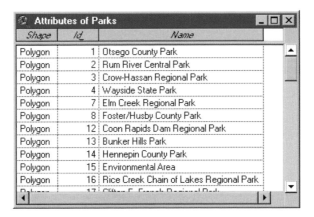

3   Turn on the *Population density* theme. The population density grid (inhabit-
    ants per square kilometer) was created from population points for the
    townships. The view gives you a sense of where the parks are located with
    respect to population.

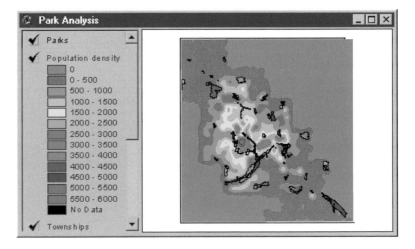

Now you'll create a distance grid to measure distances from all locations in the study area to the parks.

4   Make the *Population density* theme active and hide its legend. Turn off the *Population density* and *Townships* themes, then click on the *Parks* theme to make it active.

From the Analysis menu, choose Find Distance. In the Output Grid Specification dialog, set the output grid extent to "Same As Study area." Set the output grid cell size to "As Specified Below" and the cell size to 100 meters. Click OK.

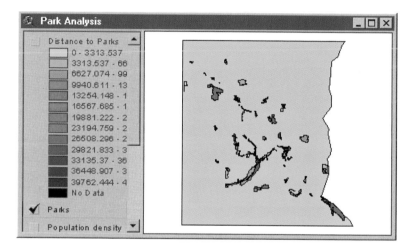

The distance grid is calculated and added to the view. The value of every grid cell is its distance (in meters) to the nearest park.

5   Double-click on the *Distance to Parks* theme to open the Legend Editor. Click the Load button and navigate to the extend\spatial\ch11 directory. Load the "distance.avl" legend file. Click Apply in the Legend Editor and close the Legend Editor.

6   Turn on the *Distance to Parks* theme. Make the *Parks* theme active and drag it to the top of the Table of Contents.

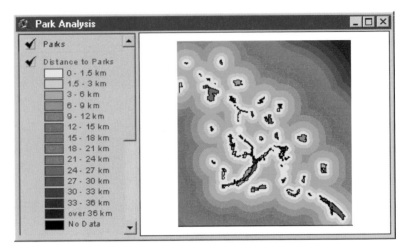

Your first objective is to find places that are crowded but close to parks. These will be called "green relief" areas. An area will be considered crowded if it has 2,000 or more people per square kilometer. It will be considered close to a park if it's within 1,500 meters.

7   From the Analysis menu, choose Map Query to open the Map Query 1 dialog. Double-click on the [Population density] layer to add it to the expression box. Click the ">=" (greater than or equal to) button, then type **2000**.

Now click the "and" button and double-click on the [Distance to Parks] layer. Click the "<=" (less than or equal to) button, then type **1500**.

Your completed expression should match the one in the graphic.

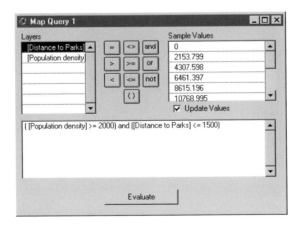

8   Click the Evaluate button. When the *Map Query 1* theme is added to the view, close the dialog.

9   Turn off the *Distance to Parks* theme and make the *Map Query 1* theme
active. In the Theme Properties dialog, change its name to **Green relief** and
click OK. Turn the theme on.

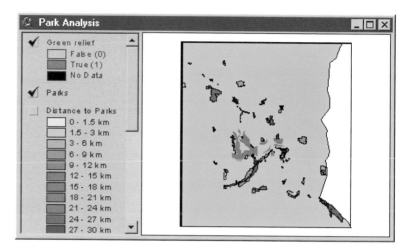

Green relief areas are shown in red. Note that in some places they
overlay the parks themselves. Had you looked for distances to parks
that were both less than 1,500 meters and greater than 30 meters,
your query would have been more accurate. But for this exercise,
it's fine as it is.

Looking at the map will give you a fair idea of which parks provide
green relief, but to get precise information you'll create and analyze
a proximity grid.

Understanding proximity. Proximity grids can be created from
active point, line, or polygon themes, or from active integer grid
themes. Every cell value in a proximity grid identifies the closest feature in the theme from which the proximity grid is created. This stored
value is typically an ID value, but it may be any attribute in the theme
table of the active feature theme. (If the active theme is an integer
grid, the integer grid's values are used.)

**Each grid cell
stores the value
of the nearest
feature.**

Proximity grids can also be used with the Summarize Zones function to
find the closest feature in one theme to each feature in another. In the
online help, use the Find tab to locate the topic *Determining proximity*.

10 Make the *Parks* theme active and drag it to the top of the Table of Contents. From the Analysis menu, choose Assign Proximity.

In the Output Grid Specification dialog, set the output grid extent to "Same As Study area." Set the output grid cell size to "As Specified Below" and the cell size to 100 meters. Click OK.

In the Proximity Field dialog, make sure the Id_ field is highlighted as the field to be used for cell values. Click OK.

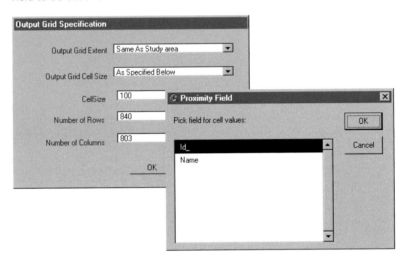

The proximity grid is calculated and added to the view.

11 Double-click on the *Proximity to Parks* theme to open the Legend Editor. From the *Color Schemes* drop-down list, choose "Minerals." Click Apply and close the Legend Editor.

Turn the theme on and hide its legend. Drag the *Parks* theme to the top of the Table of Contents.

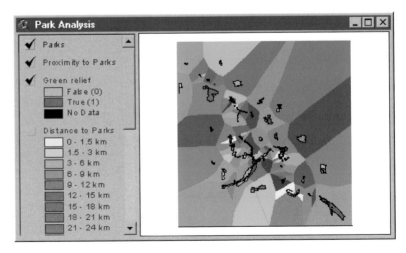

For every cell, the proximity grid identifies the nearest park. Each set of cells sharing the same nearest park forms a proximity zone and is symbolized by a unique color.

In ArcView Spatial Analyst, a zone is a set of cells in a grid theme that have the same value. The cells aren't necessarily contiguous. A zone can also describe a set of features in a feature theme that have the same attribute value.

 12   Make the *Proximity to Parks* theme active, then click the Open Theme Table button.

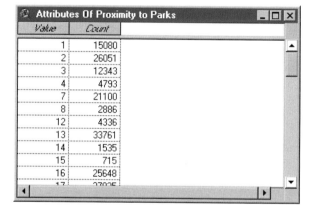

Value	Count
1	15080
2	26051
3	12343
4	4793
7	21100
8	2886
12	4336
13	33761
14	1535
15	715
16	25648
17	27035

There are 102 records in the table. A one-to-one relationship exists between parks and proximity zones. The values in this table correspond to the ID values of the parks.

Every park has a unique proximity zone. Finding the amount of green relief area in each zone will therefore tell you how much relief is provided by each park. To find this out, you'll use the Tabulate Areas function.

Tabulating areas. Tabulating areas creates a table of the amount of area in one theme's zones that falls within the zones of another theme. The themes can be integer grid or feature themes (or both). One theme is defined as the row theme and the other as the column theme. The area in each zone of the column theme is calculated for each record in the row theme. Different attributes from the row and column themes can be calculated with respect to each other. For instance, a row theme of farmland might be tabulated according to owner, soil type, amount of fertilizer applied, or some other attribute in the farmland theme table. A column theme of crops might be tabulated according to soybeans, cotton, or some other attribute in the crops theme table. Thus, one tabulation might give you the amount of soybean area belonging to each farm owner, while another might give you the amount of cotton area lying within each soil type. In the online help, use the Find tab to locate the topics *Cross tabulating areas* and *Tabulate Areas Dialog.*

13 Close the Attributes of Proximity to Parks table. Make the *Green relief* theme active and click the Open Theme Table button. With the Select tool, click on the record with a value of 1, then close the theme table.

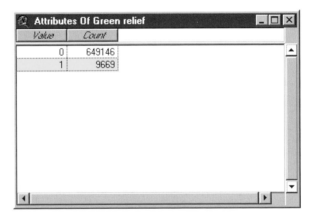

You don't see the green relief areas highlighted in the view because the proximity theme covers them.

14   From the Analysis menu, choose Tabulate Areas. In the Tabulate Areas dialog, set the row theme to "Proximity to Parks" and the row field to "Value." Set the column theme to "Green relief" and the column field to "Value." The result table will contain one record for each zone in the *Proximity to Parks* theme that has green relief area in it. Click OK.

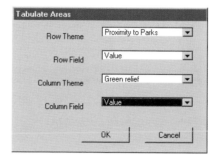

An *Areas of Green relief* table is added to the project.

Value	Value-1
28	2020000.000
37	300000.000
38	1470000.000
39	540000.000
40	270000.000
41	380000.000
43	1800000.000
44	3090000.000
45	2250000.000
48	5790000.000
49	2350000.000
50	2520000.000

Areas of Green relief Tabulated For Each Zone...

The numbers in the Value field identify the proximity zones. The numbers in the Value-1 field tell you how much green relief area, in square meters, is found in each proximity zone.

There are thirty-four records in the table. The other sixty-eight proximity zones have no green relief area.

15   In the *Areas of Green relief* table, click on the Value-1 field to highlight it, then click the Sort Descending button.

The zones are now sorted according to which ones have the most green relief area. All that remains is to join this table to the *Parks* theme table.

16   In the *Areas of Green relief* table, click on the Value field to highlight it. Make the view active and make the *Parks* theme active in the view Table of Contents. Click the Open Theme Table button. In the Attributes of Parks table, click on the ID field to make it active.

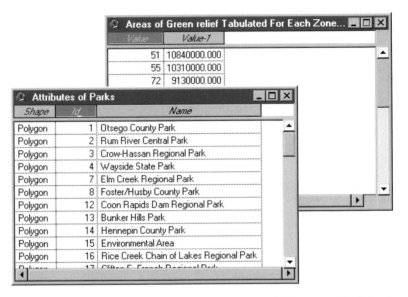

17   With the Attributes of Parks table active, click the Join button. In the joined table, highlight the Value-1 field and click the Sort Descending button.

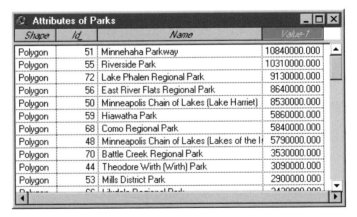

You've ranked the parks according to the amount of green relief they provide.

You might be curious about how large these parks are in proportion to their green relief values. A small park that provides as much relief as a large one might be said to be doing a better job.

18　Make sure the Attributes of Parks table is active. From the Table menu, choose Properties to open the Table Properties dialog. Make the Area and Ratio fields visible. Click OK to close the dialog.

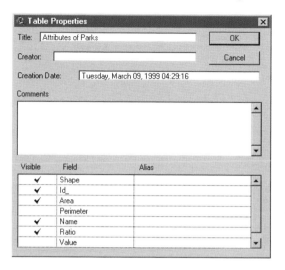

The Area field tells you the size of each park in square meters. You'll use the Ratio field to calculate each park's size in proportion to its green relief value.

19　In the Attributes of Parks table, click on the Ratio field to highlight it. From the Table menu, choose Start Editing. Click the Field Calculator button.

In the Field Calculator dialog, double-click on the [Value-1] field to add it to the expression box. Double-click the "/" (divide by) request, then double-click the [Area] field. Your completed expression should match the one in the graphic. Click OK.

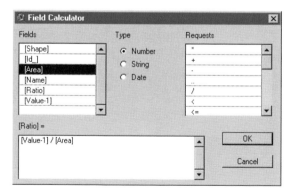

20　From the Table menu, choose Stop Editing. Click Yes to save your edits.

21 With the Ratio field highlighted in the table, click the Sort Descending button.

Area	Name	Ratio	Value-1
963.844	Pioneer Park	1525.143	1470000.000
7031.555	Gateway Park	255.989	1800000.000
34951.523	unnamed park	57.794	2020000.000
48396.914	Hennepin Island Park	41.532	2010000.000
10367.086	Prospect Terrace Park	40.513	420000.000
10908.172	unnamed park	35.753	390000.000
21685.094	Bluff Park	30.897	670000.000
440223.625	Minnehaha Parkway	24.624	10840000.000
25196.320	El Rio Vista Park	23.416	590000.000
23050.109	Main Street Park	16.486	380000.000
183677.852	Mills District Park	15.789	2900000.000

The larger the ratio, the more relief the park provides in proportion to its size. For instance, Gateway Park gives green relief to an area 256 times its own size.

Your work suggests further analysis. You could look for areas that have high population density with poor park access. You might also consider whether parks with high green relief ratios are the only parks accessible to the people who live near them. If they are, these parks might be overtaxed.

For an explanation of some potentially tricky points, open the Script document "Interpreting proximity grids" in this project.

22 From the File menu, choose Close All. Again from the File menu, choose Close Project. Click No when you're prompted to save your changes.

If you're going on to the next chapter, leave ArcView GIS running. Otherwise, choose Exit from the File menu.

12

Converting grids and setting their properties

Converting feature themes to grids

Setting grid analysis properties

Resampling grids

CONVERTING FEATURE THEMES,
especially polygon themes, to grids is a fairly common operation. Many data sets that are typically stored as integer grids (of zoning, land use, land cover, soil type, animal habitat, and so on) begin life as ArcView GIS shapefiles or ArcInfo coverages. By converting them to grids you gain two advantages: you can analyze them with other grid themes and you can apply the full range of ArcView Spatial Analyst functions to them.

You may recall from chapter 10 the process of setting output grid specifications when you interpolated a grid. These specifications, consisting of a spatial extent and a cell size, can be set from the Analysis menu and applied to all grids created from map queries or map calculations (though not to interpolated or converted grids). This lets you conveniently adjust the output properties of grids.

When analytical operations involve multiple grid themes, the grids must "line up." This means not only that they have a common spatial extent, but that their cells are of the same size and their rows and columns begin in the same places. This process of lining up grid cells is called resampling.

Converting feature themes to grids

In this exercise, you'll convert a polygon theme of cultural sites in St. Paul to a grid theme. You'll see how grid cell size affects the precision with which polygon boundaries are represented.

◆ *Exercise 12a*

1   If necessary, start ArcView GIS. Navigate to the extend\spatial\ch12 direc-
    tory and open the project "ex12a.apr." When the project opens, you see a
    view of the St. Paul metropolitan area, along with the Mississippi River and
    selected cultural sites.

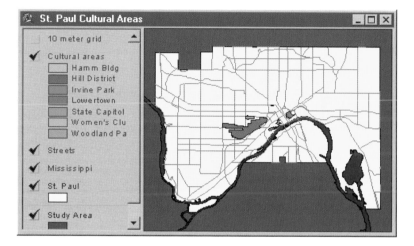

2   Make the *Cultural areas* theme active. Click the Zoom to Active Theme(s)
    button.

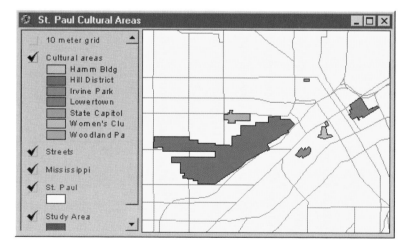

The *Cultural areas* theme contains seven polygons representing
selected historic districts and buildings in St. Paul. (The Mississippi
theme has been set not to display at this map scale.)

3   With the *Cultural areas* theme active, click the Open Theme Table button. The attributes identify the features and their historical status.

Shape	Id	Name	Brief_Name	Code_1	Cod
Polygon	127	Minnesota State Capitol	State Capitol	NRS	Nationa
Polygon	120	Lowertown Historic District	Lowertown	NRL	Nationa
Polygon	52	Woodland Park District	Woodland Park	NRL	Nationa
Polygon	116	Historic Hill District	Hill District	NRS	Nationa
Polygon	187	Hamm Building	Hamm Bldg	DOE	Determ
Polygon	143	St. Paul Women's City Club	Women's Club	NRS	Nationa
Polygon	117	Irvine Park Historic District	Irvine Park	NRS	Nationa

Attributes of Cultural areas

You'll convert these vector data features to a grid theme. You'll start with a cell size of 30 meters and see how well the polygon shapes are captured.

Converting vector data.   Converting vector data to raster data is like putting a fine net over your map features and seeing what lies in each square of the net. When you convert a point theme, each cell in the output grid is assigned the value of the point that falls within it. With a line theme, each cell gets the value of the line feature crossing it. With polygon themes, each cell gets the value of the polygon feature that covers the cell center. In all these cases, if no vector feature corresponds to a cell, the cell receives the value of No Data. If more than one feature could be assigned to a cell, ArcView Spatial Analyst makes an arbitrary choice. It's also possible to convert data in the other direction: integer grid themes can be converted to polygon feature themes. Whether the conversion is vector to raster or raster to vector, the converted theme is permanent, not temporary. In the online help, use the Find tab to locate the topics *Feature theme to grid theme* and *Grid theme to polygon theme.*

4   Close the table. From the Theme menu, choose Convert to Grid. In the Convert Cultural areas dialog, accept the default name of "nwgrd1" and click OK.

In the Conversion Extent dialog, set the *Output Grid Extent* to "Same As Cultural areas" and the CellSize to 30, then click OK. In the Conversion Field dialog, select "Brief_name" as the field to use for cell values. Click OK.

In the Attribute Join dialog, click Yes to join feature attributes to the grid theme table. Click Yes again to add the grid theme to the view.

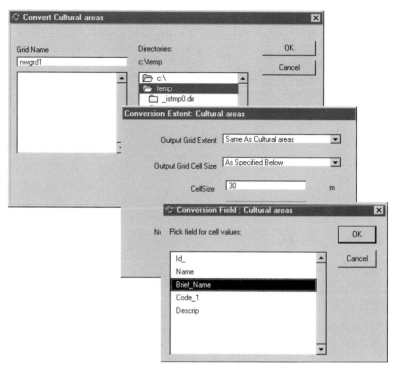

5   Make the new grid theme active. Open the Theme Properties dialog and change the theme name from *Nwgrd1* to **30 meter grid**. Click OK.

6   Double-click on the *30 meter grid* theme to open the Legend Editor. Set the color scheme to "Autumn Leaves." Click Apply, but leave the Legend Editor open. Turn the theme on.

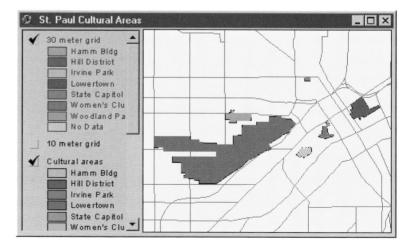

Each cultural area is represented by a set of grid cells that has a unique value.

7   In the Legend Editor, scroll to the bottom of the symbols list and double-click on the No Data symbol to open the Color Palette. Change the symbol color from transparent to black. Click Apply, but leave the Legend Editor and Color Palette open.

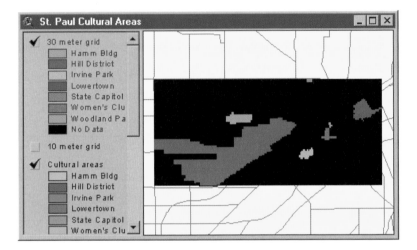

You learned in chapter 9 that every grid theme has a rectangular extent. The extent of the *30 meter grid* theme corresponds to the minimum bounding rectangle of the *Cultural areas* polygon theme. Grid cells whose centers were covered by polygon features received the values of those polygons. All other cells were assigned the No Data value.

No Data is not the same as zero, which is a legitimate mathematical value. No Data cells contain no information and are ignored in analytical operations.

---

8   In the Color Palette, change the No Data symbol back to transparent and click Apply in the Legend Editor. Close the Legend Editor and the Color Palette.

To see how well the grid theme corresponds to the polygon theme, you need to zoom in closer.

9   Select the Zoom In tool and drag a rectangle around the Lowertown Histori-
    cal District (the brown feature at the far right of the view).

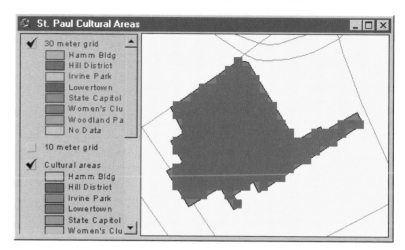

At this display scale (about 1:10,000), it's clear that rasterizing the
polygon has changed the shape of the feature. Whether or not the
change is important depends on your purposes. If you were trying
to find all St. Paul cultural sites within a kilometer of the Mississippi
River, it wouldn't make a difference. But if you wanted to know the
area in square meters of the Lowertown district, it would.

10   With the *30 meter grid* theme active, click the Open Theme Table button.

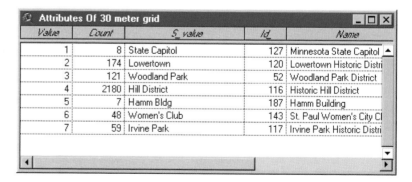

Value	Count	S_value	Id	Name
1	8	State Capitol	127	Minnesota State Capitol
2	174	Lowertown	120	Lowertown Historic Distri
3	121	Woodland Park	52	Woodland Park District
4	2180	Hill District	116	Historic Hill District
5	7	Hamm Bldg	187	Hamm Building
6	48	Women's Club	143	St. Paul Women's City Cl
7	59	Irvine Park	117	Irvine Park Historic Distri

The table, like all grid theme tables, has a Value and a Count field.
It also has a field called "S_value" (which stands for "string value").
The S_values come from the Brief_name field in the *Cultural areas*
theme table. This was the field you specified for grid cell values.
Because a grid cell can't literally hold a text string as its value, the
cells have been assigned numeric values (in this case, 1 to 7) with
which the S_values are associated.

The other fields have been joined from the *Cultural areas* theme table and don't belong permanently to the grid data set. To make them permanent, you would need to edit the grid theme table.

11   Close the theme table. Turn off the *30 meter grid* theme and turn on the *10 meter grid* theme directly below it.

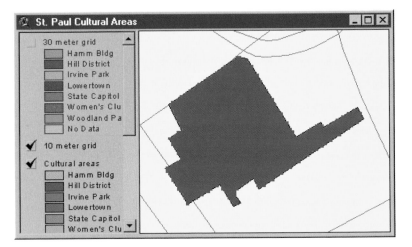

The *10 meter grid* theme was also converted from the *Cultural areas* theme, but at a smaller cell resolution. This grid better approximates the vector shapes.

Data conversion and cell resolution. Smaller cell sizes represent vector shapes more accurately, but result in larger grid files and longer processing times. Keep in mind that no matter what cell size you choose, your output grid can never be any more accurate than your input data source.

     12   Use the Zoom and Pan tools to compare the grid and vector representations of some of the other features in the view.

13   From the File menu, choose Close All. Again from the File menu, choose Close Project. Click No when you're prompted to save your changes.

In this exercise, you created a grid data set called nwgrd1 in your c:\temp directory. Use the Source Manager to delete this file.

If you want to go on to the next exercise, leave ArcView GIS running. Otherwise, choose Exit from the File menu.

Setting grid analysis properties

In this exercise, you'll set analysis properties that let you clip a large grid to a smaller area of interest. You'll start with a land use grid that covers several municipalities and single out one of these. Then, because grid extents are rectangular and municipal boundaries are not, you'll create an "analysis mask" to refine your area of interest further.

Once you have the land use grid theme you want, you'll compare it to a grid of wetlands. You'll find out whether the wetlands are being protected or encroached on by development.

◆ *E x e r c i s e   1 2 b*

1   If necessary, start ArcView GIS. Navigate to the extend\spatial\ch12 directory and open the project "ex12b.apr." When the project opens, you see a view of the region encompassing the Mississippi National River and Recreation Area. Within the region, you see the municipal boundary of Eagan, Minnesota.

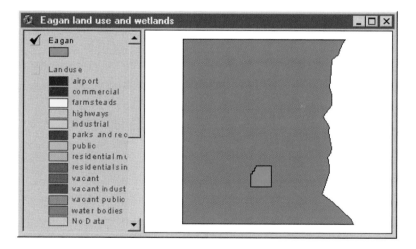

In addition to the polygon themes, the view contains two grid themes: one of land use and one of wetlands.

2   Turn on the *Landuse* grid theme.

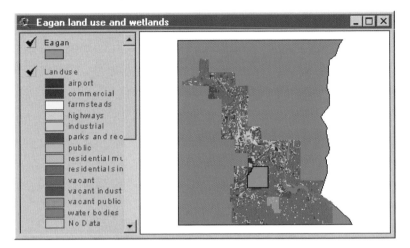

The theme shows land use categories for a number of municipalities in the study area.

3   With the *Landuse* theme active, click the Open Theme Table button.

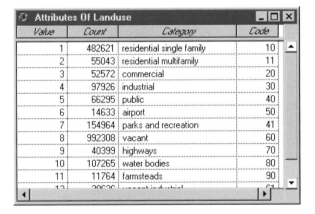

Each land use value has a descriptive category and a code.

All you want of the land use grid is the part that covers Eagan. To get it, you'll set analysis properties for the view.

4   Close the table and turn off the *Landuse* theme. From the Theme menu, choose Hide/Show Legend to hide its legend.

5   From the Analysis menu, choose Properties to open the Analysis Properties dialog. Set the Analysis Extent to "Same As Eagan." The bounding coordinates of the Eagan polygon theme are displayed. Click OK.

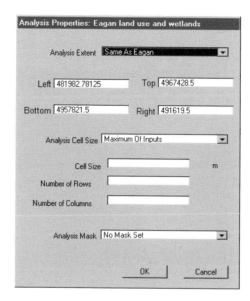

Any grids you create with map calculations or queries will have the same extent as the Eagan theme.

Setting analysis properties. The Analysis Extent property is set by default to the union of inputs (the combined extent of all grids used in a calculation or query). It can also be set to the intersection of inputs, to the extent of any theme in the view, to the extent of the view or the display, or to the extent of specific coordinates. The Analysis Cell Size property is set by default to the maximum of inputs (the largest cell size of any grid used in a calculation or query). It can also be set to the minimum of inputs, to the cell size of any grid theme in the view, or to a specified size. (You can also set the cell size indirectly by setting the number of rows and columns.) An analysis mask is a grid that sets the cell values of all output grids to No Data wherever these cells lie outside the spatial extent of the mask grid (or correspond to No Data cells in the mask grid). The analysis mask doesn't otherwise change the cell values of output grids.

In the online help, use the Find tab to locate the topics *Analysis Properties Dialog* and *What is the analysis mask?*

6 From the Analysis menu, choose Map Calculator to open the Map Calculation 1 dialog. Double-click on the [Landuse] layer to add it to the expression
   box. Your completed expression should look like this:

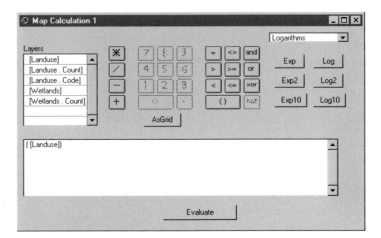

When you click Evaluate, ArcView Spatial Analyst will create a new
land use grid with values identical to those of the existing land use
grid, but clipped to the extent of the Eagan theme.

7 Click the Evaluate button. When the *Map Calculation 1* theme is added to
   the view, close the Map Calculator dialog.

8 Make the *Map Calculation 1* theme active. Open the Theme Properties and
   change its name to **Landuse clip**, then click OK.

9 Double-click on the *Landuse clip* theme to open the Legend Editor. Click the
   Load button and navigate to the extend\spatial\ch12 directory. Load the
   legend "landuse.avl," making sure that the field is set to "Value" in the Load
   Legend dialog. Click Apply and close the Legend Editor. Turn on the *Landuse
   clip* theme.

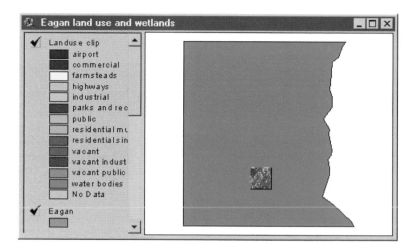

The *Landuse clip* theme has the same extent as the Eagan polygon theme.

10   With the *Landuse clip* theme active, click the Zoom to Active Theme(s) button.

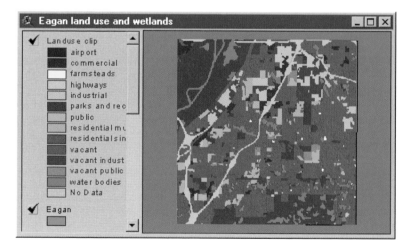

11   Click the Open Theme Table button.

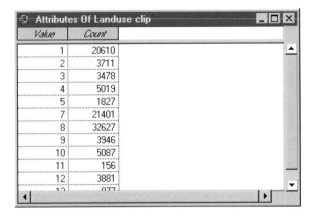

Grids created through map calculations or queries have only Value and Count fields. (The land use categories are displayed in the theme legend because they were defined in the landuse.avl legend file.)

Note that there is no value 6 in the table. This value corresponds to airport land use. It exists in the *Landuse* theme, but not in the *Landuse clip* theme, because there are no airports in Eagan.

12   Close the table and turn off the *Landuse clip* theme.

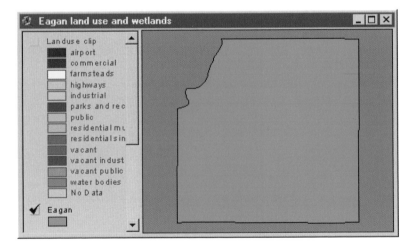

The extent of the *Landuse clip* theme is the minimum bounding rectangle of the *Eagan* polygon theme. The actual Eagan boundary, however, isn't rectangular. Eventually, you want to compare land use and wetlands in Eagan, but you can't do this accurately until you exclude areas that aren't in Eagan from the analysis.

You need to create an analysis mask. The *Eagan* polygon theme itself would make the perfect mask, except that all spatial analysis is done in the raster environment. The solution, therefore, is to convert the *Eagan* polygon theme to a grid.

13   Make the *Eagan* theme active. From the Theme menu, choose Convert to Grid. In the Convert Eagan dialog, click OK to accept the default name of "nwgrd1." (This may be nwgrd2 if you haven't deleted nwgrd1 from the previous exercise.)

Each paragraph below is part of step 13:

In the Conversion Extent dialog, set the output grid extent to "Same As Eagan." Set the cell size to 30 and click OK. In the Conversion Field dialog, choose "Name" as the field to use for cell values and click OK.

Click No at the prompt to join feature attributes to the grid. (You're only interested in the spatial extent of this grid. You don't care about its attributes.) Click Yes to add the grid theme to the view.

Analysis property settings apply only to calculated grids, not to converted grids.

14   Make the *Nwgrd1* theme active. Open the Theme Properties and change its name to **Eagan mask**, then click OK.

15   Turn on the *Eagan mask* theme.

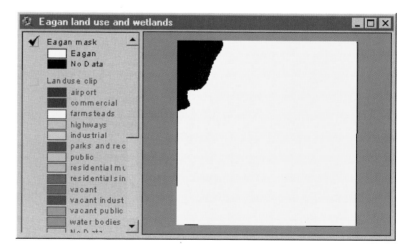

In the *Eagan mask* grid theme, cells are No Data if their centers weren't covered by the polygon in the *Eagan* feature theme.

16   From the Analysis menu, choose Properties to open the Analysis Properties dialog. (The *Analysis Extent* drop-down list displays "Current Value"—the extent of the *Eagan* theme set previously.)

17   From the *Analysis Mask* drop-down list, choose "Eagan mask" and click OK.

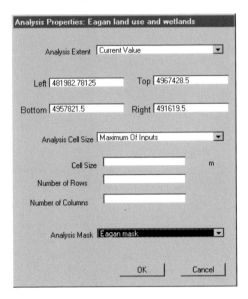

You can now mask the areas outside Eagan from the *Landuse clip* grid.

18   From the Analysis menu, choose Map Calculator. In the dialog, double-click on the [Landuse clip] layer to add it to the expression box. Your completed expression should look like this:

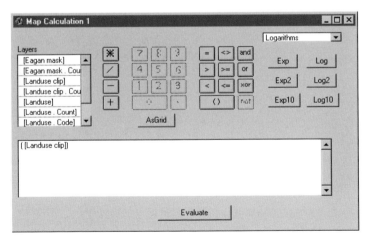

The output grid will have the same values as the *Landuse clip* grid, except that it will have No Data values where the mask grid has No Data.

19   Click the Evaluate button. When the *Map Calculation 1* theme is added to the view, close the dialog.

20   Make the *Map Calculation 1* theme active. In the Theme Properties, change its name to **Landuse Eagan** and click OK.

21   In the Legend Editor, navigate to the extend\spatial\ch12 directory and load the "landuse.avl" legend. Don't click Apply yet.

In step 11, you noticed that there is no airport land in Eagan. There is therefore no reason to keep this category symbolized in the legend.

22   In the Legend Editor, click on the blue polygon symbol representing airport land to highlight the class. Click the Delete Class button to remove it from the legend. Click Apply and close the Legend Editor. Turn on the *Landuse Eagan* theme and turn off the *Eagan mask* theme.

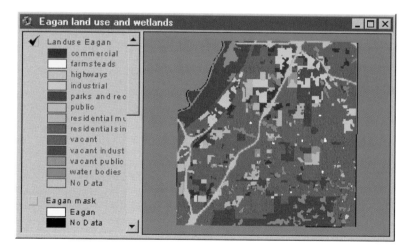

You now have a theme with land use values corresponding to the boundaries of Eagan. You're ready to look at the *Wetlands* theme and compare it to the *Landuse Eagan* theme.

23   Scroll to the bottom of the Table of Contents and make the *Wetlands* theme active. Drag it to the top of the Table of Contents and turn it on.

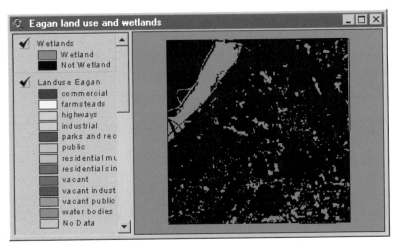

Areas shown in green are wetlands. Black areas either lie outside the Eagan boundary or are known not to be wetlands. Both types of areas are classified as No Data.

You want to find out how land is actually being used in the wetland areas. You can do this by creating a histogram that charts the values in one grid (*Wetlands*) by those in another (*Landuse Eagan*).

24   Make sure the *Wetlands* theme is active. From the Analysis menu, choose Histogram By Zone. In the first dialog, select "Value" as the field that defines zones and click OK.

In the second dialog, select *Landuse Eagan* as the theme with the values to histogram. Click OK.

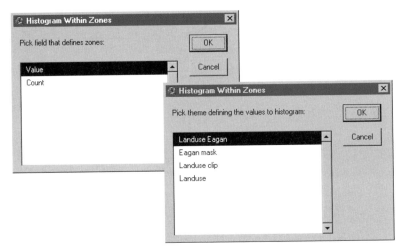

The histogram is created and added to the view.

25　Resize the histogram so that the entire legend is visible. You may need to enlarge the ArcView GIS application window.

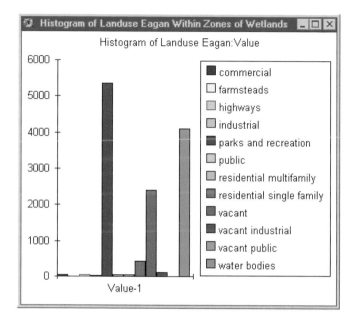

The histogram shows how land use values are distributed among wetlands. The x-axis is labeled "Value-1." (There's only one value, namely wetlands, in the *Wetlands* grid.) The y-axis tells you how many cells in each Eagan land use category fall within wetlands.

Almost all the land use falls into one of three appropriate categories: parks and recreation, vacant, and water bodies.

26　From the File menu, choose Close All. Again from the File menu, choose Close Project. Click No when you're prompted to save your changes.

In this exercise, you created a grid data set called nwgrd1 in your c:\temp directory. Use the Source Manager to delete this file.

If you want to go on to the next exercise, leave ArcView GIS running. Otherwise, choose Exit from the File menu.

Resampling grids

When grids with different cell sizes are used together in analysis, one must be resampled to the size of the other. (If there are several grids, all must be resampled to the dimensions of one.)

Normally, the finer resolution grid is resampled to the dimensions of the coarse one. Resampling a coarse grid to a finer resolution can give the false impression that your data is more detailed than it really is.

Suppose, then, that you resample a 10-meter grid to 30 meters. Each cell in the 30-meter grid covers the same area as nine cells in the 10-meter grid. How are the 30-meter grid cell values determined? ArcView Spatial Analyst has three different techniques for solving this problem. The simplest of these, the "Nearest Neighbor" method, is illustrated below. The value of the 10-meter cell that overlays the center of the 30-meter cell becomes the 30-meter cell's value.

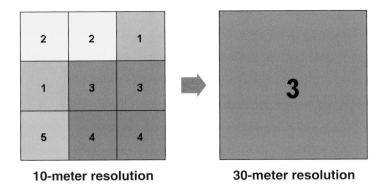

10-meter resolution   **30-meter resolution**

In this exercise, you'll resample a 30-meter land use grid to the cell size of a 90-meter elevation grid.

◆ *Exercise 12c*

1   If necessary, start ArcView GIS. Navigate to the extend\spatial\ch12 directory and open the project "ex12c.apr." When the project opens, you see a view with an elevation grid theme and a land use grid theme for the city of Eagan.

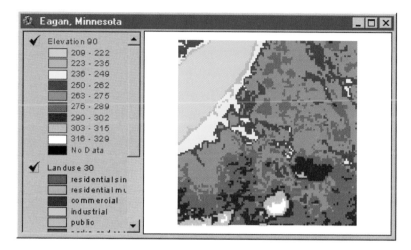

The fact that the grid extents don't conform to the Eagan boundary isn't important in this exercise. Note the large blue swath in the upper left corner of the elevation grid. This low-lying area is part of a 100-year floodplain (an area that floods every 100 years).

2   With the *Elevation 90* theme active, open the Theme Properties dialog. The cell size is 90 meters and there are 107 rows and columns. Click Cancel to close the dialog.

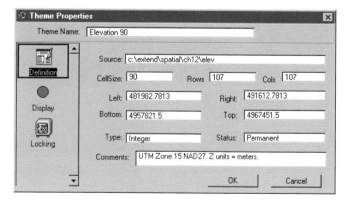

3   Make the *Landuse 30* theme active and drag it to the top of the Table of
    Contents.

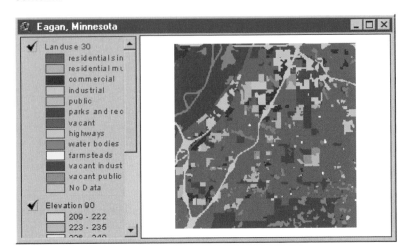

4   With the *Landuse 30* theme active, open the Theme Properties dialog. This
    theme has a cell size of 30 meters. There are 320 rows and 321 columns in
    the grid. Close the dialog.

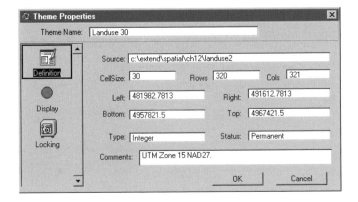

You'll use the elevation and land use themes to create a grid theme
of environmentally sensitive areas. Sensitive areas will be defined as
floodplains (elevations less than 220 meters in the *Elevation 90* grid)
and water bodies (which have a value of 9 in the *Landuse 30* grid).

You'll resample the *Landuse 30* grid cell size to 90 meters using the
Nearest Neighbor method.

Resampling methods. By default, ArcView Spatial Analyst resamples cells according to the Nearest Neighbor method. Two other methods, Bilinear Interpolation and Cubic Convolution, can be used in the Map Calculator. Each of the three methods can be used with measured data, such as elevation. (Nearest Neighbor produces the blockiest output, Cubic Convolution the smoothest.) Only the Nearest Neighbor method should be used with grids in which cell values represent codes or categories rather than measurements. The Nearest Neighbor method doesn't create any values in the resampled grid that don't exist in the input grid. The Bilinear Interpolation and Cubic Convolution methods use weighted averages of several input grid cells to determine each output cell value and may create values that don't exist in the input grid. In the online help, use the Find tab to locate the topic *Grid Resample Discussion*.

5   From the Analysis menu, choose Properties to open the Analysis Properties dialog. Make sure that the *Analysis Cell Size* is set to "Maximum Of Inputs." When you query the elevation and land use grids, the output grid will have the same resolution as the coarsest input grid (90 meters). Click OK.

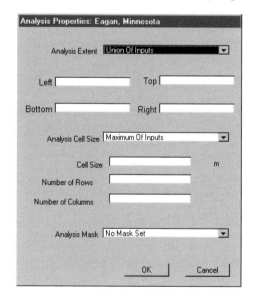

6   From the Analysis menu, choose Map Query to open the Map Query 1 dialog.

Double-click on the [Landuse 30] layer to add it to the expression box. Click the "=" button. In the *Unique Values* scrolling box, double-click "9."

Click the "or" button. Double-click on the [Elevation 90] layer. Click the "<=" (less than or equal to) button. In the *Unique Values* scrolling box, double-click "220."

Your completed expression should match the one in the graphic. Click Evaluate and close the dialog.

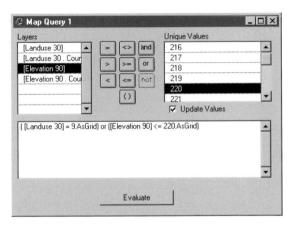

The *Map Query 1* grid theme is calculated and added to the view.

7   Make the *Map Query 1* theme active. Open the Theme Properties dialog and change the theme name to **Land sensitivity**. Note that the cell size for the *Land sensitivity* grid is 90. Click OK.

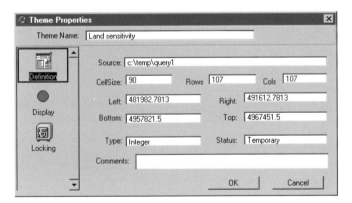

8   Double-click on the *Land sensitivity* theme to open the Legend Editor. Set the symbol for the cells with a value of 0 to a medium blue. Change their label to "Not sensitive." If necessary, set the symbol for the cells with a value of 1 to bright red. Change their label to "Sensitive." Press the Enter key to enter your changes. Click Apply, then close the Legend Editor and the Color Palette.

9 Turn on the *Land sensitivity* theme.

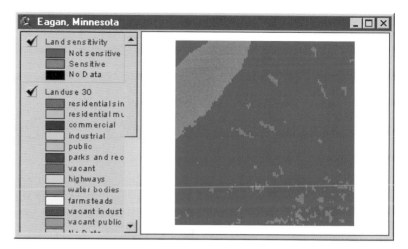

10 From the File menu, choose Close All. Again from the File menu, choose Close Project. Click No when you're prompted to save your changes.

If you're going on to the next chapter, leave ArcView GIS running. Otherwise, choose Exit from the File menu.

13

Using the
Map Calculator

Using operators

Using requests

Using conditional processing

THE MAP CALCULATOR

is the heart of ArcView Spatial Analyst. All operations can be run from it and a great many can only be run from it. You already have some experience with the Map Calculator from previous chapters. In this chapter, you'll begin to use it more systematically.

Using operators

You know more than you may think you do about map algebra operators. They're mostly the same ones that you find on a scientific calculator. Those that are used most often are the simplest: arithmetic operators like "plus," "minus," and "times"; relational operators like "equals" and "less than"; and logical operators like "and," "or," and "not."

Arithmetic operators have many purposes. In the introduction to chapter 8, you saw how grids measuring three kinds of fire risk could be added to create an overall risk analysis grid. In chapter 10, you subtracted one elevation grid from another to see where they were different. A typical use for arithmetic operators is to convert values from one measurement system to another (multiplying feet by 0.3048 to get meters, for example).

Relational and logical operators are used to find cells that meet specific conditions within a single grid or among multiple grids. In chapter 9, you used the Map Query dialog (the Map Calculator's little brother) to find vegetation "equal to" Sierra-type mixed conifer forest. In chapter 11, you found cells that satisfied conditions in two different grids: they had population density "greater than or equal to" 2,000 "and" they were "less than" 1,500 meters from a park.

In this exercise, you'll begin by converting the values in a snowfall grid of the United States from inches to centimeters. Then you'll add three different grids of monthly snowfall to create a winter snowfall grid. Finally, you'll compare the monthly snowfall grids to see which months are snowier than others.

◆ *Exercise 13a*

1   If necessary, start ArcView GIS. Navigate to the extend\spatial\ch13 directory and open the project "ex13a.apr." When the project opens, you see a
view of the United States with average January snowfall for the period 1961
to 1990.

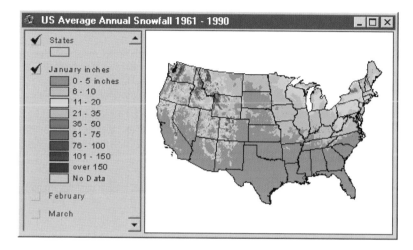

The view contains grid themes of snowfall averages for the months
of January, February, and March. The original z values (representing snowfall) were in inches, but the values in the February and
March grids have been converted to centimeters. You'll convert the
January values to centimeters as well.

2   From the Analysis menu, choose Map Calculator. In the Map Calculator dialog, double-click on the [January inches] layer to add it to the expression
box. Click the "*" (multiplication) button, then type **2.54**. Click the AsGrid
button. Your expression should match the one in the following graphic.

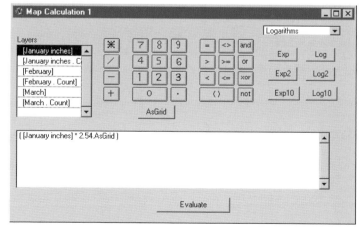

> AsGrid is a request that ensures that numbers (like 2.54) are interpreted as grid cell values or factors in grid cell values. You'll learn more about requests in the next exercise.

3   Click the Evaluate button. When the *Map Calculation 1* theme is added to the view, close the dialog.

4   Make the *Map Calculation 1* theme active. Open the Theme Properties dialog and change the theme name to **January**. Click OK.

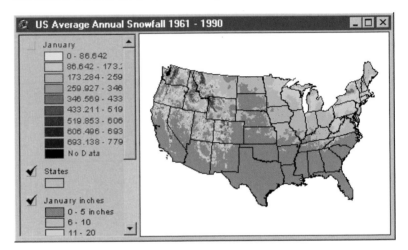

Every cell in the January grid contains the value, multiplied by 2.54, of the corresponding cell in the January inches grid. Because the multiplier contained decimal points, the new grid is a floating-point grid. There's nothing wrong with that, except that you don't need decimal point precision. You'll convert the values to integers using the Int request. (The use of requests in the Map Calculator is covered in more detail in the next exercise.)

5   Make sure the January theme is active. From the Theme menu, choose Edit Theme Expression. The Map Calculator dialog displays the expression you used to create the January theme. Place the cursor at the end of the expression and type **.Int**. Your expression should match the one in the following graphic.

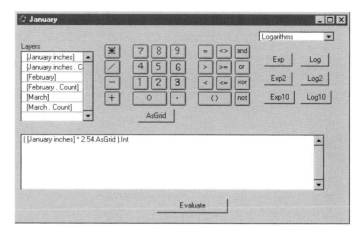

6   Click the Evaluate button. When the *January* grid is recalculated, close the dialog.

> In chapter 9, you learned that when you edit a theme expression, the output grid theme replaces the existing grid theme. (The two source data sets have different names, however. If you save a grid data set before editing its theme expression you can retrieve it from disk.)

The Int request outputs a grid in which cell values are truncated (not rounded) at the decimal place. The *January* grid is now an integer grid with a theme table.

7   Double-click on the *January* theme to open the Legend Editor. Click the Load button and navigate to the extend\spatial\ch13 directory. Load the "snow-fall.avl" legend, making sure the *Field* is set to "Value" in the Load Legend dialog. Click Apply and close the Legend Editor. Turn on the *January* theme.

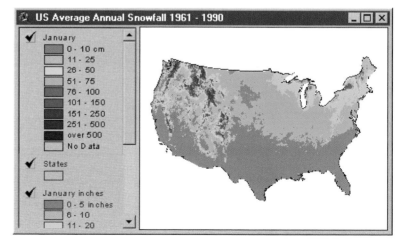

The legend is a custom classification for the centimeter values. You no longer need the *January inches* theme.

8   Make the *January inches* theme active and delete it. Make the *February* and *March* themes active. From the Theme menu, choose Hide/Show Legend to show their legends.

Now you'll add the three snowfall themes to find the average winter snowfall.

9   From the Analysis menu, choose Map Calculator. Double-click on the [January] layer to add it to the expression box. Click the "+" button. Double-click the [February] layer and click the "+" button again. Double-click the [March] layer. Your expression should match the one in the following graphic.

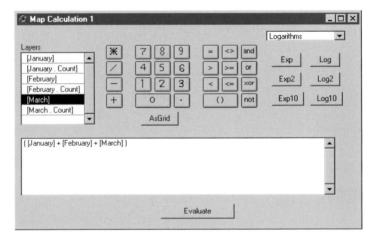

10 Click the Evaluate button. When the *Map Calculation 1* theme is added to the view, close the dialog.

11 Make the *Map Calculation 1* theme active. Open the Theme Properties dialog and change the theme name to **Winter**. Click OK.

12 Double-click on the *Winter* theme to open the Legend Editor. Click the Load button and navigate to the extend\spatial\ch13 directory. Load the "snowfall.avl" legend. Click Apply and close the Legend Editor. Turn on the *Winter* theme.

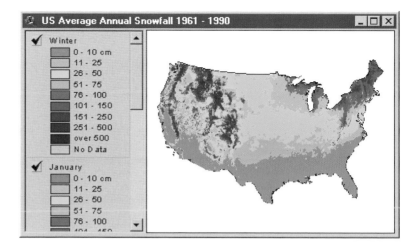

The grid shows the combined average snowfall in centimeters for the months of January, February, and March.

Suppose you want to know where snow falls late in the winter rather than early. You'll create a grid that shows where there's more snow in March than in January.

13 From the Analysis menu, choose Map Calculator. Double-click on the [March] layer to add it to the expression box. Click the ">" (greater than) button. Double-click the [January] layer. Your expression should match the one in the following graphic.

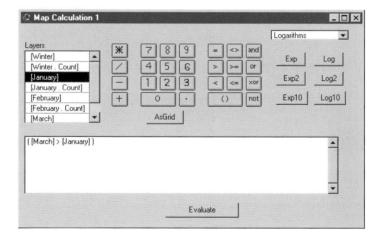

14 Click the Evaluate button. When the *Map Calculation 1* theme is added to the view, close the dialog.

The output grid is like the true/false grids you have previously created in the Map Query dialog.

Any expression you evaluate in the Map Query dialog can also be evaluated in the Map Calculator. Map queries are a convenience for expressions that test true/false conditions, because they apply a predefined legend to the output grid theme.

---

15 Make the *Map Calculation 1* theme active. Open the Theme Properties dialog and change the theme name to **March > January**. Click OK. Turn the theme on.

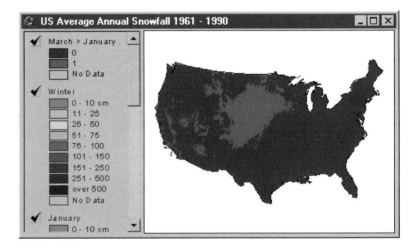

Areas with a value of 1 show where there's more snowfall in March than in January; areas with a value of 0 show where there's less or the same amount. (Your colors may be different.)

Now you'll identify parts of the country where the snowfall increases throughout the winter months.

16 From the Analysis menu, choose Map Calculator. In the dialog, create the expression:

([January] < [February]) and ([February] < [March])

Your expression should match the one in the following graphic.

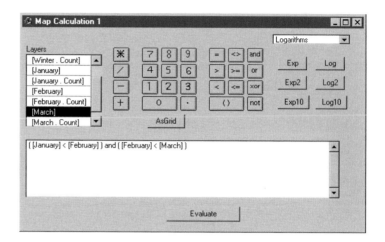

The two parts of the expression, separated by the logical operator "and," are enclosed in parentheses.

Order of evaluation. Map Calculator expressions are evaluated from left to right. You need to group your expressions properly, just as you do with ordinary math notation. If you have an uneven number of parentheses, you'll get a syntax error when you try to evaluate an expression. If you don't put parentheses in all the right places, you may get results that aren't what you want. For example, the expression $(1 + 2 * 3)$ gives a result of 9, because, moving from left to right, 1 is added to 2 and the result is multiplied by 3. On the other hand, $(1 + (2 * 3))$ is 7. The same ambiguities can occur with relational and logical operators.

17 Click the Evaluate button. When the *Map Calculation 1* theme is added to the view, close the dialog.

18 Make the *Map Calculation 1* theme active. Open the Theme Properties dialog and change the theme name to **More and more**. Click OK. Turn the theme on.

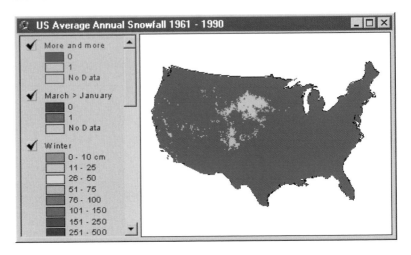

Areas with a value of 1 show where the amount of snowfall increases through each of the winter months. Areas with a value of 0 show where it does not.

19 Drag the *States* theme to the top of the Table of Contents.

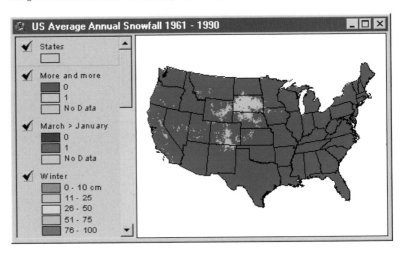

The Identify tool can tell you that the areas where snowfall increases throughout the winter lie mainly in South Dakota, Nebraska, Wyoming, and Colorado.

20 From the File menu, choose Close All. Again from the File menu, choose Close Project. Click No when you're prompted to save your changes.

If you want to go on to the next exercise, leave ArcView GIS running. Otherwise, choose Exit from the File menu.

Using requests

All Map Calculator expressions use requests. Requests are instructions in the Avenue™ scripting language, the language understood by ArcView GIS. Avenue is an object-oriented language and grids are a kind of object. That means that when you want to do something with a grid (derive its slope, change its values, or anything else), you need to send it a request. You don't have to be a programmer to use requests effectively. You just have to know how to ask.

Math and logical operators, like those you used in the previous exercise, are actually requests, but their syntax isn't typical. Most Avenue requests take the form "Object.Request (Parameter)." If you went to a restaurant where the waiter spoke only Avenue, you couldn't say, "I'll have a T-bone steak, medium-rare." Instead, you'd have to say something more like, "Steak.Make (T-bone, medium-rare)."

Every request sent to an object is an implicit instruction to make another object. (In Avenue, "doing something" and "making something" are synonymous.) For instance, when you sent the Int request to the *January* snowfall grid in the previous exercise, you made a new grid.

Most requests that are sent to grids do in fact make new grids, but some make other objects, such as numbers or lists. If you send these requests directly from the Map Calculator, you'll get a syntax error. (This explains the purpose of the AsGrid request: it confirms to ArcView Spatial Analyst that you want to make a grid object, not a number object.) The online help for any request will tell you what kind of object it makes.

In this exercise, you'll send aspect and slope requests to an elevation grid. You already know how to create slope and aspect grids with menu choices. Now you'll do it from the Map Calculator.

◆ *E x e r c i s e   1 3 b*

1   If necessary, start ArcView GIS. Navigate to the extend\spatial\ch13 directory and open the project "ex13b.apr." When the project opens, you see a
view of Yellowstone National Park and the surrounding area.

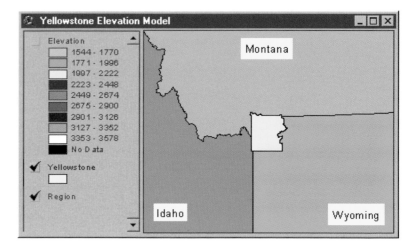

Yellowstone, located in the northwest corner of Wyoming, was
established in 1872. It's the oldest national park in the United
States.

2   With the *Yellowstone* theme active, click the Zoom to Active Theme(s) button. Turn on the *Elevation* theme.

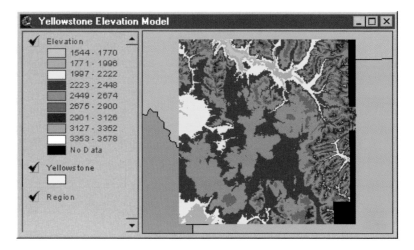

In chapter 10, you derived slope and aspect grids using choices on the Surface menu. These menu choices run Avenue scripts that use the Slope and Aspect requests. You can also derive slope and aspect by entering requests in the Map Calculator.

Why would you? The reason is that menu choices create grids with default parameter values. Running a request from the Map Calculator allows you to choose the values you want. This doesn't matter with a request like "Aspect" that has no parameters, but with most requests it does. You'll send the Aspect request from the Map Calculator, anyway, because it's an easy one. By the next exercise, you may recall it with nostalgia.

3   From the Analysis menu, choose Map Calculator. In the dialog, double-click on the [Elevation] layer to add it to the expression box. Place the cursor between the closing bracket of the Elevation layer and the closing paren-thesis of the expression and type **.Aspect**. (You can put spaces on either side of the "." if that makes it easier to see what you're doing.) Your expres-sion should match the one in the following graphic.

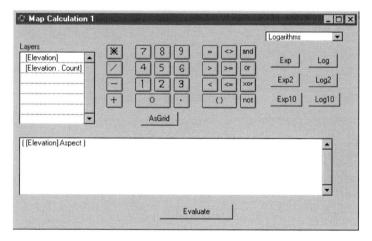

4   Click the Evaluate button. When the *Map Calculation 1* theme is added to the view, close the dialog.

You've created an aspect grid, just as if you had chosen Derive Aspect from the Surface menu. The only difference is that the menu choice gives you a predefined theme name and legend.

5   Make the *Map Calculation 1* theme active. Open the Theme Properties dialog and change the theme name to **Aspect**. Click OK.

6   Double-click on the *Aspect* theme to open the Legend Editor. Click the Load
     button and navigate to the extend\spatial\ch13 directory. Load the
     "aspect.avl" legend file, making sure that the *Field* is set to "Value" in the
     Load Legend dialog. Click Apply and close the Legend Editor. Turn the
     Aspect theme on.

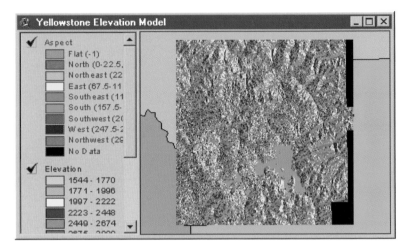

The large gray area in the southeast is Yellowstone Lake.

In a moment, you'll try the Slope request, which does have parameters with values you can set yourself. But first, you may be won-
dering how to find out which parameters a request has—and how
to get a list of all the available requests. Your main resource is the
ArcView GIS online help.

7   From the Help menu, choose Help Topics to open the online help. Click the
     Index tab. Locate and display the *Grid (Class)* help topic.

The Grid (Class) topic shows you all the requests that are understood by grids, the parameters each request takes, and the objects
that are created by running the requests. Scroll down through the
list until you come to the "Surface functions" heading (near the
end). Locate the Slope request.

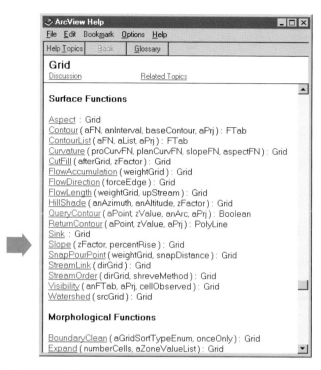

8   Click on the link to open the help page for the Slope request.

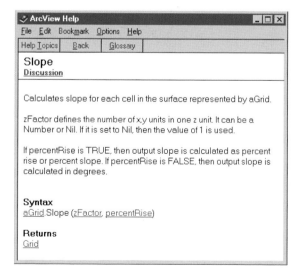

The Slope request has two parameters and returns a grid object. The first parameter is a conversion factor used to correct z values that are in a different unit of measure than the x,y values. When you derive slope from the Surface menu, ArcView Spatial Analyst assumes that your grid's x, y, and z values are in the same unit of measure. If the x,y units are meters and the z units are feet, the slope calculations will be wrong.

The second parameter defines whether the output grid values will be in degrees or percent of slope.

9   Close the Help window. From the Analysis menu, choose Map Calculator. In the dialog, double-click on the [Elevation] layer to add it to the expression box. Place the cursor between the closing bracket of the Elevation layer and the closing parenthesis of the expression and type **.Slope (NIL, TRUE)**. Your expression should match the one in the following graphic.

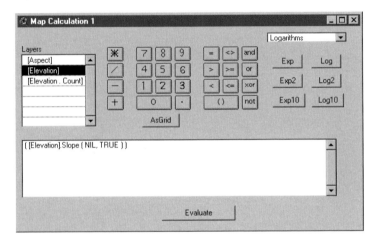

The NIL parameter means that your z values are already in the same unit of measure as your x,y values. The TRUE parameter specifies an output grid of slope by percent rather than slope in degrees.

10   Click the Evaluate button. When the *Map Calculation 1* theme is added to the view, close the dialog.

11   Make the *Map Calculation 1* theme active. Open the Theme Properties dialog and change the theme name to **Slope by percent**. Click OK.

12   Double-click on the *Slope by percent* theme to open the Legend Editor. Click the Load button and navigate to the extend\spatial\ch13 directory. Load the "slope.avl" legend file. Click Apply and close the Legend Editor. Turn the *Slope by percent* theme on.

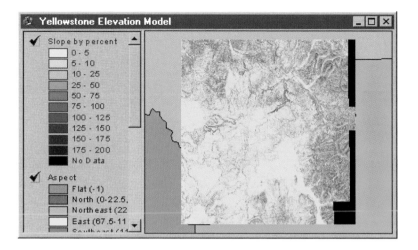

The values are classified in shades of brown. A slope of 100 percent corresponds to 45 degrees. As the slope angle approaches vertical (90 degrees), the percent of slope approaches infinity.

13 From the File menu, choose Close All. Again from the File menu, choose Close Project. Click No when you're prompted to save your changes.

If you want to go on to the next exercise, leave ArcView GIS running. Otherwise, choose Exit from the File menu.

Using conditional processing

In this exercise, you'll work with the Con ("Condition") request. Most requests leave no room for alternatives once their parameters are set; the Con request tells ArcView Spatial Analyst to do either one thing or another, depending on the conditions it finds in a particular grid.

If a typical request asked someone to buy a pound of Swiss cheese, then the Con request might ask them, for example, to check the price first and then buy Swiss or cheddar, depending on which was cheaper.

What conditions the Con request checks, and what alternatives it follows, are up to you. In this exercise, you'll work with a grid of Yellowstone fire data in which all areas not burned by the summer fires of 1988 are classified as No Data. Information from a second grid, however, will tell you that many of these No Data areas definitely did not burn. With the Con request, you'll check for these unburned areas and tell ArcView Spatial Analyst to change No Data cells in the fire data grid as appropriate.

◆ *E x e r c i s e   1 3 c*

1   If necessary, start ArcView GIS. Navigate to the extend\spatial\ch13 directory and open the project "ex13c.apr." When the project opens, you see a view of the Yellowstone National Park boundary. A polygon theme of water bodies is also turned on.

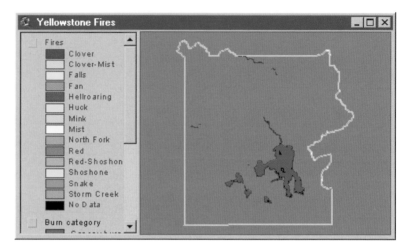

In the summer of 1988, wildfires burned large areas of the park. The view contains a grid theme of the burned areas, classified by the names of the fires.

2   Turn on the *Fires* theme.

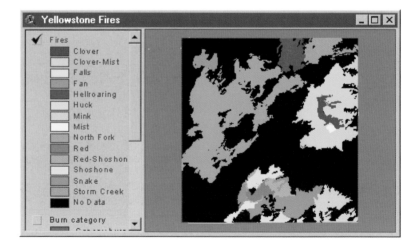

The No Data values represent areas where there were no fires. For some of these areas there's no information, but others are known not to have burned (and some, like Yellowstone Lake, couldn't have burned). You will distinguish the No Data that means "no information" from the No Data that means "no fire."

3   With the *Fires* theme active, click the Open Theme Table button.

Value	Count	Name	Date
1	450	Storm Creek	August 20, 1988
2	14	Storm Creek	September 7, 1988
3	114	Hellroaring	August 19, 1988
4	2870	Storm Creek	August 30, 1988
5	286	Hellroaring	August 18, 1988
6	317	Storm Creek	August 24, 1988
7	140	Hellroaring	August 22, 1988
8	1591	Storm Creek	August 31, 1988
9	650	Hellroaring	August 30, 1988
10	63	Storm Creek	September 5, 1988
11	25	Hellroaring	September 2, 1988

Each value in the table is associated with a fire name and a date.

4   Close the table. Turn off the *Fires* theme and the *Water* theme. Make the *Burn category* theme active and turn it on.

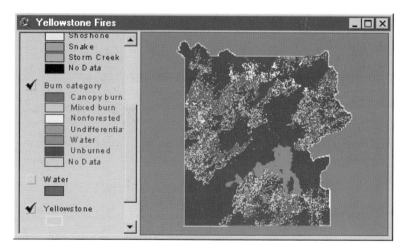

The *Burn category* grid doesn't have attribute information for the names and dates of fires, but it does identify which parts of the park did and didn't burn.

Your Con request will test each cell in the *Burn category* grid to see whether it falls into either the "Water" or "Unburned" categories. If it does, its corresponding No Data cell in the *Fires* grid will be replaced with a new value. If it doesn't (that is, if the cell belongs to one of the other burn categories), it shouldn't correspond to a No Data cell in the *Fires* grid—it should correspond to a cell representing a particular fire. In any case, a No Data cell in the *Fires* grid will remain No Data unless it corresponds to a Water or Unburned cell in the *Burn category* grid.

What value should you use to replace No Data cells in the *Fires* grid? It really doesn't matter, as long as it's not a value that already exists somewhere in the *Fires* grid. A number like −999 will do.

In order to create the Con expression, you need to know the numeric values for the Water and Unburned categories.

5   With the *Burn category* theme active, click the Open Theme Table button. Water has a value of 5 and Unburned has a value of 6. Close the table.

6   From the Analysis menu, choose Map Calculator. Because the structure of Con requests is often complicated (and this one will be no exception), it's helpful to create a template expression and then fill it in with grid names and values.

In the dialog, with the cursor between the parentheses, type
aGrid.Con (yesGrid, noGrid)

Your expression should match the one in the following graphic.

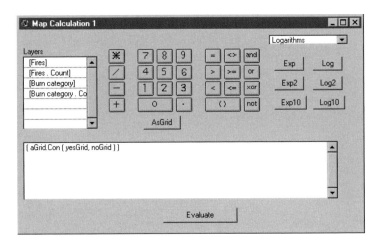

Now you'll replace the placeholders. The condition you're evaluating is whether or not the cell values of the Burn category grid are equal either to 5 or 6. If they are, you want the corresponding output grid cells to have the value −999. Otherwise, you want the output grid values to be the same as the values in the *Fires* grid.

7 Highlight and delete the term "aGrid." Replace it with
(([Burn category] = 5) or ([Burn category] = 6))

Replace the term "yesGrid" with
−999.AsGrid

Replace the term "noGrid" with
[Fires]

Your completed expression should be:
((([Burn category] = 5) or ([Burn category] = 6)).Con (−999.AsGrid, [Fires]))

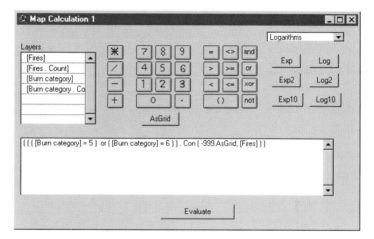

Check your syntax carefully before proceeding. The outermost set of parentheses is optional, but the rest are necessary. (It may be reassuring to know that this is the longest Map Calculator expression you'll create in this book.)

8 Click Evaluate. When the *Map Calculation 1* theme is added to the view, close the dialog.

9   Make the *Map Calculation 1* theme active. Open the Theme Properties dialog and change the theme name to **Final fires**. Click OK. Turn the theme on.

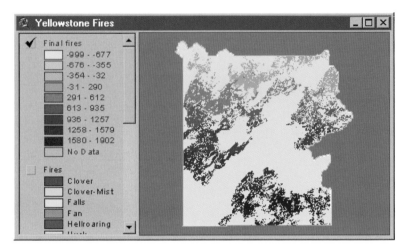

Most of the areas that were No Data in the *Fires* grid are assigned the value −999 in the *Final fires* grid. You now have the information you want, but not the legend you want.

   10 With the *Final fires* theme active, click the Open Theme Table button.

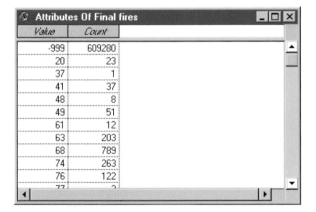

You'd like to display this grid according to the name of each fire (just like the *Fires* grid). Unfortunately, the *Final fires* grid has no name or date attributes. You could open the *Fires* theme table and join its attributes to the *Final fires* table, but this won't help you display values of −999 according to a name attribute (it doesn't have one).

Instead, you'll open a table in the project that contains name attributes for both the fires and the unburned areas.

One way to preserve attributes for calculated grids is to export your original grid theme table as a .dbf file. In this exercise, a table called fire-code.dbf was exported from the *Fires* theme table. The original Value field was recalculated to a field called ID and the original Count field was deleted. A record with an ID of −999 and the name attribute "Unburned or Water" was added in anticipation of the *Final fires* grid.

11 Make the Project window active and make sure the Tables icon is selected. Double-click on the firecode.dbf table to open it.

The ID field in this table contains values that correspond to the grid values. You'll join this table to the *Final fires* grid theme table.

12 In the firecode.dbf table, click on the ID field to highlight it. Make the *Attributes of Final fires* table active and click on its Value field to highlight it. With the *Attributes of Final fires* table active, click the Join button.

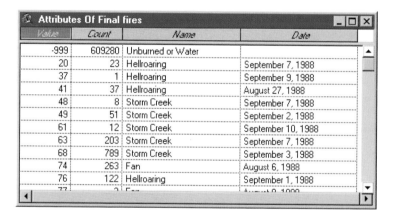

Value	Count	Name	Date
-999	609280	Unburned or Water	
20	23	Hellroaring	September 7, 1988
37	1	Hellroaring	September 9, 1988
41	37	Hellroaring	August 27, 1988
48	8	Storm Creek	September 7, 1988
49	51	Storm Creek	September 2, 1988
61	12	Storm Creek	September 10, 1988
63	203	Storm Creek	September 7, 1988
68	789	Storm Creek	September 3, 1988
74	263	Fan	August 6, 1988
76	122	Hellroaring	September 1, 1988
77	2	Fan	August 9, 1988

All the values have their original attributes from the *Fires* grid theme table. The value of −999 has the name Unburned or Water.

13 Close the table. With the *Final fires* theme active in the view, double-click to open the Legend Editor. Click the Load button and navigate to the extend\ spatial\ch13 directory. Load the "final.avl" legend file, making sure that *Field* is set to "Name" in the Load Legend dialog. Click Apply in the Legend Editor and close the Legend Editor.

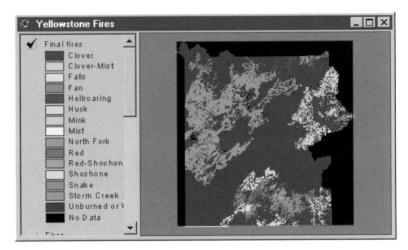

You now have your result: a grid theme of fires in which unburned areas are distinguished from areas of No Data. Most of the remaining No Data areas lie outside the grid analysis area, but not all of them. There are some small, speckled No Data areas within the analysis area as well. These are areas that weren't defined as fires in the *Fires* grid, but were nonetheless defined as burned in the *Burn category* grid.

By comparing the *Final fires* grid to the original *Fires* grid, you will also see that some areas classified as "Unburned or Water" in the final grid have fire values in the *Fires* grid.

What this means is that your two original grids (*Fires* and *Burn categories*) don't always agree on what's what. Without knowing how the source data was created, or what may have been done to it since, you can't say which of the two grids more accurately describes reality. It's quite possible that the *Fires* grid data was generalized to give it a more homogeneous appearance and avoid the speckled, "noisy" effect of the *Final fires* grid.

In the next chapter, you'll see how to generalize and smooth grid data in this way to make it easier to interpret.

Understanding conditional processing. The syntax of the Con request is aGrid.Con (yesGrid, noGrid). In this context, "aGrid" really means "a condition of a grid," or "a possible value of the cells in a grid" (for example, [Elevation] > 1000). The logic is that each cell in an input grid is tested for a given condition. If the cell tests true, the value from the corresponding cell in the yesGrid is assigned to the output grid cell. If the cell tests false, the value from the corresponding noGrid cell is assigned. Suppose a zoning grid is being consolidated. Values of 500 and 510, representing two residential housing density codes, are being replaced by the single value of 500. The appropriate Con request would be

$$(([Zoning] = 510).Con (500.AsGrid, [Zoning]))$$

Each cell in the input zoning grid is tested to see whether it has a value of 510. If it does, the corresponding output grid cell is given a value of 500 (specified in the yesGrid parameter). If it doesn't, the output grid cell gets whatever value currently exists in the Zoning grid (the noGrid parameter). The effect is to replace values of 510 with 500 and to leave other values unchanged. Con requests can be nested inside one another to make increasingly complex evaluations. In the online help, use the Find tab to locate the topic *Con (Grid)*.

14 From the File menu, choose Close. Again from the File menu, choose Close Project. Click No when you're prompted to save your changes.

If you're going on to the next chapter, leave ArcView GIS running. Otherwise, choose Exit from the File menu.

14

Creating statistics and generalizing data

Creating neighborhood and zonal statistics

Generalizing grid data

Advanced generalizing techniques

IN THIS CHAPTER,

you'll create a statistical grid that shows you where the variety of land cover types is high and low within Yellowstone National Park. (In other words, you'll find out where lots of different kinds of trees grow together and where one or two types stick to themselves.) Then you'll look for a correlation between land cover variety and slope. Finally, you'll apply several editing techniques to a land cover grid of Yellowstone to simplify the data and make it easier to interpret.

Creating neighborhood and zonal statistics

Statistics are aggregate information about the cells in a grid. You can get basic statistics, like the minimum, maximum, and mean values in a grid, by clicking the Statistics button in the Legend Editor.

With a little more work, you can also get statistics for the zones and neighborhoods within a grid. Zones are sets of cells with the same value. With a grid of land use, for example, you could get statistics like the amount of area belonging to each land use type.

Neighborhoods are sections of grids that can be defined in almost any way you want. A neighborhood can be a three-cell by three-cell square or a 2-kilometer by 4-kilometer rectangle. It can be a circle with a radius of 1.5 miles or twenty-five cells. It can be a wedge, a doughnut, or an irregular shape that you define. Neighborhoods can be overlapping or discrete. (When neighborhoods overlap, the statistics you get are called focal statistics; when neighborhoods are discrete, the statistics are called block statistics.) With a grid of vegetation, for example, you could find the majority vegetation type in each neighborhood—or the minority type, or the number of different types.

It's also possible to get statistics about one grid in terms of another. For instance, with a grid of elevation and another of vegetation, you could determine the maximum elevation at which each vegetation type is found—or the minimum elevation or the mean.

Zonal statistics are normally output as tables. Neighborhood statistics are output as grids. If, for example, you ask ArcView Spatial Analyst to find the majority cell value in each neighborhood (that is, the value held by the majority of cells), it will create an output grid in which each cell is assigned the majority value for its neighborhood.

In the following example, both block and focal majority statistics have been created for a three-cell by three-cell neighborhood. In block statistics, neighborhoods are discrete. For the neighborhood outlined in red, 2 is the majority value in the input grid (five of the nine cells have this value). In the output grid, all cells in the red neighborhood are changed to 2. For the neighborhood outlined in blue, 3 is the majority value in the input grid and all cell values in the output grid are changed to 3.

In focal statistics, neighborhoods overlap and each cell's neighborhood is unique. For the neighborhood outlined in red, the majority value is still 2 in the input grid, but only the cell whose neighborhood it is— in this example, the center cell—gets that value in the output grid. (Because this cell's value was already 2, it didn't change.) In the blue neighborhood, the majority value in the input grid is again 2. This time, the center cell's value is changed from 3 to 2.

Block neighborhood statistics   **Focal neighborhood statistics**

Input grid

In block statistics, every cell within a neighborhood gets the same value. In focal statistics, a unique neighborhood is defined for every cell and each output cell value is potentially different.

In this exercise, you'll create neighborhood (focal) statistics to find the variety of land cover types within Yellowstone. Then you'll create zonal statistics to find the average slope for each variety zone.

◆ *E x e r c i s e   1 4 a*

1   If necessary, start ArcView GIS. Navigate to the extend\spatial\ch14 directory and open the project "ex14a.apr." When the project opens, you see a view of land cover in Yellowstone National Park.

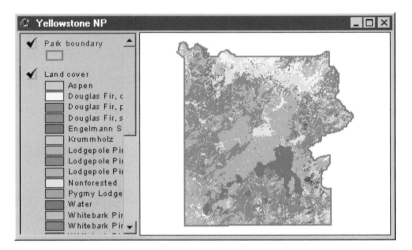

You'll get Variety statistics for neighborhoods in the *Land cover* theme. The output grid will have cell values like 2, 3, 4, and so on, where each value tells you how many different land cover types were found in that cell's neighborhood.

2   Make sure the *Land cover* theme is active. From the Analysis menu, choose Neighborhood Statistics to open the Neighborhood Statistics dialog.

From the *Statistic* drop-down list, choose "Variety." From the *Neighborhood* drop-down list, choose "Rectangle." In the Units field, make sure that the Cell radio button is selected and that the Width and Height values are both set to 3. You're defining a neighborhood of three cells by three cells.

3   Click OK. When the *NbrVariety of Land Cover* grid is added to the view, click on it to make it active. In the Theme Properties dialog, rename the theme **Land cover variety** and click OK. Turn the theme on.

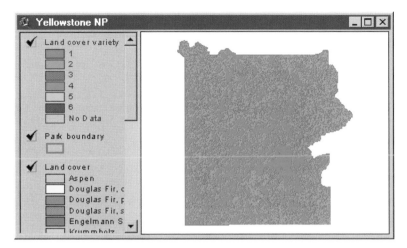

The theme is displayed according to a randomly chosen Unique Value color scheme. Although it may not strike you that you're looking at statistics, in a sense that's what you're doing. The legend tells you how many different land cover types are found among the neighborhoods (as you defined them) of the *Land cover* grid. Some neighborhoods have one land cover type; others have as many as six.

The statistical grid will be easier to interpret with a Graduated Color legend.

4   Double-click on the *Land cover variety* theme to open the Legend Editor.
Set the legend type to "Graduated Color," the classification field to "Value,"
and the number of classes to "6."

Set the color ramp to "Yellow to Green to Dark Blue," then click the Flip
Symbols button, so that the value 1 is dark blue and the value 6 is bright
yellow. Click Apply and close the Legend Editor.

It's not easy to single out the high-variety areas. They are inter-
mixed with low-variety areas throughout the park, though they
seem more conspicuous near the park boundaries.

Understanding neighborhood statistics. The Neighborhood Statistics dialog allows you to define four different types of neighborhoods: rectangle, circle, doughnut, and wedge. (Using a script
available in the online help, you can define a fifth type: an "irregular"
neighborhood.) You can also specify the size of the neighborhood,
either in number of cells or in map units. Many different kinds of statistics can be generated: minimum, maximum, mean, median, sum,
range, standard deviation, majority, minority, and variety. Neighborhood statistics can be created for point feature themes as well as for
grid themes. (The output is still a grid theme.) When you run neighborhood functions from the Analysis menu, you're creating focal statistics rather than block statistics. Both focal and block statistics can be
created using Map Calculator requests. In the online help, use the Find
tab to locate the topics *BlockStats (Grid), Calculating neighborhood
statistics, FocalStats (Grid), MakeIrregular (NbrHood),* and *Neighborhood Statistics Dialog.*

Now that you have the *Land cover variety* grid, you can use zonal
statistics to find slope values within each of the six zones. This will
let you see if land cover variety is correlated with slope.

5   Turn off the *Land cover variety* and *Land cover* themes. Scroll down in the
    Table of Contents and turn on the *Slope* theme.

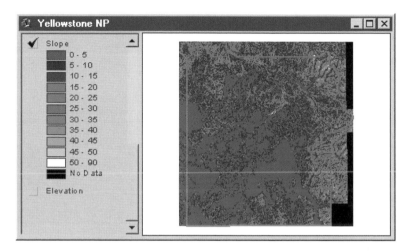

The grid shows slope values in degrees.

6   Make sure the *Land cover variety* theme is still active. From the Analysis
    menu, choose Summarize Zones. In the first Summarize Zones dialog, select
    "Slope" as the theme with variables to summarize. Click OK to generate a
    table of zonal statistics.

    In the second Summarize Zones dialog, select "Mean" as the statistic to
    chart. Click OK to create a chart that displays land cover variety by mean
    slope value.

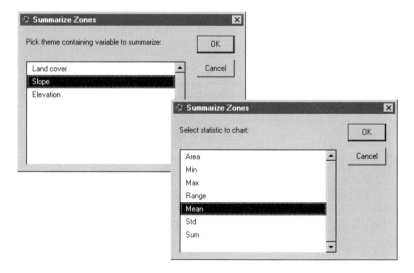

7   Enlarge the Chart document window.

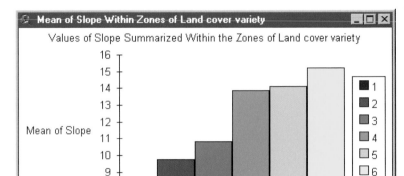

The chart shows a correlation between slope and land cover variety. For zones with one land cover variety, the average slope is just over 7 degrees. The average slope gets steeper for each succeeding zone, until, for zones with six varieties, the average slope is slightly over 15 degrees. This is an interesting result. In a moment, you'll consider whether it might be misleading.

8   Close the chart. Make the *Stats of Slope Within Zones of Land cover variety* table active. Scroll through the table.

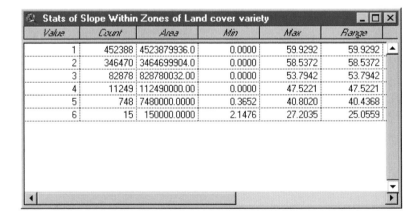

Value	Count	Area	Min	Max	Range
1	452388	4523879936.0	0.0000	59.9292	59.9292
2	346470	3464699904.0	0.0000	58.5372	58.5372
3	82878	828780032.00	0.0000	53.7942	53.7942
4	11249	112490000.00	0.0000	47.5221	47.5221
5	748	7480000.0000	0.3652	40.8020	40.4368
6	15	150000.0000	2.1476	27.2035	25.0559

You chose mean slope as the statistic to chart, but many other statistics are provided in the table.

Understanding zonal statistics. The Summarize Zones process creates a table of statistics on a values theme for each zone in a zone theme. (In this exercise, *Slope* was the values theme and *Land cover variety* was the zone theme.) The zone theme can be either an integer grid theme, where zones are defined by sets of cells with the same value, or it can be a feature theme, where zones are defined by record values in a selected field of the attribute table. The value theme can be either an integer or a floating-point grid theme. The resulting statistics table can be joined to the zone theme, allowing you to classify the theme by any of the statistical fields in the table. It's also possible to output a grid theme, rather than a table, for a particular statistic. A script is provided to do this in the online help. In the online help, use the Find tab to locate the topics *Calculating summary attributes for features using a grid theme, Summarize Zones, Zonal-Stats (Grid),* and *ZonalStatsTable (Grid).*

9   Close the table. In the view, turn off the *Slope* theme and turn on the *Land cover* theme.

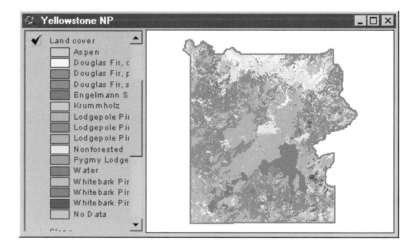

A fair amount of the *Land cover* grid's surface area is taken up by water, which has a slope of zero and a land cover variety value of 1 (except along shorelines). To see how much the effect of water influenced your results, it would be worthwhile to repeat the analysis after setting values of water in the *Land cover* grid to No Data.

There are a couple of ways to change values to No Data. You can do it in the Map Calculator using the SetNull request (you'll use this method in exercise 14c) or you can do it by reclassifying values from the Analysis menu.

10 Make the *Land cover* theme active and click the Open Theme Table button. Scroll down and note that water has a value of 12. Close the table.

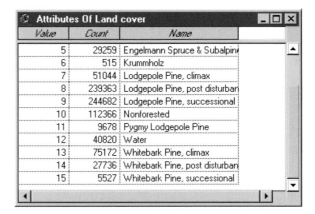

11 From the Analysis menu, choose Reclassify to open the Reclassify Values dialog.

By default, the Classification Field is set to "Value." The scrolling box shows you the existing values in the active grid theme (Old Values) and the corresponding values they'll have in the reclassified grid (New Value). At the moment, these values are the same.

12 Scroll down to "12" in the Old Values column. In the corresponding New Value cell, highlight the value "12" and type **No Data**, then press Enter on your keyboard.

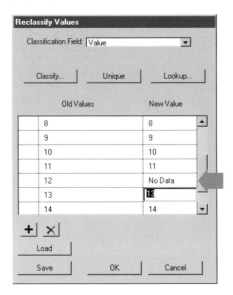

13   Click OK. When the *Reclass of Land cover* theme is added to the view, make it active. In the Theme Properties dialog, change its name to **No water** and click OK.

14   Double-click on the *No water* theme to open the Legend Editor. Click the Load button and navigate to the extend\spatial\ch14 directory. Load the "cover1.avl" legend, making sure that *Field* is set to "Value" in the Load Legend dialog. Click Apply in the Legend Editor and close the Legend Editor. Turn the *Land cover* theme off and turn the *No water* theme on.

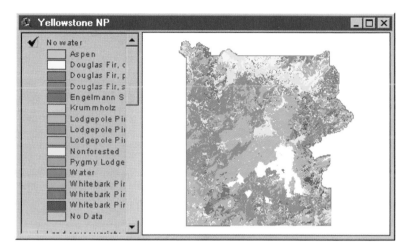

All areas of water have been changed to No Data and are transparent. These areas will be excluded from analysis performed on the *No water* grid.

Reclassifying grids.   There are several reasons to reclassify grid cell values. One is to set specific values to No Data to exclude them from analysis. Others are to change values in response to new information or classification schemes, or to replace one set of values with an associated set (for example, to replace values representing soil types with pH values). Still another reason is to assign values of preference, priority, sensitivity, or similar criteria to a grid theme. This may be done with a single grid (a grid of animal habitat may be assigned values of 1 to 10 that represent degree of endangerment), or with several grids to create a common scale of values. In an agricultural site selection project, for example, grids of soil type, slope, aspect, and so on might each be reclassified on a suitability scale of 1 to 10. These grids, which originally held values belonging to different measurement scales, could then be added to find the most suitable site. In the online help, use the Find tab to locate the topic *Reclassifying the cell values of a grid theme.*

15   On your own, calculate neighborhood variety statistics for the *No water* theme. Then summarize the output grid zones by slope, just as you did for the *Land cover variety* theme.

You'll find that the outcome of the analysis isn't significantly different. The mean slope values do increase somewhat for the lower variety zones (especially for the value 1) after water is taken out of the analysis. The overall trend, however, is the same.

16 From the File menu, choose Close All. Again from the File menu, choose Close Project. Click No when you're prompted to save your changes.

If you want to go on to the next exercise, leave ArcView GIS running. Otherwise, choose Exit from the File menu.

Generalizing grid data

In this exercise, you'll work with a small grid of land cover clipped from the larger Yellowstone land cover grid. You'll learn various techniques for generalizing your data, a process often called "cleaning." The point is to take data sets that have lots of different values sprinkled throughout a grid, and homogenize them to make the data easier to interpret.

◆ *E x e r c i s e   1 4 b*

1 If necessary, start ArcView GIS. Navigate to the extend\spatial\ch14 directory and open the project "ex14b.apr." When the project opens, you see a view of the Yellowstone National Park boundary. A small land cover grid, covering about 100 square kilometers, is located in the northwest section of the park.

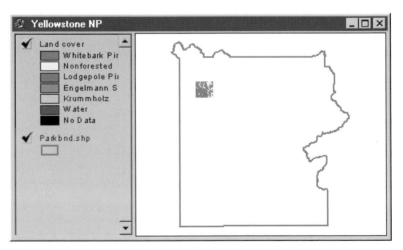

2   With the *Land cover* theme active, click the Zoom to Active Theme(s) button.

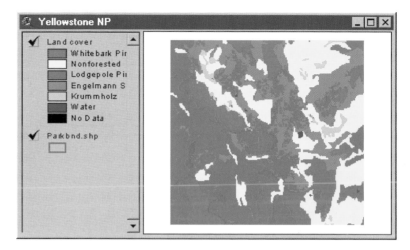

You'll make a first pass at cleaning the grid with the MajorityFilter request in the Map Calculator. MajorityFilter replaces the value of each cell in a grid with the value that belongs to the majority of its adjacent cells.

3   From the Analysis menu, choose Map Calculator. In the dialog, create the expression:

([Land cover].MajorityFilter (TRUE, FALSE))

By setting the first parameter to true, you specify that you want all eight neighbors, not just the four orthogonal ones, to be included in the process. By setting the second parameter to false, you are telling ArcView Spatial Analyst that a majority must be a clear majority (50 percent doesn't count.)

If you like, open the online help and examine the syntax of the MajorityFilter request. Your expression should match the one in the following graphic.

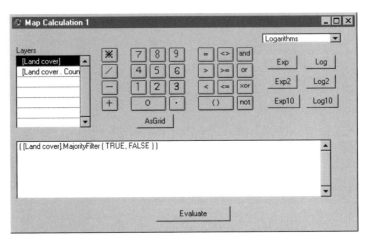

Click Evaluate. When the *Map Calculation 1* theme is added to the view, close the dialog. Make the new theme active. In the Theme Properties dialog, change its name to **Edit1** and click OK. Turn the theme on.

With the randomly selected colors in your legend, it's hard to tell what you've accomplished.

4   Double-click on the *Edit1* theme to open the Legend Editor. In the Legend Editor, click the Load button and navigate to the extend\spatial\ch14 directory. Load the "cover2.avl" legend, making sure that *Field* is set to "Value" in the Load Legend dialog. Click Apply in the Legend Editor and close the Legend Editor.

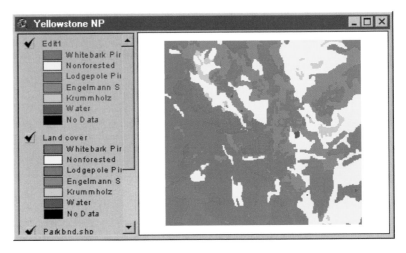

5   Turn the *Edit1* theme off and on a few times so you can compare it with the *Land cover* theme underneath.

You can probably tell that the grid is a little smoother, but the difference is not dramatic. That's because the size of the neighborhood used by MajorityFilter is small.

You can use neighborhood statistics to accomplish smoothing effects as well. And because you define the size of the neighborhood, you have much greater control over how much smoothing occurs.

6   Make sure the *Edit1* theme is active. From the Analysis menu, choose Neighborhood Statistics.

In the *Statistic* drop-down list, choose "Majority." In the *Neighborhood* drop-down list, choose "Circle." Make sure that the Cell radio button is selected. In the Radius input box, type **3**.

Your output will be a grid in which each cell is assigned the majority value in its circular neighborhood.

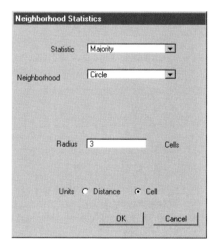

7   Click OK. When the *NbrMajor of Edit1* theme is added to the view, make it active. In the Theme Properties dialog, change its name to **Edit2** and click OK.

8   Double-click on the *Edit2* theme to open the Legend Editor. Load the
    "cover2.avl" legend. Click Apply in the Legend Editor and close the Legend
    Editor. Turn the *Edit2* theme on.

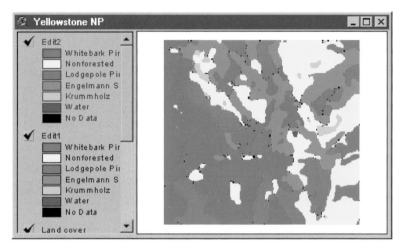

9   Turn the *Edit2* theme off and on a few times so you can compare it with the
    Edit1 theme.

    The different land cover areas have grown distinctly more homoge-
    neous. At the same time, you'll notice some little black speckles in
    the *Edit2* grid that weren't there before.

10 Make the Zoom In tool active and zoom in close on any part of the view
    where there are black speckles.

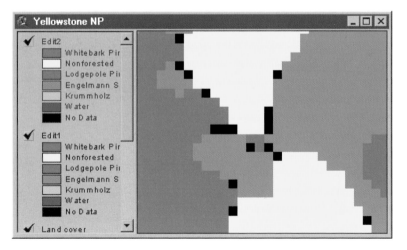

Sure enough, they are No Data cells. A side effect of using neighborhood majority statistics to do your grid cleaning is that if there's no clear majority in a cell's neighborhood, the cell will be assigned the No Data value. You can fix this problem with a Con statement.

11   Click the Zoom to Active Theme(s) button. From the Analysis menu, choose Map Calculator. In the dialog, create the expression:

([Edit2].IsNull.Con ([Edit1], [Edit2]))

"IsNull" is just a condition, like "=3" or ">100," which may be true of a grid cell. It means the cell has the No Data value. Translated into English, your map algebra expression says, "Wherever *Edit2* grid cells have the No Data value, replace them with the values these cells had in the *Edit1* grid. Otherwise, leave the *Edit2* values alone." Your expression should match the one in the following graphic.

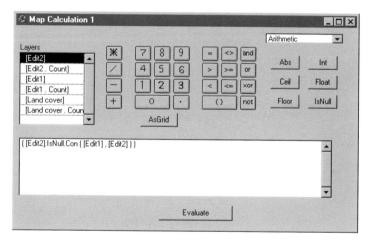

12   Click Evaluate. When the *Map Calculation 1* theme is added to the view, close the dialog. Make the new theme active. In the Theme Properties dialog, change its name to **Edit3** and click OK.

13 Double-click on the *Edit3* theme to open the Legend Editor. Load the "cover2.avl" legend. Click Apply in the Legend Editor and close the Legend Editor. Turn the *Edit3* theme on.

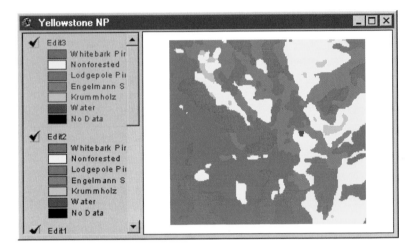

The No Data speckles have been removed.

14 Turn the *Edit3* theme off and on to compare it with the *Edit2* theme. The values are the same, except where the *Edit2* grid has No Data cells. Turn off the *Edit2* and *Edit1* themes and compare the *Edit3* theme to the original *Land cover* theme.

The *Edit3* grid is more homogeneous and easier to interpret. In the next exercise, you'll look at techniques for generalizing the *Edit3* grid even further.

15 From the File menu, choose Close All. Again from the File menu, choose Close Project. Click No when you're prompted to save your changes.

If you want to go on to the next exercise, leave ArcView GIS running. Otherwise, choose Exit from the File menu.

Advanced generalizing techniques

In this exercise, you'll learn how to break zones into regions, spatially contiguous cells that have the same value. Creating regions gives you more flexibility in grid cleaning, because you can eliminate particular regions, or regions of particular sizes.

◆ *E x e r c i s e   1 4 c*

1   If necessary, start ArcView GIS. Navigate to the extend\spatial\ch14 directory and open the project "ex14c.apr." When the project opens, you see a view with two themes: the *Land cover* theme you began the previous exercise with and the *Edit3* theme you ended it with.

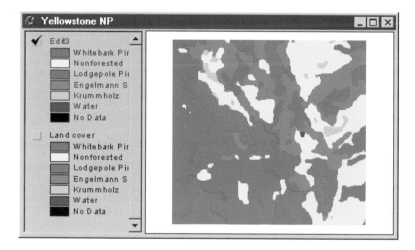

Thus far, you haven't gotten to a smaller level of analysis than the zone, which is any set of cells with the same value. Now you'll divide zones into regions with the RegionGroup request in the Map Calculator.

2   From the Analysis menu, choose Map Calculator. In the dialog, create the expression:

([Edit3].RegionGroup (TRUE, FALSE, NIL))

By setting the first parameter to true, you are specifying that only orthogonally connected cells be considered contiguous. By setting the second parameter to false, you stipulate that every region must consist of cells with the same value. By setting the third parameter to nil, you specify that you don't want any cells to be assigned the No Data value unless they are No Data already.

If you like, open the online help and examine the syntax of the RegionGroup request. Your expression should match the one in the following graphic.

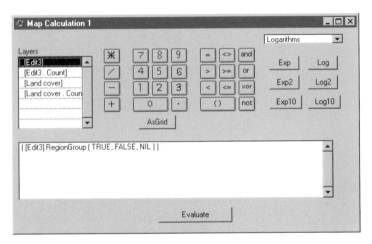

3   Click Evaluate. When the *Map Calculation 1* theme is added to the view, close the dialog. Make the new theme active. In the Theme Properties dialog, change its name to *Edit3 regions* and click OK. Turn on the *Edit3 regions* theme.

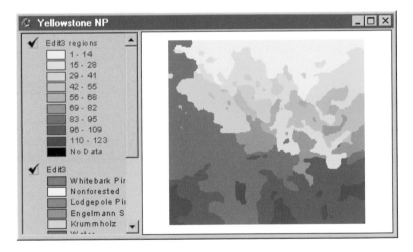

It doesn't look like anything recognizable, but it's not supposed to. The one thing you can tell from the legend is that the *Edit3* grid has been divided into 123 different regions.

4   With the *Edit3 regions* theme active, click the Open Theme Table button.

Value	Count	Link
1	1062	9
2	34	8
3	13	7
4	213	2
5	240	9
6	588	2
7	249	9
8	6	9
9	15	34
10	2435	7
11	4	34
12	207	2

Attributes Of Edit3 regions

The Value field assigns a unique value to each region. The Count field tells you how many cells each region contains. The Link field identifies which zone in the *Edit3* grid each region corresponds to.

5   Scroll down through the table and notice the values in the Count field. Some of the regions consist of thousands of cells; others of only a few. When you're finished, close the table.

You'll eliminate very small regions, consisting of fifteen or fewer cells, by replacing their values with the values of neighboring cells from larger regions. To do this, you must first create an edit mask (similar to the analysis mask you created in chapter 12) that contains No Data values for the unwanted regions.

6   From the Analysis menu, choose Map Calculator. In the *Layers* scrolling list, double-click on [Edit3 regions. Count] to add it to the expression box. Go on to create the expression:

(([Edit3 regions . Count] <= 15).SetNull (1.AsGrid))

Your expression should match the one in the following graphic.

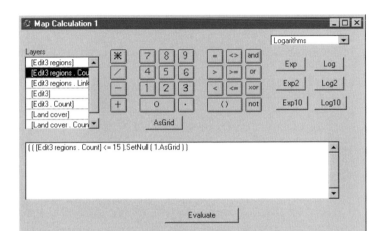

Your expression will create a grid in which regions with a Count value of 15 or less in the *Edit3 regions* grid are replaced with No Data values. All other cells will be assigned a value of 1. The output grid will be the edit mask you use to eliminate the unwanted regions.

7   Click Evaluate. When the *Map Calculation 1* theme is added to the view, close the dialog. Make the new theme active. In the Theme Properties dialog, change its name to **Mask3** and click OK. Turn on the *Mask3* theme.

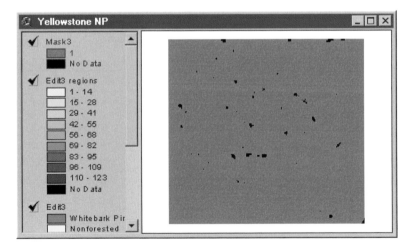

The black No Data speckles are the regions of fewer than fifteen cells. You will replace them using the Nibble request. Nibble replaces No Data cells in a mask grid with their nearest neighboring cells from another grid (in this case, the *Edit3* grid).

8   From the Analysis menu, choose Map Calculator. In the dialog, create the expression:

([Edit3].Nibble ([Mask3], TRUE))

Your expression should match the one in the following graphic.

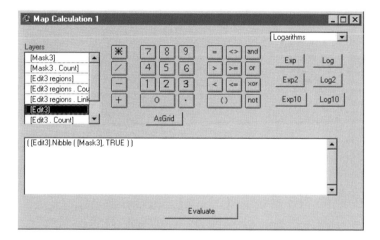

By setting the first parameter to [Mask3], you specify the mask grid. This tells the *Edit3* grid where the nibbling is to be done. By setting the second parameter to true, you specify that only neighboring cells in the *Edit3* grid which are not themselves No Data get to be nibblers.

9   Click Evaluate. When the *Map Calculation 1* theme is added to the view, close the dialog. Make the new theme active. In the Theme Properties dialog, change its name to **Edit4** and click OK.

10 Double-click on the *Edit4* theme to open the Legend Editor. Load the "cover2.avl" legend. Click Apply in the Legend Editor and close the Legend Editor. Turn the *Edit4* theme on.

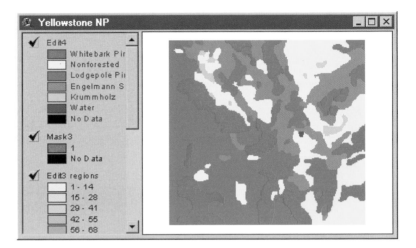

There are no regions in the *Edit4* grid with fewer than fifteen cells. They have all been nibbled away.

11 Turn off the *Mask3* and *Edit3 regions* themes. Turn the *Edit4* theme off and on a few times to compare it with *Edit3*. You can see how the small regions in *Edit3* disappear when you look at *Edit4*.

You'll apply one more cleaning technique to your grid. The BoundaryClean request smooths boundaries between adjacent zones by expanding and shrinking them. The request lets you specify that large zones gain at the expense of small zones or the other way around (or that zones not be favored by size).

12 From the Analysis menu, choose Map Calculator. In the dialog, create the expression:

([Edit4].BoundaryClean (#GRID_SORTTYPE_DESCEND, FALSE))

Your expression should match the one in the following graphic.

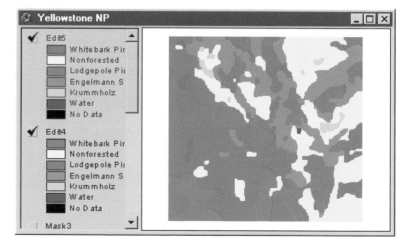

By setting the first parameter to #GRID_SORTTYPE_DESCEND, you are helping small zones expand. By setting the second parameter to false, you specify that boundary cleaning takes place twice instead of once. Repeating the operation increases the smoothing effect.

13 Click Evaluate. When the *Map Calculation 1* theme is added to the view, close the dialog. Make the new theme active. In the Theme Properties dialog, change its name to **Edit5** and click OK.

14 Double-click on the *Edit5* theme to open the Legend Editor. Load the "cover2.avl" legend. Click Apply in the Legend Editor and close the Legend Editor. Turn the *Edit5* theme on.

15 Turn the *Edit5* theme off and on a few times to compare it with *Edit4*.

The effects of BoundaryClean are subtle, but noticeable, particularly in areas where a small region is squeezed in between two large ones (it may disappear) or where there are small gaps between regions with the same value (the gaps will usually be filled in).

In addition to BoundaryClean, there are specific Expand and Shrink requests that allow you to expand and shrink zones by a specific number of cells. There's also a Thin request that can be used to shrink line features to the width of one cell.

16 Turn off the *Edit4* and *Edit3* themes. Compare *Edit5* to the original *Land cover* grid.

The small, speckled, discontinuous areas of the *Land cover* grid have been filled in and the overall shapes of the zones are smoother.

17 From the File menu, choose Close All. Again from the File menu, choose Close Project. Click No when you're prompted to save your changes.

The next chapter introduces ModelBuilder, an ArcView Spatial Analyst 2 enhancement. There are no exercises to do in chapter 15, so you may want to exit ArcView GIS.

15

Introducing the ESRI ModelBuilder

How ModelBuilder works

ModelBuilder components

Build your own model

By now you know

that most ArcView Spatial Analyst sessions involve a series of analytical procedures and many different data sets. So far, the only way to keep track of these projects has been to take good notes and keep your data well organized. In this chapter, you'll learn about a new tool that automates selected spatial processes in an ArcView Spatial Analyst 2 session and keeps them in a working model that you can run as often as you like. The model can then be distributed to others, who can easily alter it to fit their needs.

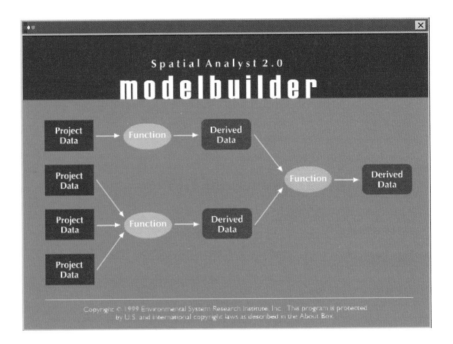

How ModelBuilder works

ModelBuilder operates in conjunction with ArcView Spatial Analyst 2, and is designed to work primarily with grid data sets. It groups selected ArcView Spatial Analyst functions into eleven wizards that guide you step by step through the procedures necessary to create a final map. As you work through the wizards, ModelBuilder also creates a model diagram, or flow chart, of the session that captures the geographic data, the spatial functions that operate on the data, and the order of those functions. When you run the model, all of the spatial functions in the project created by ModelBuilder are executed in sequence, so that the project essentially runs itself. You can add, delete, or replace any data set, any spatial operation, or any variable within a spatial operation, then run the model again. You can retain the model for future use or distribute it to others, who can then use it to analyze their own data sets or alter it as they see fit.

A process is a complete spatial operation, such as buffering streams or overlaying vegetation and rainfall data. Each process is divided into three parts: project data, a spatial function performed on the project data, and derived data. The derived data from one process can become the project data for another process. As with any ArcView GIS project, all data is stored on disk and referenced through the ArcView GIS project file.

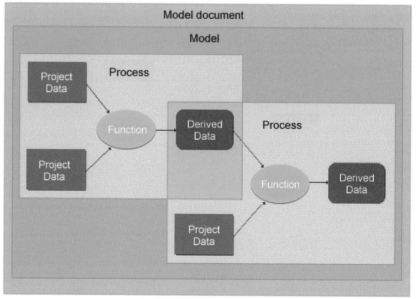

A model is a collection of processes. A process is a spatial function that accepts project data and produces derived data.

ModelBuilder components

The Model Document   The Model Document is a new type of ArcView GIS document, and is accessed from the View GUI when ArcView Spatial Analyst is loaded.

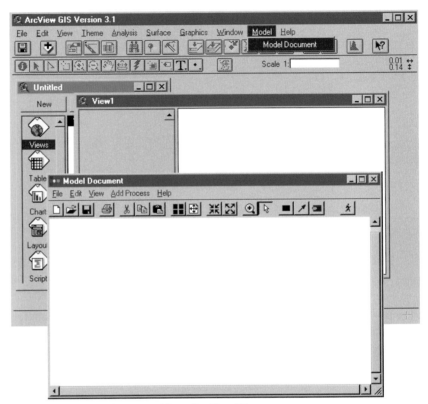

The Model Document is accessed from the View GUI.

Every ModelBuilder operation is initiated from the Model Document window. Here, you construct individual processes from project data, spatial functions, and derived data, and then link the processes together to create a working model. Each process is symbolized in the Model Document window by one or more Input icons, one Function icon, and one Output icon. The arrows on the lines connecting the icons indicate the flow of data through the model. When you run the model, the processes are executed to produce the final maps as grid themes in ArcView GIS.

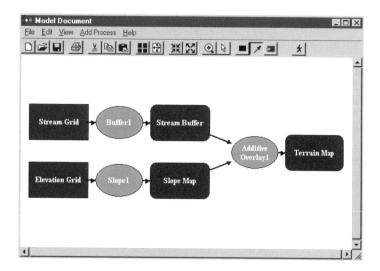

Say that you want to find out which bear, mountain lion, and deer habitats are most in need of conservation management. You don't want to
create a conservation area that's too close to roads, and you don't need
to consider habitat that's already being managed inside national parks.
For the analysis, you'll need geographic data sets of the roads and the
national parks in your study area, and individual data sets of the bear,
mountain lion, and deer habitats.

First, you create buffer zones around the roads to keep the conservation
areas away from them.

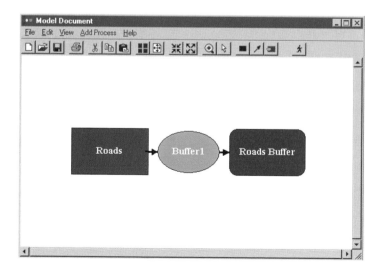

Next, you overlay your maps of the bear, mountain lion, and deer habitats to create a Habitat Range map of the areas that are critical for all three species.

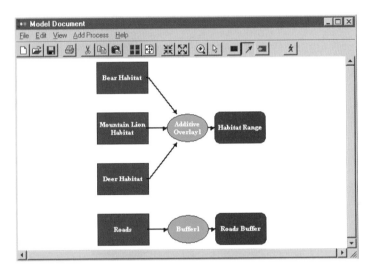

Habitat areas within national parks are already being managed, so you overlay the Habitat Range map, Roads Buffer map, and National Parks map to show areas lying outside the national parks and away from roads.

The model is complete. If you were to click the Run button, the processes would be activated in the ArcView GIS interface and you'd get a set of output maps showing the road buffers, the total habitat range for all three species, and a final map of the selected habitat areas that most need attention.

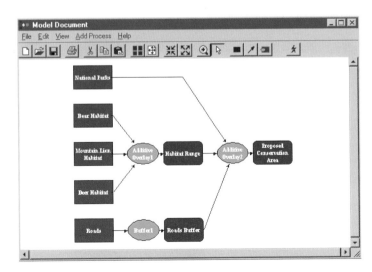

Properties

Each Input, Output, and Function icon has its own set of variables, or properties, that must be defined before a process can run. A full list of properties is beyond the scope of this chapter, but an Input icon requires information such as a grid or DEM name, and a field in the grid theme's table that can be used to classify the grid for analysis. The Output icon requires a grid extent, grid output cell size, legend color, legend table, and output file name. The information that you supply for each Function icon depends on the type of spatial operation you're using. The following table describes the spatial operations available.

Spatial operation category	Function	Description
Data conversion	Vector to integer grid	Converts a point, line, or polygon theme to an integer grid
	DEM to floating-point grid	Converts a Digital Elevation Model file to a floating-point grid
	Point interpolation to floating-point grid	Converts a point theme to a floating-point grid
Reclassification	Reclassification	Groups the values in a grid theme into new classes and assigns them new values
Terrain	Contour	Converts a floating-point elevation grid to a contour line theme
	Slope	Converts a floating-point elevation grid to a slope grid
	Aspect	Converts a floating-point elevation grid to an aspect grid
	Hillshade	Converts a floating-point elevation grid to a hillshade grid
Distance	Buffer zones	Reclassifies all cells within a specified distance from a feature into a single buffer zone
Overlay	Additive overlay	Multiplies the values of two or more input themes by influence factors, then adds the values to produce an output grid
	Weighted overlay	Reclassifies the cell values of two or more input themes to a common scale, then multiplies the reclassified values by influence factors and adds the values to produce an output grid

Wizards

ModelBuilder provides wizards that allow you to add complete processes to the Model Document. The wizards, located in the Add Process menu, reflect the categories listed in the preceding table. Each wizard presents a series of dialogs that ask for the input properties of the process first, the function properties next, and the output properties last. When the wizard finishes, it adds the new process to the Model Document.

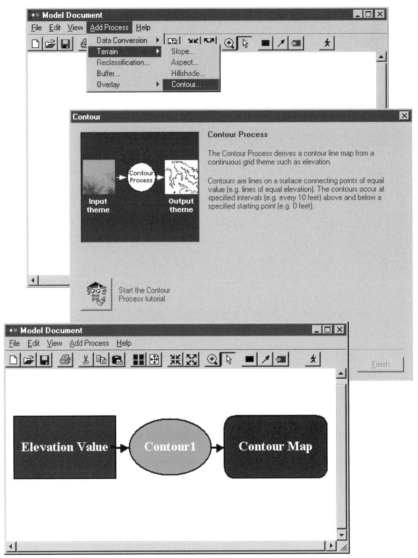

From the Add Process menu in the Model Document you select a wizard, which prompts you for the properties of each icon in the process. When it finishes, the process is added to the Model Document.

To change one or more properties of an existing process, right-click on the Function icon for that process to bring up the wizard again.

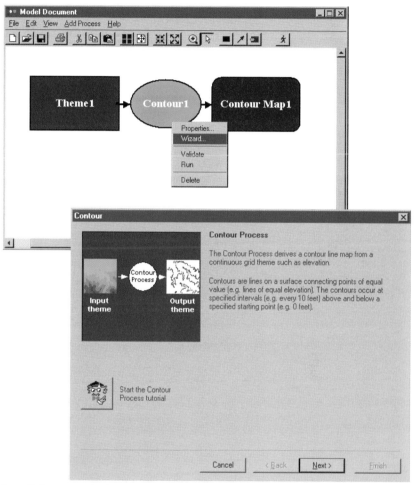

To edit the properties for an existing process with its wizard, right-click on the Function icon and select Wizard from the menu.

Drag-and-drop tools

When you become comfortable with the way ModelBuilder works, you may want to bypass the wizards and build parts of your model piece-meal, adding processes icon by icon without setting the properties of an entire process right away. This is very convenient if you're not sure what the properties are going to be, or if you don't want to go through an entire wizard to edit one property.

To create processes without using the wizards, drag and drop individual icons onto the Model Document with the Add Data tool and the Add Function tool. You can place as many icons as you need in the Model Document, anywhere you like.

Next, connect the Input icons to the Function and Output icons with the Add Connection tool. For each process, you can have several Input icons, but only one Function icon and one Output icon.

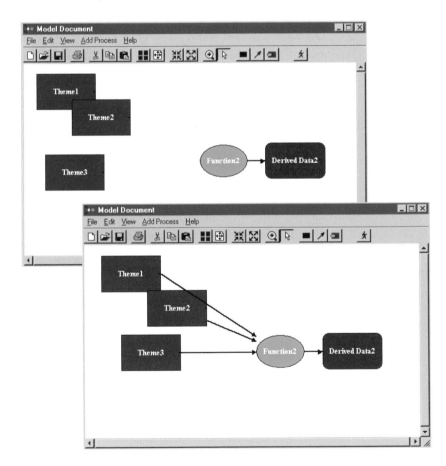

When you're finished, click the Auto Layout tool to arrange the way the processes are displayed in the Model Document.

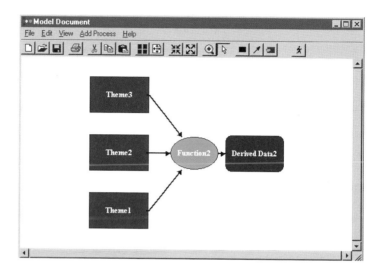

Property sheets

When you add an icon using the drag-and-drop tools, you can define its properties right away, or you can add it as an "empty" icon and set its properties later. Before you can run a model, however, you have to set the properties for each icon in the Model Document. You can use the wizards to do this, as you saw in the last section, or you can use the ModelBuilder property sheets. The property sheets resemble the wizards in that they present dialogs from which to set an icon's properties. Each icon—Input, Function, and Output—has its own property sheet, which can be accessed by right-clicking on that icon. A wizard, on the other hand, only applies to an entire process, and can only be accessed by right-clicking on the Function icon for that process.

To set the properties for any icon, right-click it, select Properties, and open its property sheet.

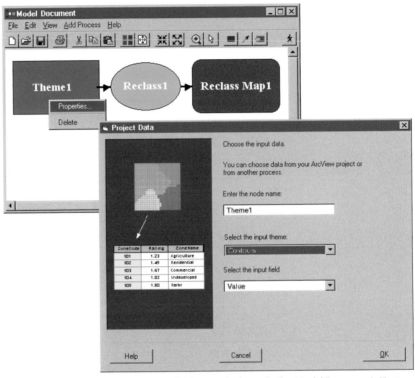

Access the property sheets by right-clicking on the icons in the Model Document. Here, the property sheet for the Input icon has been selected.

Validating the model

If you're not sure that you've defined all the properties in your model, select Validate Model from the File menu. It will tell you whether or not the model is ready to run. If you right-click on the Function icon of a single process and select Validate, it will tell you if all the processes up to and including that process are ready to run.

Build your own model

Creating a model begins with deciding what question you're trying to answer, what factors will affect the answer, and what data is needed to measure those factors.

Suppose you're buying land to build homes. You want to make sure that the land you buy isn't prone to soil erosion or landslides. Your goal is to determine which areas are suitable for building and which ones should be avoided.

To find the areas that are safe to build on, you need to identify the factors that weaken soil and estimate their influences across the site. The factors that affect erosion in this area are the slope and the type of soil. You can't build on slopes greater than 20 degrees, and you prefer slopes less than 10 degrees. The site has clay soil, sandy soil, gravel, and bedrock. Clay soil doesn't drain well and is prone to landslides. Sandy soil drains well and is less difficult to grade than gravel or bedrock. Therefore, the most desirable areas will have a slope of less than 10 degrees and a sandy soil type. Less desirable areas will have a slope of 10 to 20 degrees and clay, gravel, or bedrock soil types. Areas with slopes greater than 20 degrees are not suitable.

You already have an elevation grid for the site, but no slope data. Though the elevation data isn't what you need, you can use ModelBuilder to convert it to a slope grid.

To get the soil data, you send a geologist to the site to map the soil types. You store the soil data as an ArcView GIS polygon shapefile.

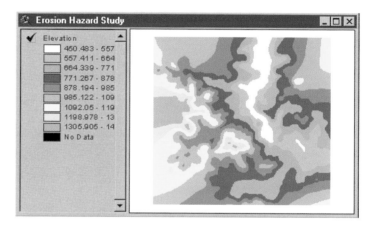

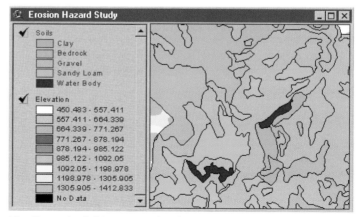

Elevation and soil data are stored as themes in ArcView GIS.

Now you can use ModelBuilder to process the elevation and soil data so you can see which areas are suitable for building.

First, you start ModelBuilder and use the Slope wizard to create a process that will convert the elevation grid to a slope grid. In the wizard, you define which project data will be used, how the slope will be measured (percent or degrees), and what the output theme will look like. When the wizard finishes, a slope process is added to the Model Document. The slope theme won't be created in ArcView GIS until you run the model.

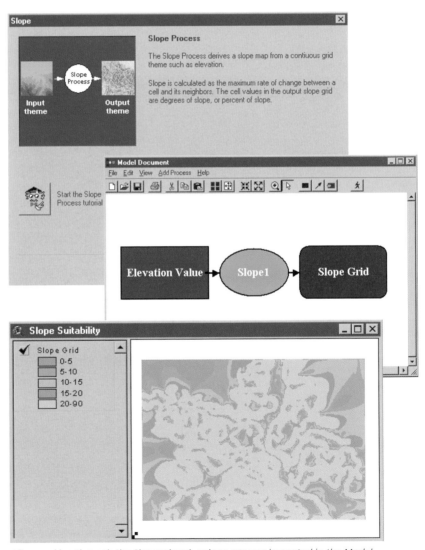

After working through the Slope wizard, a slope process is created in the Model Document. Right-click on the Function icon to run the process.

ModelBuilder requires grid themes for most operations. Since the soil data is stored as a shapefile, you use the Data Conversion wizard to convert it to a grid.

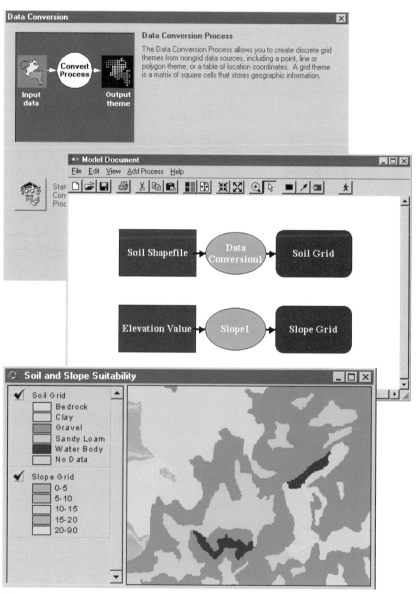

There are now two processes in the Model Document: the Slope process that converts the elevation grid to a slope grid and the Data Conversion process that converts the soil shapefile to a soil grid.

Now you want to combine the slope and soil data to map the suitability for building across the site. Combining different themes of geographic data is called overlay. But how do you overlay data that isn't alike? The slope data is measured in degrees, and the soil data defines soil type. With ModelBuilder you can assign a common suitability scale to each type of data, then add the suitability values together. For example, you might choose a scale of one to three, three being highly suitable for building, one being the least suitable. You assign the slope and soil data suitability values as shown in the two tables below.

Soil	Suitability value
Sandy soil	3 (highly suitable)
Bedrock	2 (suitable)
Gravel	2 (suitable)
Clay	1 (somewhat suitable)
Water body	Restricted (not suitable)

Slope	Suitability value
0–10 degrees	3 (highly suitable)
11–15 degrees	2 (suitable)
15–20 degrees	1 (somewhat suitable)
Greater than 20	Restricted (not suitable)

Once the slope and soil data are converted to a common scale, the values can be combined to establish an overall suitability rating. If the slope and soil data were equally important to you, you could just add their values and divide by two to get an overall rating. But you determined earlier that although you prefer sandy soil, you could build on any of the four soil types. Slopes steeper than 10 degrees are undesirable, however, and those greater than 20 degrees are unacceptable. The incline of the land has more influence on erosion than soil type. Therefore, you want slope data to weigh more heavily than soil data in your model.

You use the Weighted Overlay wizard in ModelBuilder to add a process to the Model Document. It asks you to define the common scale, the suitability values for the data, and the weight assigned to each data type. You assign a weight factor of 75 percent to the slope suitability values, and a weight factor of 25 percent to the soil suitability values.

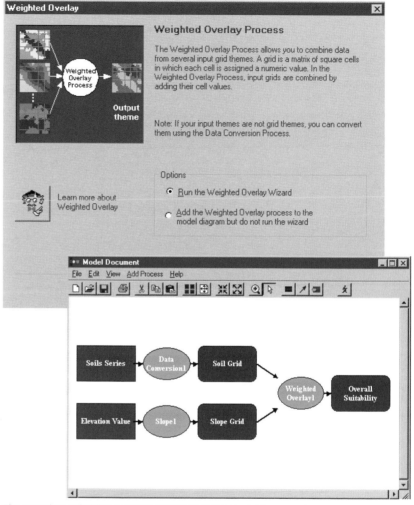

The complete suitability model is displayed in the Model Document.

When you run the model, the slope and overlay processes are applied to the project data to create an overall suitability map. The map shows how prone each area is to erosion and landslides. Now you can choose those areas with the highest suitability value as the best sites to build on. If you like, you can change the weighting factors, suitability values, and other processing properties to produce several possible outcomes.

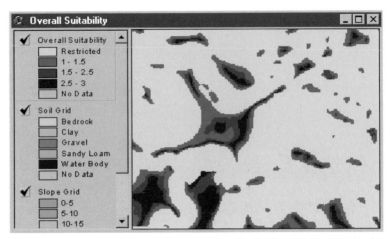

When you run the model, the results are displayed in ArcView GIS. The Weighted Overlay process created an overall suitability map that shows you where it's safe to build.

16

Introducing ArcView 3D Analyst

Displaying data in three dimensions

3D shapefiles and TINs

Choosing a data structure

Exploring ArcView 3D Analyst

ArcView 3D Analyst

makes spatial data look like the world it represents. Mountains are tall, cliffs are steep, roads rise and fall as they wind through the hills, buildings cast shadows. Seeing your data in three-dimensional perspective makes it easy to grasp relationships that remain abstract in two dimensions.

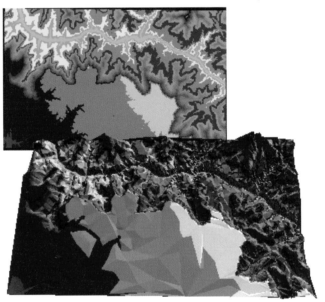

ArcView 3D Analyst displays elevation surfaces, like this theme of part of the Grand Canyon, in detailed 3D perspective.

Displaying data in three dimensions

3D Analyst lets you choose the perspective you want, so you can look at your data from any direction, angle, or zoom level. You can start with a large area, then zoom in for a closer look. You can approach from a different direction or get a bird's-eye view.

Mt. Rainier, as seen from the west.

A close-up of the summit.

A view from the northeast.

Looking straight down at the peak.

If you have aerial or satellite photographs that align with your elevation data, you can display these images in 3D.

An aerial photograph of Gillette, Wyoming, draped over an elevation model.

3D Analyst displays vector data in 3D as well, allowing you to model urban neighborhoods.

A view of downtown Seattle, Washington.

Or even smaller structures.

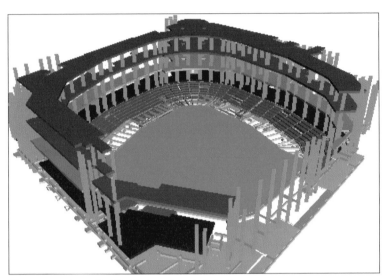

The proposed new Seattle Mariners baseball stadium.

For that matter, you can create three-dimensional models of surfaces other than elevation.

Population density around Minneapolis–St. Paul, Minnesota. Peaks show concentrations of population.

3D Analyst does more than display data. It analyzes information, too. You can evaluate visibility to determine what can and can't be seen from any given point on a surface. You can draw steepest paths to predict the course that water will take downhill. You can find the area and volume of a spatial model and compare the volumes of different models to measure the changes made by excavation or erosion.

Tracing the downhill flow of water from selected points.

3D shapefiles and TINs

You don't need special data to create 3D displays—you can use ordinary shapefiles and grid themes. 3D Analyst also uses two new data types: 3D shapefiles and TINs.

3D shapefiles resemble ordinary 2D shapefiles, except that they have elevation values. An ordinary shapefile stores x,y coordinates that define the position of features in planar space. A 3D shapefile stores z values as well, to locate features in three-dimensional space. (A 3D point feature has one z coordinate; 3D line and polygon features have a z coordinate for every vertex.)

Because ordinary shapefiles can be displayed in three-dimensional perspective, 3D shapefiles are a convenience rather than a necessity. 2D shapefiles can easily be converted to 3D.

The other data type used by 3D Analyst is the triangulated irregular network, or TIN. In the preceding section of this book, you used raster data to model continuous surfaces. TINs model continuous surfaces with vector data. Instead of representing a surface as a matrix of square cells, they represent it as an arrangement of contiguous, nonoverlapping triangles.

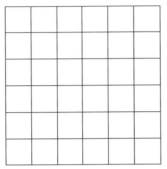 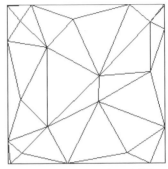

A grid divides a surface into square cells. A TIN divides it into triangles of different sizes and angles.

Like a grid, a TIN interpolates surface elevation values from a set of sample points.

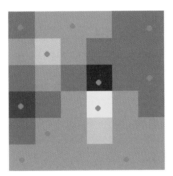 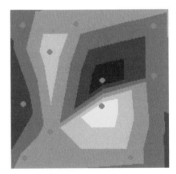

A grid and a TIN interpolated from the same sample data.

Unlike a grid, a TIN is a variable-resolution model. Where your sample data is dense, your surface is detailed. Where your data is sparse, your surface is simpler.

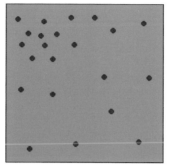 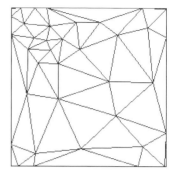

Sample data points are more abundant in the northwest part of the study area. The TIN model interpolated from the points has more triangles in this area than elsewhere on the surface.

A TIN is composed of triangle nodes, lines, and faces. Each sample data point becomes a triangle node, or end point. Additional nodes are placed as needed along the boundary of the model to complete triangles. An elevation value is interpolated for every x,y location on the surface.

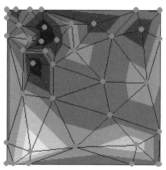 *Every triangle has a single slope and aspect value. Elevation values, however, are interpolated for each unique location on the surface.*

TINs can be constructed from combinations of points, lines, and polygons, allowing you to model surfaces with greater accuracy than is possible with points alone. Line features representing streams, roads, or other landscape features can be built into the TIN structure. These lines, called breaklines, can't be crossed by any triangles in the TIN. (Another way of saying this is that breaklines are enforced as triangle edges.) Because each triangle has its own slope and aspect value, breaklines let you model the effects on terrain of roads, rivers, ridgelines, and similar features.

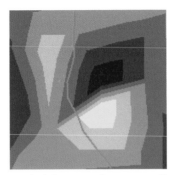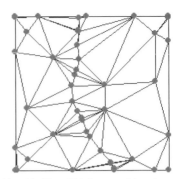

On the left, a green line representing a road is added to a TIN. Because triangles can't cross the breakline, the triangle structure is more complex than it would be otherwise. Slope and aspect values are affected. If the line feature has elevation information, this will also be incorporated into the TIN.

Choosing a data structure

Because 3D Analyst creates, displays, and analyzes grid and TIN themes with equal facility, whether you use grid or TIN data often depends on your sample data and the nature of the surface you're modeling.

If the complexity of your surface is highly variable, and if this variability is reflected by the irregular distribution of your sample data, a TIN will depict the surface more effectively than a grid. And because a TIN can incorporate lines and polygons in its structure, it's a better data model for representing the influence of features like streams, roads, and lakes on the terrain.

On the other hand, if your surface is fairly uniform and your sample data is evenly distributed, a grid is probably better—it will be just as accurate while taking less time to build and using less disk space. Grids are also better for large study areas because of these same processing advantages. And if you want to do analysis on your surface in ArcView Spatial Analyst, you will need to use a grid. Choosing one data structure or another isn't an irrevocable commitment, however. In 3D Analyst, you can convert grid themes to TINs or TIN themes to grids.

In this section of the book, you'll work with TIN themes rather than grids. In most respects, the procedures are the same for both, and the few differences have been noted. 3D Analyst also shares certain functions—such as the ability to interpolate grids from sample data points—with ArcView Spatial Analyst. In cases of overlap, operations that have been discussed earlier in the book aren't repeated.

Exploring 3D Analyst

ArcView 3D Analyst introduces a new document type: the 3D scene. Although most analytical operations take place in View documents, 3D scenes are where you display your data in 3D perspective.

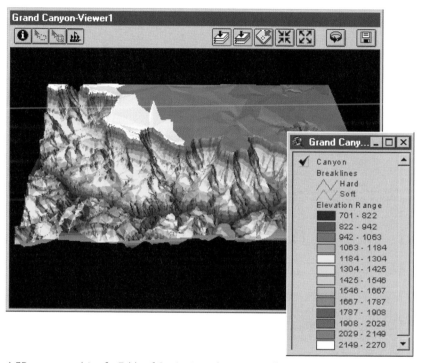

A 3D scene consists of a Table of Contents and a separate display window called a viewer. A viewer has its own buttons and tools and can be moved outside the ArcView GIS application window.

In this exercise, you'll learn how to navigate your way around a 3D scene. You'll identify elevation, slope, and aspect values for a TIN theme, and select features in a 3D scene.

◆ *Exercise 16a*

1 If necessary, start ArcView GIS. In the Welcome to ArcView GIS dialog, make sure that "Create a new project with a new View" is selected. Click OK. Click No when you're prompted to add data to the view. (If ArcView GIS is running and you've already dismissed the Welcome dialog, open a new project from the File menu and create a new view.)

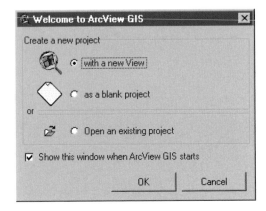

Now you'll load the 3D Analyst extension to see how the ArcView GIS interface changes.

2 From the File menu, choose Extensions to open the Extensions dialog. Scroll through the list of available extensions and make sure none of them is turned on. Scroll back to the top and click on the 3D Analyst check box to turn it on. Click OK.

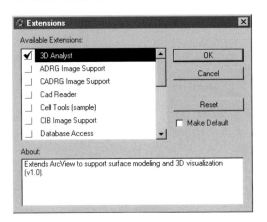

In the remaining exercises in this section, the 3D Analyst extension will already be loaded when you open a project.

When the extension is loaded, the ArcView GIS interface changes. There's a new menu, the Surface menu, which is similar to the ArcView Spatial Analyst Surface menu. There are also two new drop-down tools. (Both are presently disabled.)

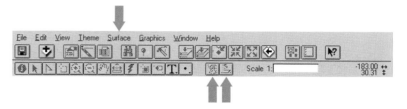

The Contour drop-down tool includes a Contour tool for drawing elevation contours, a Line of Sight tool for analyzing visibility, and a Steepest Path tool for finding the steepest downhill path from a given point. The Interpolate drop-down tool lets you create 3D graphics and theme features on grid and TIN surfaces.

Now you'll open a project in which 3D Analyst is already loaded.

3   From the File menu, choose Close All. Again from the File menu, choose Open Project. Click No at the prompt to save changes to your untitled project. In the Open Project dialog, navigate to the \extend\3d\ch16 directory and open the project "ex16a.apr."

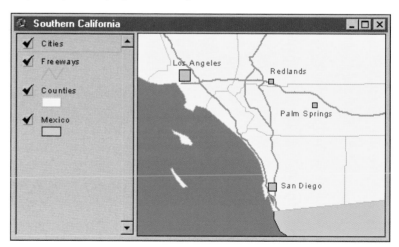

When the project opens, you see a view of southern California. Located between Los Angeles and Palm Springs is the city of Redlands, where ESRI is headquartered.

4 Close the view and scroll to the bottom of the Project window. When the 3D Analyst extension is loaded, a new document type, 3D Scenes, is available. Click on the 3D Scenes icon to select it, then click the Open button to open the Redlands, CA 3D scene.

The 3D scene contains three themes. A TIN theme of elevation is displayed in the 3D scene window (called a "viewer"). Two feature themes, one of land parcels and one of streets, are not turned on.

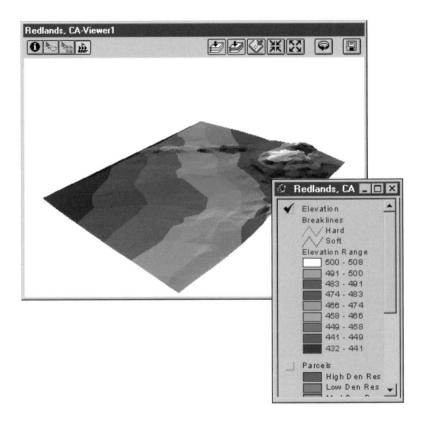

The background color of your 3D scene will be black, the 3D Analyst default. In the graphics in this book, it's been changed to white. Leave your background color as it is, unless you have a strong preference for another color. You'll learn how to change the background color in the next chapter.

5 On the viewer control bar, select the Navigation tool.

Navigation lets you control the perspective of a 3D scene by rotating, zooming, and panning.

6 Press and hold the left mouse button. Drag the mouse pointer slowly to the left and back to the right. The TIN theme rotates on its horizontal axis. Drag the mouse pointer slowly up and down. The theme rotates on its vertical axis. You can get a bird's-eye view or even look at it from below.

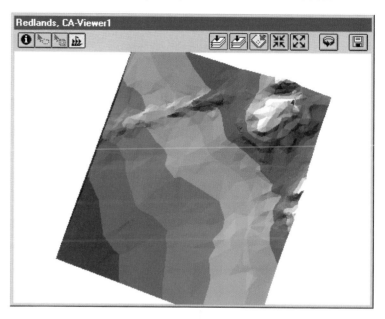

7 On the viewer control bar, click the Zoom to Active Theme(s) button to return the scene to its default perspective. In the Table of Contents, turn on the *Parcels* theme and the *Streets* theme.

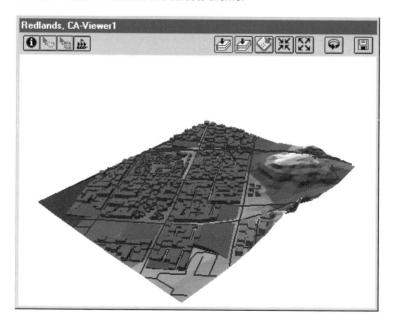

The buildings in the *Parcels* theme are displayed in 3D on the TIN theme surface, as are the streets. Note that, unlike in a view, the display isn't affected by the order of themes in the Table of Contents. In a 3D scene, theme features are displayed according to their elevation values.

8   With the Navigation tool still active, place the mouse pointer over the viewer window. Press and hold the right mouse button and drag the pointer slowly up and down. Dragging the pointer downward zooms you in on your data. Dragging it upward zooms you out. Zoom in until the data fills most of the viewer.

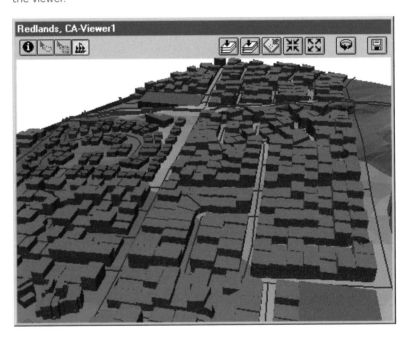

As you zoomed in and out, the buildings may have disappeared and been replaced by a transparent box with white lines. During navigation, data sets that are too large to be redrawn quickly are temporarily replaced by white boxes.

9   Place the mouse pointer over the viewer window. Press and hold both the right and left mouse buttons (or the middle button on a 3-button mouse). Drag the pointer slowly up and down, then slowly left and right.

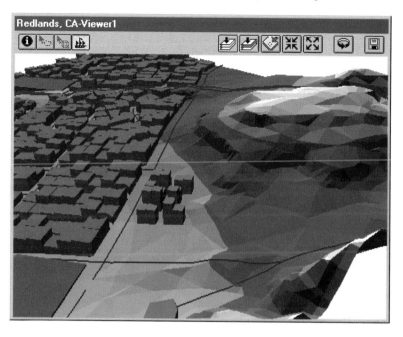

Using both mouse buttons lets you pan to different parts of the display.

Navigation.   In addition to the mouse buttons, you can navigate with the control bar buttons. The various zoom buttons work just like the ones on the ArcView GIS button bar. (The zoom buttons on the button bar work, too. They control zoom operations for all open viewers rather than just the active one.) The Rotate Viewer button, second from the right on the viewer control bar, sets your data in automatic counter-clockwise rotation that continues until you press the Escape key on the keyboard or the Stop button on the application window status bar. Although it's natural to think and speak of the data in a viewer as moving when you navigate, it's more correct to think of the position of the data as fixed and of your point of view as changing in relation to it. Your default point of view in a 3D scene is always from the southwest. In the online help, use the Find tab to locate the topic *Navigating*.

10   On the ArcView GIS application window button bar, click the New Viewer button. A new viewer opens and displays the same data in the default perspective. Move Viewer2 out of the way of Viewer1. With Viewer2 active and the Navigation tool selected, navigate to a new perspective in Viewer2.

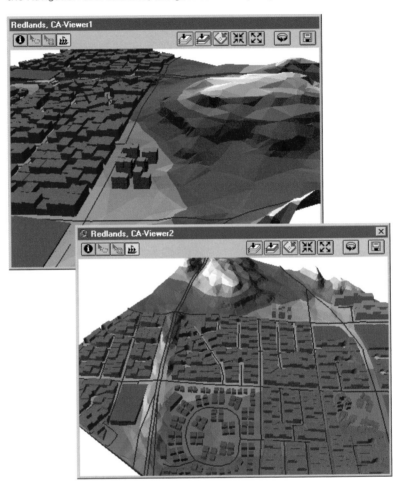

11 Close Viewer2. Click on the title bar of Viewer1 to make it active and make sure the Navigation tool is selected. Navigate to a perspective in which you're zoomed in close on some of the purple buildings. (The exact perspective doesn't matter.) If you get lost, you can always click the Zoom to Active Theme(s) button and begin again.

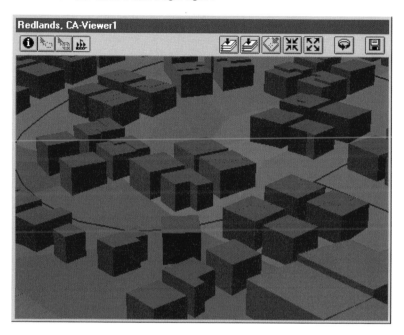

12 In the 3D Scene Table of Contents, make sure the *Elevation* theme is active. On the viewer control bar, select the Identify tool. Click on any spot of ground to identify it.

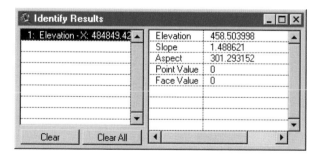

The Identify Results box shows you the elevation, slope, and aspect for the location you clicked on.

If you happen to click on a feature, such as a building, you still get the values for the underlying TIN theme. Only one active theme can be identified at a time in a 3D scene.

13   Click on a few additional locations. When you're finished, close the Identify Results box.

14   In the Table of Contents, make the *Parcels* theme active, then click on any building to identify it. The Identify Results window shows you the attributes of the Parcels theme table, including area, perimeter, zoning, and number of stories. Close the Identify Results window.

15   With the *Parcels* theme active, click on the Select Feature tool on the viewer control bar. Click on any purple building to select it. Click on another purple building. (The first building is deselected.) With the second building selected, hold down the Shift key and click on a third building.

The Select Feature tool is disabled when a TIN, grid, or image theme is active in a 3D scene.

16   On the viewer control bar, click the Zoom to Selected button.

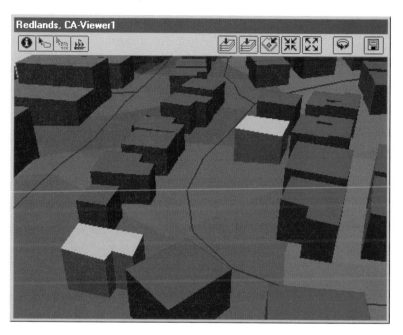

The view zooms to the extent of the selected features. It also reori-
ents your perspective so that you're looking at the data from the
southwest.

17   On the ArcView GIS application button bar, click the Clear Selected Features
button.

18   From the File menu, choose Close All. Again from the File menu, choose
Close Project. Click No when you're prompted to save your changes.

17

Displaying data in 3D

Setting 3D scene properties

Setting 3D properties for feature themes

Setting 3D properties for image themes

WHEN YOU DISPLAY DATA in a 3D scene viewer, some properties apply to all the data in the scene. Sun position is one. The sun can't be in two places at once, blazing down with midday light on the landscape while leaving the buildings in twilight shadow. Display properties that apply to all data in a 3D scene are set in the 3D Scene Properties dialog.

Other properties are specific to themes within a 3D scene. A building, for instance, may be ten stories tall, but streets won't be. Display properties that apply to individual themes within a 3D scene are set in each theme's 3D Theme Properties dialog.

Setting 3D scene properties

The position of the sun is defined by azimuth and altitude. Azimuth, or compass position, is measured clockwise in degrees from 0 (due north) to 360. The default setting is in the northeast at 33.69 degrees. Altitude, or angle above the horizon, is measured in degrees ranging from 0 (level with the horizon) to 90 (directly overhead). You can use negative altitude values to put the sun below the horizon. The default setting, called "Low," is 29.02 degrees.

Changing the sun position affects the display of a 3D scene. If you're looking at the southwest face of a mountain, with the sun in the northeast, the face of the mountain will be in shadow and some surface details will be lost. As you move the sun to different azimuths and altitudes, light and shadow fall differently on the terrain, heightening surface details in some places and obscuring them in others.

Vertical exaggeration defines the relationship of x,y values to z values in a 3D scene. The default vertical exaggeration factor is "none," which means that data is displayed in its true geographic proportions. When there's little change in elevation over a large spatial extent, these true proportions can look a little dull. Applying a vertical exaggeration factor multiplies the z values of data in a 3D scene to give the surface a more striking appearance. (The effect is purely visual and doesn't influence analysis.)

In this exercise, you'll set a vertical exaggeration for a 3D scene, give the scene a new background color, and change the sun position.

◆ *E x e r c i s e   1 7 a*

1   If necessary, start ArcView GIS. Navigate to the \extend\3d\ch17 directory and open the project "ex17a.apr." When the project opens, you see a view containing the area around Big Bear Lake, a popular recreation spot in the San Bernardino Mountains east of Los Angeles. The city of Redlands is visible in the southwest corner of the view.

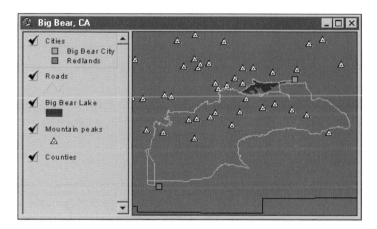

2   Close the view and open the Big Bear Lake 3D scene.

The 3D scene contains a TIN theme of the area around Big Bear Lake and a 3D polygon theme of the lake itself.

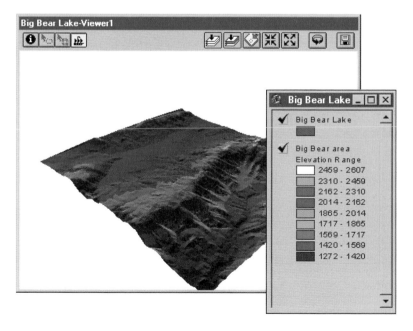

3   From the 3D Scene menu, choose Properties to open the 3D Scene Proper-
    ties dialog.

Besides the settings for vertical exaggeration and sun position, the
dialog contains much of the same information you find in a View
Properties dialog.

Projecting data in 3D Analyst. ArcView GIS can't project TIN
themes by projecting a view or a 3D scene. TIN data sets are assumed
to be in projected coordinates. 3D Analyst can display unprojected
TIN or grid data by calculating an appropriate vertical exaggeration factor, but most analysis on this data isn't valid. The 2D projection box in
the 3D Scene Properties dialog is used to make unprojected feature
themes align with projected TIN or grid data. For more information,
see appendix B, "Aligning your data."

4   In the *Vertical exaggeration factor* drop-down list, set the vertical exaggeration to "3." Click the Apply button.

The 3D Scene Properties dialog remains open and the change is applied to the viewer. The steepness of the mountains is accentuated.

Applying a vertical exaggeration factor.   To emphasize surface variation, use a vertical exaggeration factor greater than 1. To deemphasize variation, use a fraction between 0 and 1. Negative numbers are appropriate when the surface's z-values represent depth (a lake bed, for instance). A value of 0.0 renders the surface completely flat. The Calculate button automatically selects an appropriate vertical exaggeration factor. Automatic calculation is especially useful for displaying unprojected geographic data or data in which the z values represent an attribute other than elevation (like population density).

5   In the dialog, click on the Background color Select button. In the Color
    Picker, scroll to the bottom and select the sky blue square shown in the
    graphic. Click OK.

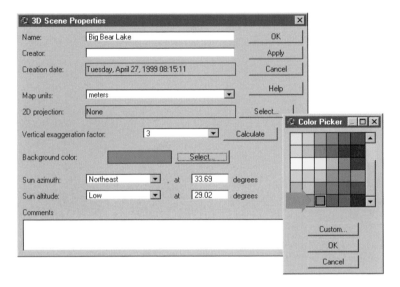

The *Background color* box is updated.

6   In the 3D Scene Properties dialog, click Apply to change the color in the
    viewer.

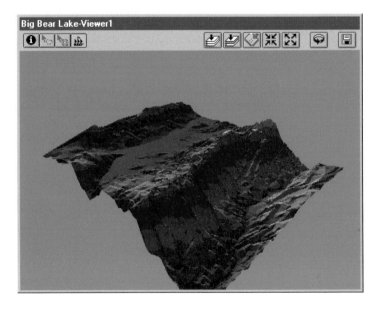

7   In the *Sun azimuth* drop-down list, set the azimuth to "Southwest"
    (225 degrees). In the *Sun altitude* drop-down list, set the altitude to "High"
    (50 degrees). You can also set values by typing numbers directly into the
    input boxes. Click OK to apply your changes and close the 3D Scene Proper-
    ties dialog.

Much of the terrain that was in shadow before is now brightly lit.

8   From the File menu, choose Close All. Again from the File menu, choose
    Close Project. Click No when you're prompted to save your changes.

If you want to go on to the next exercise, leave ArcView GIS running. Otherwise, choose Exit from the File menu.

Setting 3D properties for feature themes

Three-dimensional properties that belong to individual themes, rather than the entire 3D scene, are set in the 3D Theme Properties dialog for each theme. Among these are base heights ("base heights" is just another name for elevation values); offset heights, which position features slightly above (or below) a surface to make them stand out distinctly; and extrusion, which gives features three-dimensional solidity.

Only TIN and 3D feature themes are displayed according to their base heights (that is, in 3D perspective) by default. A grid theme's base heights are simply its cell values, but these values aren't applied by default. Instead, you must tell 3D Analyst to use them.

Two-dimensional feature themes don't have base height information. (That's why they're two-dimensional.) To be displayed in 3D perspective, a 2D theme must borrow base heights from another source. The source can be a field in its own attribute table or it can be the elevation values of a TIN or grid theme.

Image themes can be displayed in 3D perspective only by using the base heights of a TIN or grid theme.

When a feature theme uses a TIN or grid theme as the source of its base heights, the features will display at the same height as the surface. This may be geographically accurate (for instance, roads really do run along the ground), but in 3D display, it can make the features hard to see. By setting an offset height for the theme, you raise its features slightly above the surface and make them easy to distinguish.

Extrusion gives features solidity and spatial extension. Points become vertical lines, lines become walls, and polygons turn into blocks. (Only feature themes can be extruded.) There are two extrusion properties: an extrusion value, which defines how far a feature will be extruded, and an extrusion method.

Setting an extrusion value is straightforward: you take a line feature, for instance, and tell 3D Analyst to extrude it into a wall 2 meters high. Choosing an extrusion method is a bit more complicated. The four methods are "Adding to min z value," "Adding to max z value," "Adding to base height," and "Using as absolute."

No extrusion

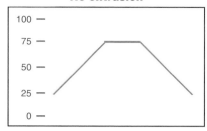

The lowest base height value in the line at left is 25 and the highest is 75. In each of the other four graphics, the line is extruded by a value of 25, using a different extrusion method.

Adding to base height

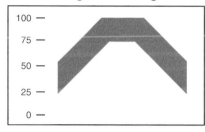

Every z value in the line is extruded upward by 25.

Adding to max z value

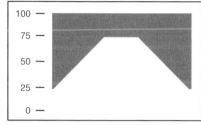

The maximum z value of 75 is extruded upward to 100. All other z values are extruded upward to the same horizontal plane.

Adding to min z value

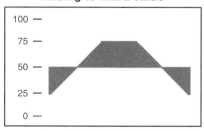

The minimum z value of 25 is extruded upward to 50. All other z values are extruded upward or downward to the same horizontal plane.

Using as absolute

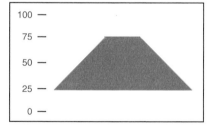

Every z value in the line is extruded to the absolute value 25. This means that z values of 75 are extruded downward to 25 and z values of 25 aren't extruded at all.

In this exercise, you'll display 2D streets and buildings in 3D perspective by using a TIN theme as a source of base heights. You'll offset the features from the TIN surface and extrude the buildings to change them from flat rectangles to solid blocks.

◆ *E x e r c i s e   1 7 b*

1   If necessary, start ArcView GIS. Navigate to the \extend\3d\ch17 directory
     and open the project "ex17b.apr."

When the project opens, you see a view of Redlands that contains a
TIN theme of elevation and *Streets* and *Parcels* feature themes. The
data is familiar to you from the previous chapter.

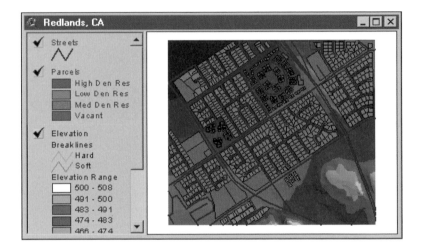

You'll create a 3D scene and copy all three themes into it.

2   Make all three themes active in the view. From the Edit menu, choose Copy
     Themes. Close the view. With the Project window active, double-click on the
     3D Scenes icon to create a new 3D scene.

3   From the Edit menu, choose Paste to add the themes to the 3D scene. On the viewer control bar, click the Zoom to Full Extent button.

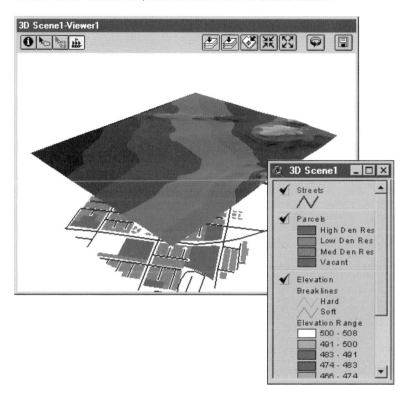

The themes are added to the 3D scene Table of Contents and displayed in the viewer. The *Streets* and *Parcels* themes appear well below the surface of the *Elevation* theme. That's because these are 2D feature themes with no z values. By default, 3D Analyst assigns them base heights (elevation values) of 0. They lie 432 meters below the lowest elevation on this TIN theme.

Although the feature themes contain no height information, 3D Analyst can display them in 3D perspective by assigning them elevation values from the TIN surface.

4   In the Table of Contents, click on the *Streets* theme to make it the only active theme. From the Theme menu, select 3D Properties to open the 3D Theme Properties dialog.

5   In the *Assign base heights by* panel, click the Surface radio button. In the *Surface* drop-down list, the path to the *Elevation* TIN theme's location on disk is already specified. (The name of the *Elevation* theme's data set is "redtin.")

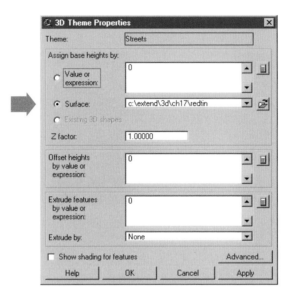

3D Analyst knows that the *Streets* theme and the *Elevation* theme are georeferenced to one another (that they "line up," just as they lined up in the view). It will use this knowledge to assign appropriate elevation values to the streets from the TIN surface.

Understanding base heights.   TIN themes have base height (elevation) values for every measurable location on their surface. Grid themes have one base height value for each grid cell. Point themes have one base height value for each feature. Line and polygon themes have one base height value for each feature vertex and additional values wherever a feature crosses a triangle edge (if the feature theme's base heights are set to a TIN theme) or at intervals equal to the grid cell size (if the base heights are set to a grid theme). Since polygons have vertices only along their boundaries, they have no height variation across their interiors. This means that if you try to display a large polygon feature on a hilly surface, the center of the polygon will often be submerged in the terrain. (You can avoid this problem by converting the polygon theme to a grid theme.) In the online help, use the Find tab to locate the topics *3D Properties (Dialog box)* and *Base height default settings*.

6 Click Apply to apply your change to the viewer without closing the 3D Theme Properties dialog.

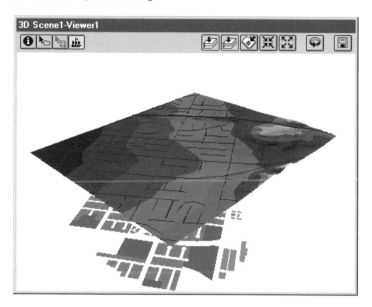

The streets are displayed on the TIN theme surface. But because their elevation values are identical to the corresponding surface locations, the streets don't stand out as well as they might.

7 In the *Offset heights by value or expression* panel of the dialog, type **2**. Click OK to close the 3D Theme Properties dialog.

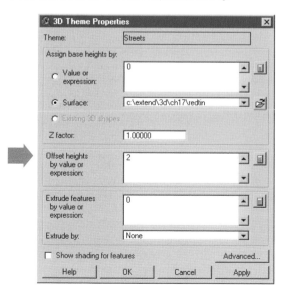

The streets are now better delineated. The offset value raises the features 2 meters above the surface of the TIN. (The values are meters because the z units of the TIN theme are meters.)

8 In the Table of Contents, make the *Parcels* theme active. From the Theme menu, choose 3D Properties to open the 3D Theme Properties dialog.

Like the *Streets* theme, the *Parcels* theme has a default base height of zero.

9 In the *Assign base heights by* panel, click the Surface radio button. In the *Surface* drop-down list, the path to the *Elevation* TIN theme's location on disk is correctly set.

10 In the *Offset heights by value or expression* panel of the dialog, type **2**. Click Apply to apply your change to the viewer without closing the dialog.

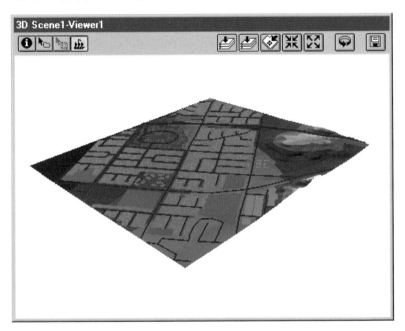

In the viewer, the parcels now appear on the surface of the TIN theme. They're offset from the surface to stand out clearly. One thing, however, still isn't right. The buildings are completely flat. You'll fix this by extruding them.

11 In the *Extrude features by value or expression* panel of the dialog, click the Calculator button to open the Expression Builder.

The *Fields* scrolling list displays all numeric fields in the attribute table of the *Parcels* theme. One of these is a field called "Stories." This field contains values like "1" and "2" that designate the number of stories each building has. (Vacant lots have a value of 0 in this field.)

12   Double-click on the [Stories] field to add it to the expression box. Click the "*" (multiplication) operator. Type **4**. Your completed expression should match the one in the graphic. Click OK to close the Expression Builder and update the 3D Theme Properties dialog.

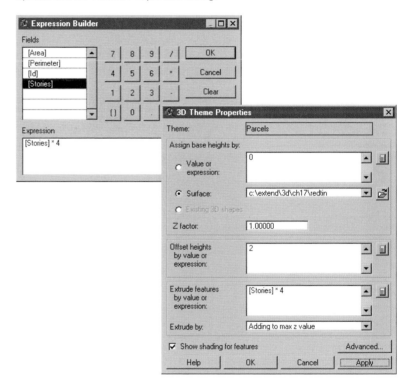

The *Extrude features by value or expression* box contains the expression you just created. Every building in the parcels theme will be extruded by the number of stories it has times 4 meters. The *Extrude by* method defaults to "Adding to max z value." (All base heights in a building will be extruded to the same level as its highest base height. This ensures that the buildings will have level roofs.)

Notice that the "Show shading for features" check box has been turned on. The buildings will display light and shadow according to the sun position setting.

13   Click OK to apply the changes and close the 3D Theme Properties dialog. With the Navigation tool selected in the viewer, zoom in for a close look at the effects of the extrusion.

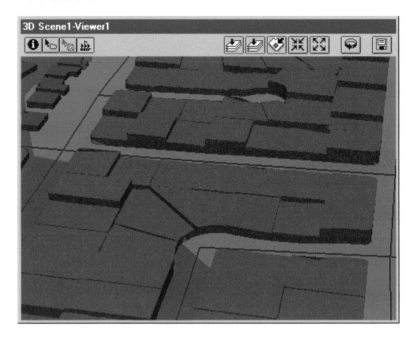

All the buildings are now solid blocks. They're extruded according to the number of stories they have.

The feature themes are now positioned correctly on the TIN surface. The TIN theme itself, however, is rather flat. You'll apply a vertical exaggeration factor to the scene, as you did in the previous exercise.

14   On the viewer control bar, click the Zoom to Full Extent button. Open the 3D Scene Properties dialog and click the Calculate button to calculate an appropriate vertical exaggeration factor. Click OK to apply the change and close the dialog.

15   Navigate around the display to see it from various perspectives.

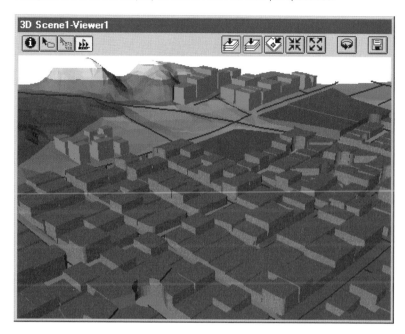

16   From the File menu, choose Close All. Again from the File menu, choose Close Project. Click No when you're prompted to save your changes.

If you want to go on to the next exercise, leave ArcView GIS running. Otherwise, choose Exit from the File menu.

Setting 3D properties for image themes

In this exercise, you'll set 3D theme properties for an image theme to "drape" it over a TIN surface.

◆ *E x e r c i s e   1 7 c*

1 If necessary, start ArcView GIS. Navigate to the \extend\3d\ch17 directory and open the project "ex17c.apr."

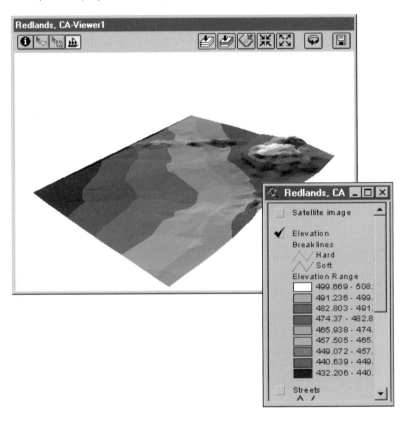

When the project opens, you see a 3D viewer containing the familiar TIN elevation theme for Redlands. The Table of Contents also includes a satellite image theme of the area as well as street and parcel themes. Only the elevation theme is turned on.

2   Turn on the *Satellite image* theme. The image is quite detailed and may take a few moments to display. When it does, click the Zoom to Full Extent button.

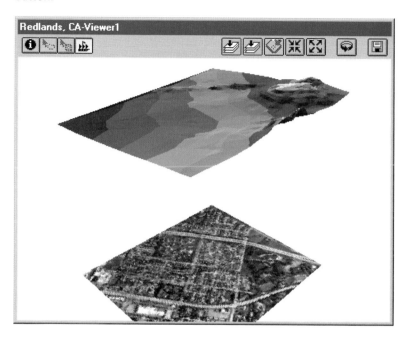

Like the 2D feature themes in the previous exercise, the image theme is assigned a default base height of zero and displays underneath the TIN theme. As you did with the feature themes, you'll assign base heights to the image from the TIN surface. In this case, however, you don't want to display both the image and the TIN theme. You want to display only the image theme.

3   In the Table of Contents, turn off the *Elevation* theme. Click on the *Satellite image* theme to make it active. From the Theme menu, choose 3D Properties to open the 3D Theme Properties dialog.

4   In the *Assign base heights by* panel, click the Surface radio button. In the *Surface* drop-down list, the path to the *Elevation* TIN theme's location on disk is already specified.

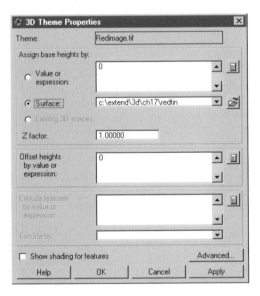

5   Click OK to apply the new base heights and close the dialog. Again, it may take a few moments. When the process is finished, click the Zoom to Active Theme(s) button on the viewer control bar.

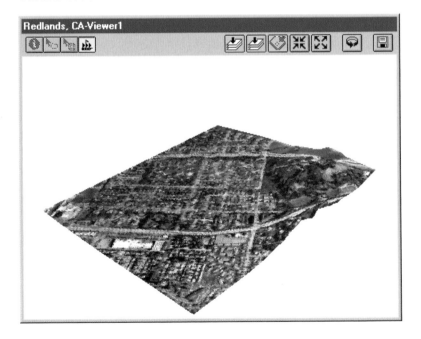

The image is draped over the TIN surface and displayed in 3D perspective.

6   With the Navigation tool selected in the viewer control bar, navigate in the viewer.

As you navigate, you'll probably exceed the redraw time and the image will be temporarily replaced by a white bounding box.

By clicking the Advanced button in the 3D Theme Properties dialog, you can change the amount of time 3D Analyst allocates for redrawing a theme before switching to a simplified version. The default value is one second.

7   In the Table of Contents, turn on both the *Streets* and *Parcels* themes.

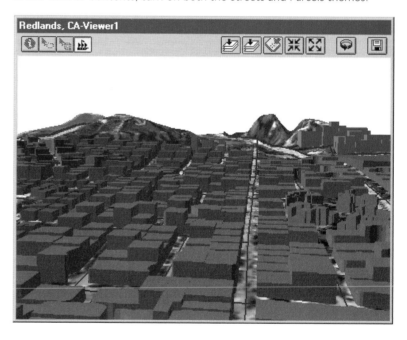

You don't need to set 3D theme properties for the *Streets* and *Parcels* themes. These themes have been converted to 3D shapefiles, and display according to the correct base heights by default. Their other 3D theme properties (offset and extrusion values) have been set for you in this project. You'll learn how to create 3D shapefiles in chapter 19, "Creating 3D feature data."

8   From the File menu, choose Close All. Again from the File menu, choose Close Project. Click No when you're prompted to save your changes.

If you're going on to the next chapter, leave ArcView GIS running. Otherwise, choose Exit from the File menu.

18

Symbolizing TIN themes

Symbolizing TIN theme points and lines

Symbolizing TIN theme faces

TIN SYMBOLOGY

is controlled through the TIN Legend Editor. The TIN Legend Editor is a kind of super Legend Editor containing three standard Legend Editors embedded within it: one for triangle points (nodes), one for lines (triangle edges), and one for faces.

Points can be symbolized by three different legend types. The default is "Single Symbol." Points can also be symbolized by their elevation values or by attribute values that can be assigned to them during TIN creation or editing. (The "Value" legend type isn't available unless attribute values have actually been assigned.) The color and size of points, but not the marker type, can be changed in the Symbol Palette.

Lines can also be symbolized by three different legend types. The default type is "Breakline Features," which displays hard and soft breaklines. Lines can also be symbolized according to "All Feature Types," which displays regular and outside lines in addition to breaklines. Finally, lines can be symbolized with a single symbol.

TIN faces can be symbolized by five legend types. By default, they're displayed according to their elevation values. They can also be displayed by slope or aspect. The "Value" legend displays faces according to attribute values that may be assigned when the TIN is created or edited. (You'll learn how to do this in chapter 20, "Creating TIN data.") Like points and lines, triangle faces can also be symbolized with a single symbol.

Symbolizing TIN theme points and lines

In this exercise, you'll use different point and line legends to display the structure of a TIN theme.

◆ *Exercise 18a*

1   If necessary, start ArcView GIS. Navigate to the \extend\3d\ch18 directory and open the project "ex18a.apr." When the project opens, you see a 3D scene containing a TIN theme of the Big Bear area.

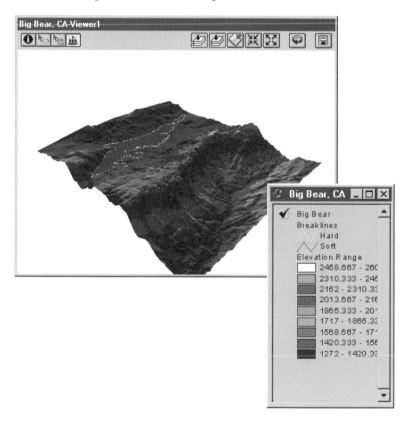

The TIN theme shows the area around Big Bear Lake. The lake boundary itself is represented in the TIN as a hard breakline.

2   In the 3D scene Table of Contents, double-click on the *Big Bear* theme to open the TIN Legend Editor.

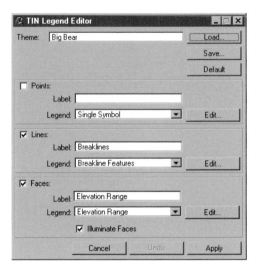

The TIN Legend Editor consists of separate panels for symbolizing points, lines, and triangle faces. Each panel contains an embedded Legend Editor.

3   In the TIN Legend Editor, click on the Lines and Faces check boxes to turn them off. Click on the Points check box to turn it on. Click the Apply button.

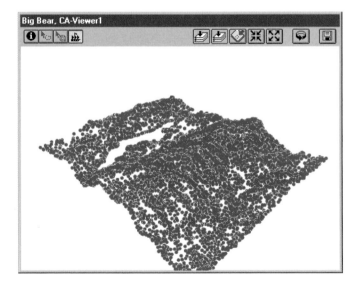

You see the individual nodes that make up the TIN. Each is an end point of a triangle.

4   With the Navigation tool selected in the viewer control bar, zoom in until you can distinguish individual points.

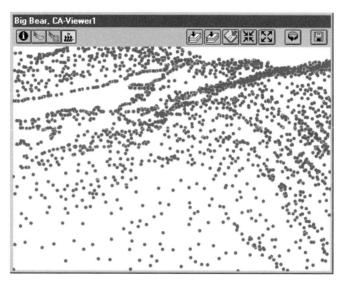

5   In the *Points* panel of the TIN Legend Editor, the legend is set to Single Symbol. From the drop-down list, set the legend to "Elevation Range" and click Apply. On the viewer control bar, click the Zoom to Active Theme(s) button.

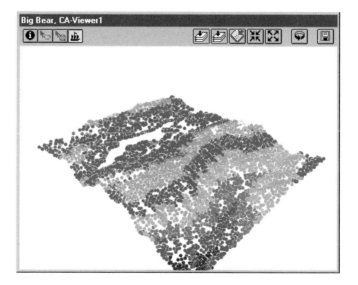

The points are symbolized by their elevation values according to the "Terrain Elevation #1" color ramp.

ArcView 3D Analyst adds three new terrain elevation color ramps to the predefined color schemes in ArcView GIS. The Terrain Elevation #1 ramp is the default used to symbolize TIN themes.

6   In the *Points* panel of the TIN Legend Editor, click the Edit button to open the embedded Legend Editor. From the *Color Ramps* drop-down list, choose "Terrain Elevation #3." If necessary, click the Flip Symbols button to associate white with the highest elevation range and dark green with the lowest. Click Apply and close the Legend Editor to return to the TIN Legend Editor.

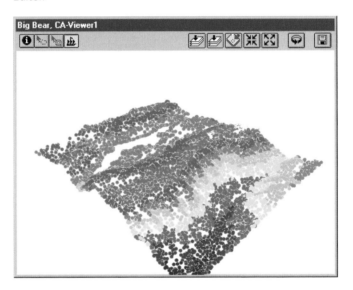

7   In the *Points* panel of the TIN Legend Editor, reset the legend to Single Sym-
     bol and click on the Points check box to turn it off.

8   In the *Lines* panel, click on the Lines check box to turn it on. The legend is
     set to Breakline Features. From the *Legend* drop-down list, set the legend
     to "All Feature Types" and click Apply.

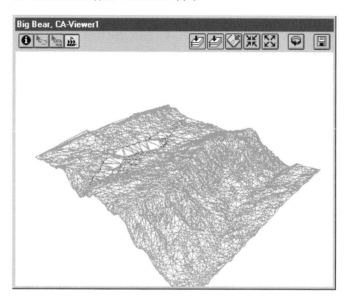

The lines that compose the TIN triangle edges and the hard breaklines of the lake boundary are displayed in randomly chosen colors. The lake boundary isn't easy to discern.

TIN lines are triangle edges and can be of four kinds. Most lines are *regu-*
lar lines. *Hard breaklines* are added to a TIN to mark distinct changes in
slope, such as the shore of a lake. *Soft breaklines* mark other surface
boundaries. *Outside* lines belong to triangles for which no values are
interpolated. (These triangles are similar to No Data cells in a grid.)

9   In the *Lines* panel of the TIN Legend Editor, click the Edit button to open the embedded Legend Editor. A unique symbol is assigned to all four types of lines. This TIN theme, however, has only regular lines and hard breaklines.

In the Legend Editor, change the symbol for regular lines to bright red and the symbol for hard breaklines to bright blue. Change the line thickness for the hard breaklines to 5.

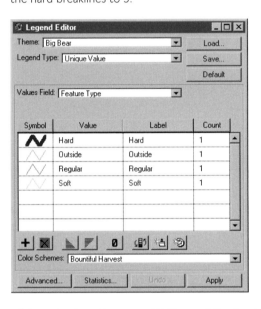

10 Click Apply. Close the Legend Editor and the Symbol Palette to return to the TIN Legend Editor.

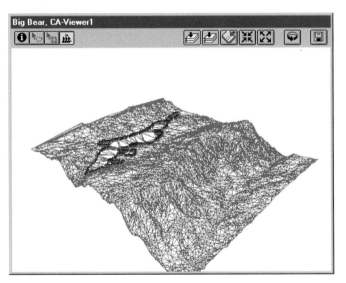

11   In the *Points* panel of the TIN Legend Editor, click on the Points check box to turn it on. Click Apply, then close the TIN Legend Editor.

12   With the Navigation tool active on the viewer control bar, zoom in and navigate to different perspectives.

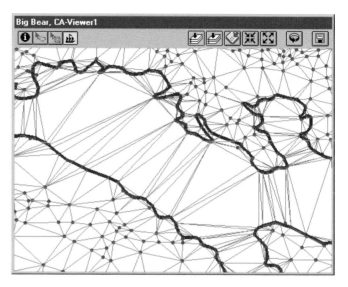

13   From the File menu, choose Close All. Again from the File menu, choose Close Project. Click No when you're prompted to save your changes.

If you want to go on to the next exercise, leave ArcView GIS running. Otherwise, choose Exit from the File menu.

Symbolizing TIN theme faces

In this exercise, you'll display a TIN theme by its slope, aspect, and value legends.

◆ *Exercise   18b*

1   If necessary, start ArcView GIS. Navigate to the \extend\3d\ch18 directory and open the project "ex18b.apr."

When the project opens, you see a 3D scene containing the TIN theme of Big Bear that you worked with in the last exercise.

2   Double-click on the *Big Bear area* theme to open the TIN Legend Editor.

In the *Faces* panel, the legend is set to "Elevation Range." The "Illuminate Faces" check box is turned on by default to take into account the effects of sun position.

3   In the *Faces* panel of the TIN Legend Editor, change the legend to "Slope" and click Apply.

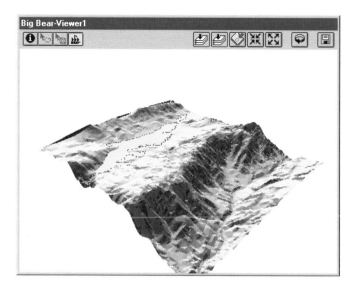

The TIN theme is displayed by slope values according to a randomly selected color ramp.

4　In the *Faces* panel of the TIN Legend Editor, click the Edit button to open the embedded Legend Editor. The default classification into equal intervals of 10 degrees is too broad. You'll change the default legend to a more appropriate one.

Click the Load button. Navigate to the \extend\3d\ch18 directory and load the TIN legend file "slope.avl." In the Load Legend dialog, make sure the *Field* drop-down list is set to "Slope." Click Apply and close the Legend Editor to return to the TIN Legend Editor.

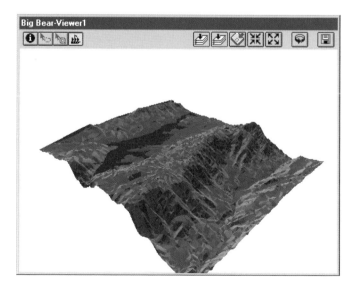

Slopes increase in steepness from blue to cyan to green. The surface of the lake has a slope of zero.

5   In the *Faces* panel of the TIN Legend Editor, change the legend to "Aspect." Click the Edit button to open the embedded Legend Editor, where you can preview the legend.

Again, a custom legend will make for a better map.

6   Click the Load button. Navigate to the \extend\3d\ch18 directory and load the TIN legend file "aspect.avl." In the Load Legend dialog, make sure the *Field* drop-down list is set to "Aspect." Click Apply and close the Legend Editor to return to the TIN Legend Editor.

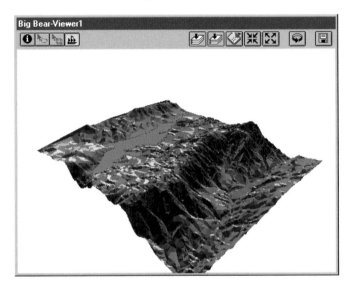

The TIN is symbolized according to its aspect values.

7   In the *Faces* panel of the TIN Legend Editor, change the legend to "Value" and click Apply.

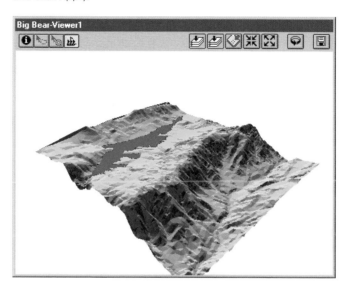

The TIN is displayed according to attributes representing land and water that were assigned to the triangle faces when the TIN theme was created. The colors are randomly selected.

8   In the *Faces* panel of the TIN Legend Editor, click the Edit button to open the embedded Legend Editor. Double-click the symbol for 0 and change it to a greenish-gray. Change the symbol for 1 to a bright blue. In the Label field, replace the label "0" with **Land**. Replace the label "1" with **Water**.

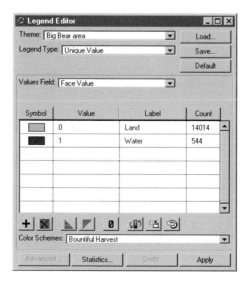

9   Click Apply. Close the Legend Editor, the Symbol Palette, and the TIN Legend Editor.

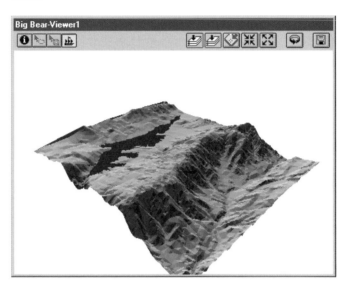

10 From the File menu, choose Close All. Again from the File menu, choose Close Project. Click No when you're prompted to save your changes.

If you're going on to the next chapter, leave ArcView GIS running. Otherwise, choose Exit from the File menu.

19

Creating 3D feature data

Creating 3D themes

Converting 2D themes to 3D

Y OU CAN CREATE 3D FEATURE THEMES

in two ways. You can start from scratch, drawing points, lines, or polygons on top of an elevation surface. Or you can convert existing 2D themes to 3D by specifying a source of elevation values for the 2D features.

You don't have to use 3D feature themes at all, since 3D Analyst can display 2D themes in three-dimensional perspective. But if you use a data set frequently for 3D display, it's convenient to have it saved as a 3D shapefile. That way, it will display at the proper elevation without your having to set base heights in the 3D Theme Properties dialog. (You'll still have to set offset and extrusion values manually.)

Creating 3D themes

In this exercise, you'll create a 3D theme and add features to it with the Interpolate tool. You'll then display the new theme in a 3D scene.

◆ *Exercise 19a*

1   If necessary, start ArcView GIS. Navigate to the \extend\3d\ch19 directory and open the project "ex19a.apr."

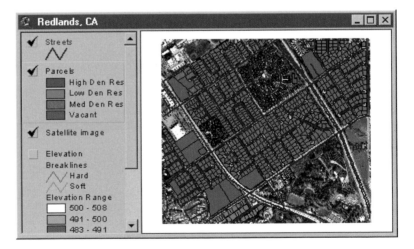

When the project opens, you see a view of a section of Redlands containing feature themes of streets and parcels, a satellite image theme, and a TIN of elevation values (turned off).

The *Streets* and *Parcels* themes are 3D shapefiles, which means that z values are defined as part of their shape geometry. That's not apparent from the view, where 2D and 3D shapefiles look the same, but it is apparent from their theme tables.

2 With both the *Streets* and *Parcels* themes active, click the Open Theme Table button. The Shape field values for the two themes end in "Z"—this tells you that they're 3D shapefiles. Close both tables.

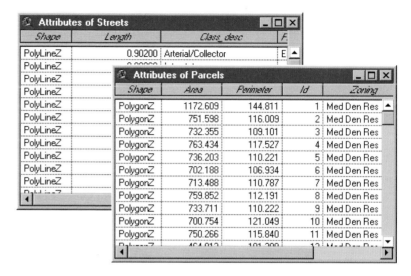

You'll create a new 3D theme of some Redlands High School buildings. You'll use the satellite image as a background on which to digitize the features. Although they're created in the two-dimensional drawing environment of a view, the features will be three-dimensional.

3 Make sure the view is active. From the View menu, choose New 3D Theme to open the dialog. In the *Feature type* drop-down list, choose "PolygonZ." Click OK.

4   By default, the new theme is called *thmz1.shp*. In the New 3D Theme dialog, click OK to save the theme to your c:\temp (or working) directory.

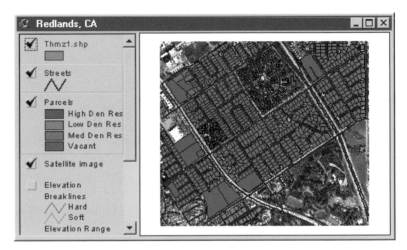

The new 3D theme is added to the view and is editable. If you don't like the randomly assigned color, you can change it now in the Legend Editor.

Three-dimensional features are created with the tools on the *Interpolate tool* drop-down list. Because the features derive their z values from an elevation surface, the Interpolate tool is enabled only when a grid or TIN theme is active in the view. It isn't necessary, however, that the surface theme be turned on.

5   Make the *Elevation* TIN theme the only active theme.

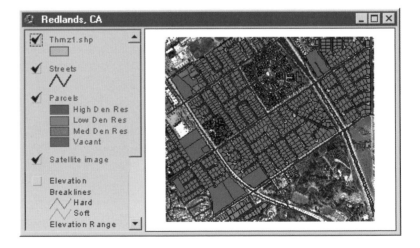

6 Select the Zoom In tool. Zoom in close on the northwest corner of the view until your map scale is about 1:3,000. You'll see some Redlands High athletic buildings. Two swimming pools and a baseball diamond should be visible.

7 From the *Interpolate tool* drop-down list, select the Interpolate Polygon tool. Draw three polygons to trace the outlines of the buildings, as shown in the following graphic. (If you don't like your first try, you can use the Pointer tool to select and delete a polygon.)

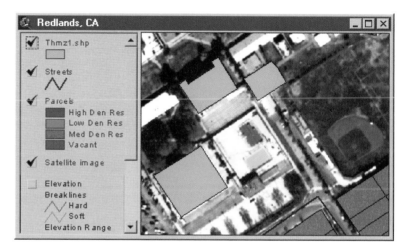

Elevation values are assigned to the polygon boundaries from locations on the active TIN theme.

8 Click on *Thmz1.shp* to make it active. From the Theme menu, choose Stop Editing. Click Yes to save your edits.

3D features and 3D graphics. You can create either 3D theme features or 3D graphics when a grid or TIN theme is active in a view. If the view contains an editable 3D theme, a figure drawn with the Interpolation tool becomes a theme feature; otherwise, it becomes a 3D graphic. Unlike 2D graphics, 3D graphics can be pasted into a 3D scene. Their 3D properties are limited, however. They can't be offset or extruded, although you can offset a TIN or grid surface by a small negative value to make a 3D graphic display better. Nor can they be moved in a 3D scene. If you need to move a 3D graphic, you can return to the view document, move it there, then copy and paste it again into the 3D scene. In the online help, use the Find tab to locate the topic *Feature Interpolation Tools*.

9 Make sure *Thmz1.shp* is the only active theme. From the Edit menu, choose Copy Themes.

10 Close the view and open the Redlands 3D scene. From the Edit menu, choose Paste.

The theme is displayed in the 3D scene. Because its features have built-in z values, they automatically appear at the correct elevation.

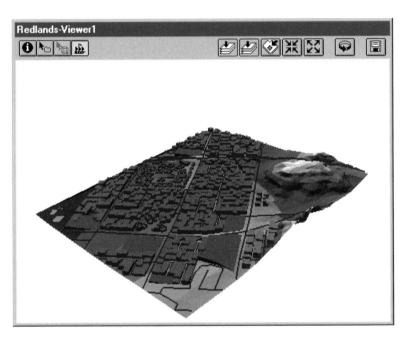

11 In the 3D Scene Table of Contents, click on *Thmz1.shp* to make it the only active theme. From the Theme menu, choose 3D Properties to open the 3D Theme Properties dialog.

In the *Assign base heights* panel of the dialog, the base heights for the theme are set by default to "Existing 3D shapes."

12   In the *Offset heights* panel, set the offset value to **2**. In the *Extrude features* panel, set the extrusion value to **4**. (The z values for the 3D theme are in meters because they were derived from an elevation theme with z values in meters.) The extrusion method defaults to "Adding to max z value." Click OK.

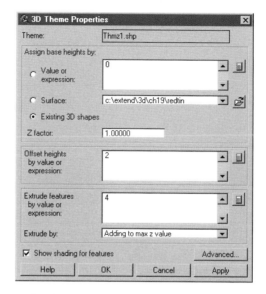

13   In the viewer control bar, click the Zoom to Active Theme(s) button. Navigate to look at the buildings from different perspectives.

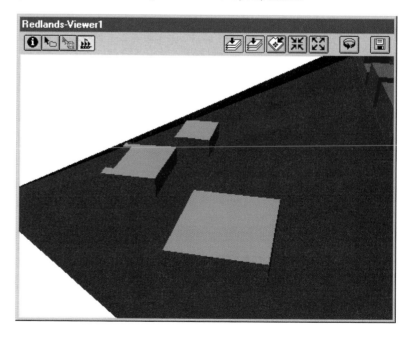

14 From the File menu, choose Close All. Again from the File menu, choose Close Project. Click No when you're prompted to save your changes.

In this exercise, you created a shapefile called thmz1.shp in your c:\temp directory. Use the Source Manager to delete this file. If ArcView GIS continues to reference the file after the project is closed, delete it at another time.

If you want to go on to the next exercise, leave ArcView GIS running. Otherwise, choose Exit from the File menu.

Converting 2D themes to 3D

Any 2D shapefile can be converted to 3D (while preserving the original 2D shapefile) as long as a source of z values for the 3D shapes is specified.

Z values can be derived from a grid or TIN surface theme. If the surface theme isn't already in your project, you can browse to its location on disk. Z values can also be derived from a numeric field in the theme table of the 2D shapefile being converted. A third option is to specify z values as a constant (for instance, 100). In this case, all theme features will have the same base height.

If z values are derived from a TIN theme, a value is assigned to every vertex in the line or polygon theme. (A point feature receives one z value.) Additional z values are assigned wherever a line segment in a line or polygon feature intersects a TIN triangle edge.

If z values are derived from a grid theme, a value is again assigned to every vertex in the line or polygon theme. Additional values are placed along the lengths of line segments at intervals equal to the grid cell size. The length of the interval can be decreased to assign more z values to the 3D features. (However, the accuracy with which features are represented doesn't improve once the interval becomes smaller than half the grid cell size.)

In this exercise, you'll convert a 2D theme to 3D using values from a TIN theme. You'll then display the theme in a 3D scene.

◆ *E x e r c i s e   1 9 b*

1   If necessary, start ArcView GIS. Navigate to the \extend\3d\ch19 directory and open the project "ex19b.apr."

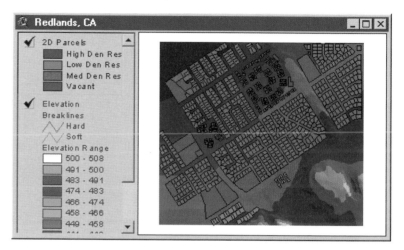

When the project opens, you see a parcels theme and a TIN theme of elevation. The *2D Parcels* theme is active.

2   Click the Open Theme Table button to open the Attributes of 2D Parcels table.

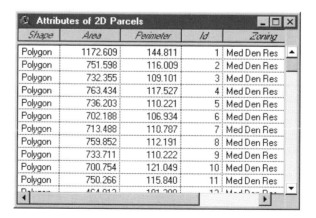

Shape	Area	Perimeter	Id	Zoning
Polygon	1172.609	144.811	1	Med Den Res
Polygon	751.598	116.009	2	Med Den Res
Polygon	732.355	109.101	3	Med Den Res
Polygon	763.434	117.527	4	Med Den Res
Polygon	736.203	110.221	5	Med Den Res
Polygon	702.188	106.934	6	Med Den Res
Polygon	713.488	110.787	7	Med Den Res
Polygon	759.852	112.191	8	Med Den Res
Polygon	733.711	110.222	9	Med Den Res
Polygon	700.754	121.049	10	Med Den Res
Polygon	750.266	115.840	11	Med Den Res

The value in the Shape field is "Polygon," which tells you that the theme is a 2D theme.

3   Close the table and make sure that *2D Parcels* is the only active theme.
From the Theme menu, choose Convert to 3D Shapefile.

In the Convert 2D Parcels dialog, make sure the *Get Z values from* drop-
down list is set to "Surface." Click OK. In the Select Surface dialog, the only
available surface theme, *Elevation,* is highlighted. Click OK.

In the Output Shapefile dialog, click OK to accept the default name of
thmz1.shp (or *thmz2.shp,* if you haven't deleted the 3D shapefile from
the previous exercise) and save it to your c:\temp directory. Click Yes to
add the 3D shapefile as a theme to the view.

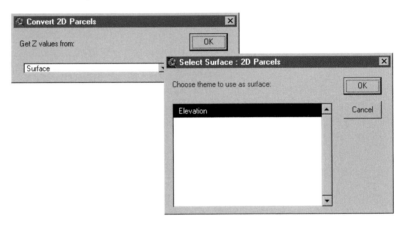

If there are no surface themes in the view, the Select Surface dialog lets
you browse to TIN or grid data sets on disk.

4   Make the new 3D theme active. From the Theme menu, choose Properties.
In the Theme Properties dialog, change the theme name to **3D Parcels** and
click OK. Turn the *3D Parcels* theme on.

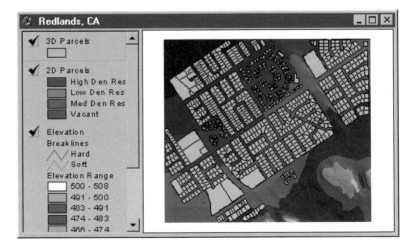

The *3D Parcels* theme covers the *2D Parcels* theme exactly, as it should. All features in the two themes have the same x,y values.

You'll classify the 3D theme according to the same zoning values that the 2D theme displays. Then you'll delete the 2D theme.

5   Double-click on the *3D Parcels* theme to open the Legend Editor. Click the Load button and navigate to the \extend\3d\ch19 directory. Load the "parcel.avl" legend file, making sure the *Field* drop-down list is set to "Zoning." Click Apply in the Legend Editor and close it.

6   Make the *2D Parcels* theme the only active theme. From the Edit menu, choose Delete Themes. At the prompt, click Yes to delete the *2D Parcels* theme.

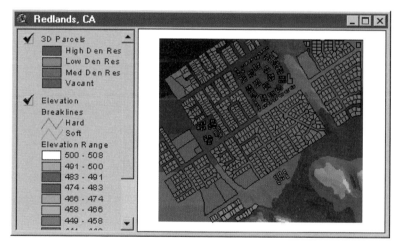

7   Make the *3D Parcels* theme active. Click the Open Theme Table button to open the Attributes of 3D Parcels theme table.

Shape	Area	Perimeter	Id	Zoning
PolygonZ	1172.609	144.811	1	Med Den Res
PolygonZ	751.598	116.009	2	Med Den Res
PolygonZ	732.355	109.101	3	Med Den Res
PolygonZ	763.434	117.527	4	Med Den Res
PolygonZ	736.203	110.221	5	Med Den Res
PolygonZ	702.188	106.934	6	Med Den Res
PolygonZ	713.488	110.787	7	Med Den Res
PolygonZ	759.852	112.191	8	Med Den Res
PolygonZ	733.711	110.222	9	Med Den Res
PolygonZ	700.754	121.049	10	Med Den Res
PolygonZ	750.266	115.840	11	Med Den Res
PolygonZ	464.913	101.200	12	Med Den Res

The Shape field contains values of "PolygonZ."

8   Close the table and make sure the *3D Parcels* theme is active in the view. From the Edit menu, choose Copy Themes. Close the view.

9   From the Project window, open the Redlands 3D scene. From the Edit menu, choose Paste.

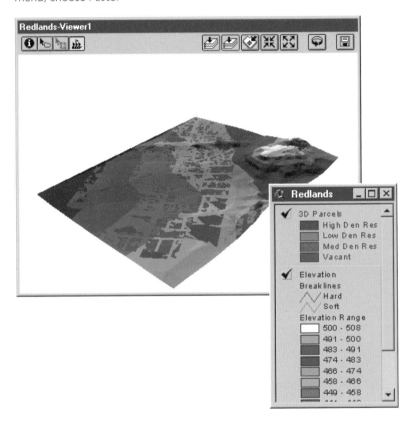

The *3D Parcels* theme is displayed on the surface of the *Elevation* theme.

10 Click on *3D Parcels* to make it the only active theme. From the Theme menu, choose 3D Properties to open the 3D Theme Properties dialog.

By default, the theme's base heights are set to "Existing 3D shapes."

11 In the *Offset heights* panel, type **2** in the expression box to raise the features 2 meters above the surface.

12   In the *Extrude features* panel, click the Calculator button to open the Expression Builder dialog. In the *Fields* scrolling list, double-click on [Stories] to add it to the expression box. Click the "*" (multiplication) operator, then type **4**. Your completed expression should match the one in the graphic. Click OK.

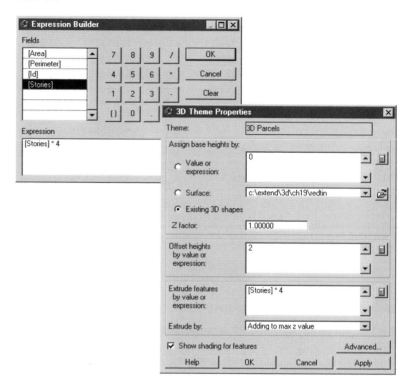

The expression is added to the 3D Theme Properties dialog. The extrusion method defaults to "Adding to max z value."

13   Click OK to apply your changes and close the 3D Theme Properties dialog.

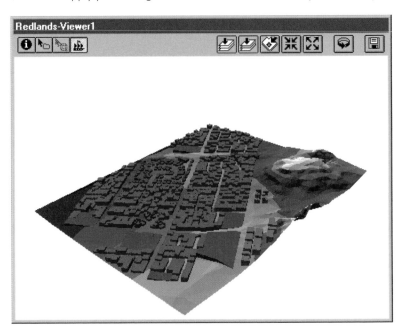

14   Select the Navigation tool and navigate to various perspectives.

15   From the File menu, choose Close All. Again from the File menu, choose
       Close Project. Click No when you're prompted to save your changes.

In this exercise, you created a shapefile called thmz1.shp in your c:\temp
directory. Use the Source Manager to delete this file.

If you're going on to the next chapter, leave ArcView GIS running.
Otherwise, choose Exit from the File menu.

20

Creating
TIN data

Creating a TIN from elevation points

Creating a TIN from elevation contours

Modifying TINs

YOU CAN CREATE TIN DATA SETS
from vector features, like points or contour lines, that contain elevation values. You can also convert existing grid themes to TINs.

When you create a TIN from features, or when you edit an existing TIN, you can include features that define prominent characteristics of the landscape, such as shorelines and roads. And you can assign values to triangle nodes and faces to represent properties other than elevation, such as land cover, land ownership, or zoning codes. The TIN theme can then be symbolized according to these values.

In addition to creating TINs, 3D Analyst can interpolate grids from sample points and convert feature themes to grids and grids to feature themes. These functions are shared by 3D Analyst and ArcView Spatial Analyst and are described in the ArcView Spatial Analyst section of this book.

Creating a TIN from elevation points

TINs can be created (interpolated) from point, line, or polygon themes, used singly or in combination. The themes can be either 2D or 3D, but at least one of them must have z values.

If a point theme is the source of z values, each point location becomes a triangle node, and the point's z value is assigned to the node. If lines or polygons are used, each feature vertex becomes a triangle node.

 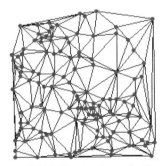

On the left is a set of elevation points. On the right is the structure of a TIN created from the points. Every elevation point becomes a triangle node. Elevation values for locations on the triangle faces are interpolated from the values of nearby nodes.

Line and polygon themes can contribute to the definition of a surface in other ways, for example as breaklines. Hard breaklines represent distinct changes in slope on a surface: a stream, a road, a lakeshore, or something similar. In the TIN triangulation process, no triangle is allowed to cross a breakline. Because each triangle has a single slope value, a breakline enforces a change in slope.

Soft breaklines form the same barrier to triangulation. They're used to mark boundaries that aren't physical features of the landscape: the edge of the TIN, for instance, or a political boundary, or physical changes that don't affect slope, such as vegetation or soil type.

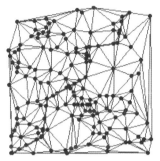 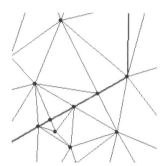

On the left, a breakline has been added to an existing TIN. The TIN is retriangulated and new nodes are added. On the right is a zoomed-in view. No triangles cross the breakline.

Polygon themes can refine the TIN surface in additional ways. A "clip" polygon defines a zone of interpolation by excluding everything outside its boundary from the analysis area. The area outside the zone of interpolation is like a No Data area in a grid theme. An "erase" polygon functions like a clip polygon, except that it excludes areas that are inside its boundaries from the zone of interpolation.

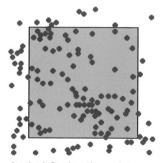 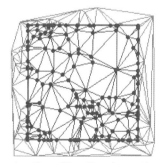

On the left, elevation points are used in conjunction with a clip polygon. On the right is the resulting TIN structure. The polygon boundary becomes a soft breakline that marks the zone of interpolation. Areas outside the zone are triangulated, but have no nodes and no values.

You'll learn about some other specialized uses for polygons in exercise 21c.

In this exercise, you'll create a TIN from a set of elevation points in the Grand Canyon.

◆ *E x e r c i s e   2 0 a*

1   If necessary, start ArcView GIS. Navigate to the \extend\3d\ch20 directory
and open the project "ex20a.apr."

When the project opens, you see a view of Arizona. The study area,
covering a small section of the Grand Canyon, is marked by a small
green rectangle.

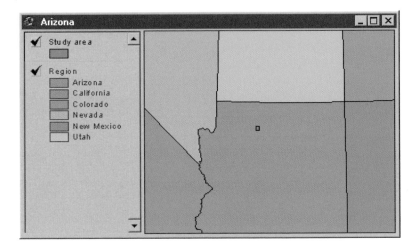

2   Close the view and open the Grand Canyon Area view.

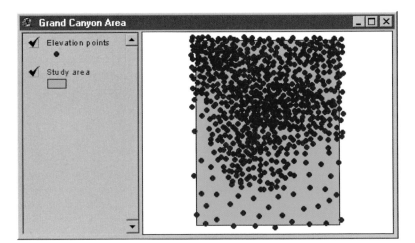

The view displays the study area and a theme of elevation points.
The points are unevenly distributed—dense in areas where there
are sharp changes in elevation and sparse where the surface is flat.

A TIN is a variable resolution model. Where z values are dense, the surface will be detailed. Where z values are scarce, there will be few triangles. Grids, in contrast, have a uniform structure. You can't infer from the surface how the input data is distributed.

3   Click the Open Theme Table button. The theme is a 2D theme and the z value of each point is stored in the Elevation field. Close the table.

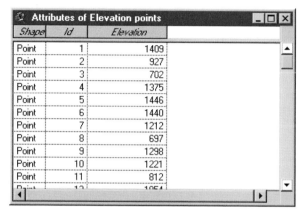

4   With the *Elevation points* theme active, hold down the Shift key and click on the *Study area* theme to make it active as well. From the Surface menu, choose Create TIN from Features to open the Create new TIN dialog.

5   In the dialog, the *Active feature themes* scrolling list shows you the themes that will be used to create the TIN. Click on each theme in turn to see its default settings.

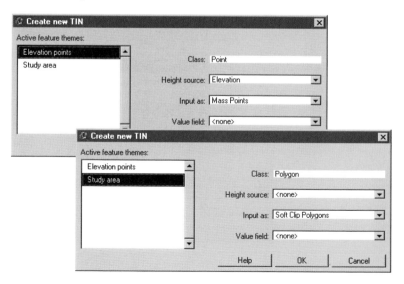

Both themes will be used to create the TIN. The *Elevation points* theme is input as mass points, which means that the elevation points will become triangle nodes. The height source is the Elevation field in the *Elevation points* theme table. The z value of each TIN triangle node will be taken from the appropriate record in this table.

The *Study area* theme is input as a soft clip polygon with no height source. It will define the zone of interpolation for the TIN. (Any points lying outside its boundary won't become triangle nodes.)

6   In the Create new TIN dialog, click OK. In the Output TIN Name dialog, accept the default name of crtin1 and click OK to save the new TIN to your c:\temp (or working) directory. The TIN is created and added to the view.

7   Make the *Crtin1* theme active. From the Theme menu, choose Properties. Rename the theme **Grand Canyon** and click OK. Turn the theme on.

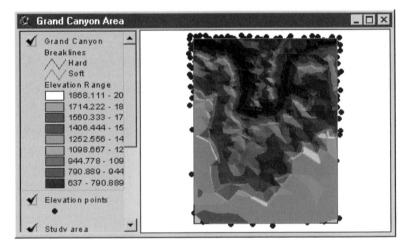

The reason for the uneven distribution of elevation points is clear when you look at the TIN. You need lots of samples to represent the canyon adequately. You don't need many to model the rim.

8   Make sure the *Grand Canyon* theme is the only active theme. From the Edit menu, choose Copy Themes. Close the view.

9   In the Project window, open the Grand Canyon 3D scene. From the Edit
    menu, choose Paste to paste the theme into the viewer.

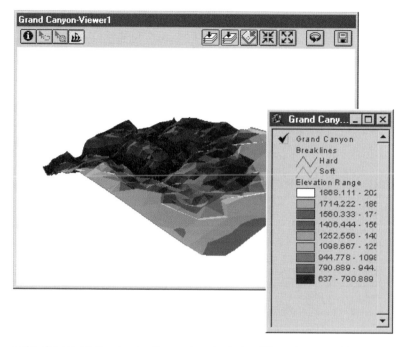

10 Make the Navigation tool active and navigate to different perspectives.
    When you're finished, click the Zoom to Active Theme(s) button.

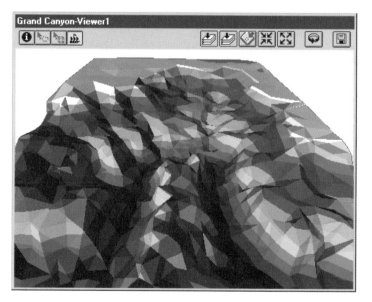

11 In the 3D Scene Table of Contents, double-click on the *Grand Canyon* theme
    to open the TIN Legend Editor. In the Lines panel, set the *Legend* drop-
    down list to "All Feature Types." Turn off the display of Faces. Click Apply
    and leave the TIN Legend Editor open. Make the viewer active.

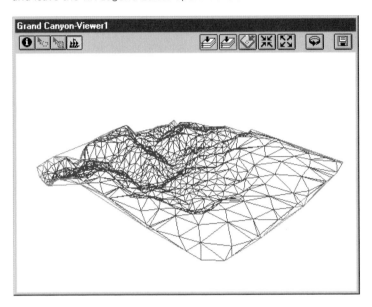

The regular lines (blue in the graphic) form the triangles that
belong to the zone of interpolation. The outside lines (gold) are
outside the zone of interpolation. A soft breakline (purple) marks
the boundary. Depending on the colors assigned to your line features, the breakline may be hard to see.

12 Make the TIN Legend Editor active. In the *Lines* panel, click the Edit button
    to open the embedded Legend Editor. Double-click on the symbol for soft
    breaklines. In the Pen Palette, set its size to 3. In the Color Palette, set its
    color to bright red.

    If you like, change the colors of your regular and outside lines as well. Click
    Apply in the Legend Editor. Close the Legend Editor, the Symbol Palette, and
    the TIN Legend Editor.

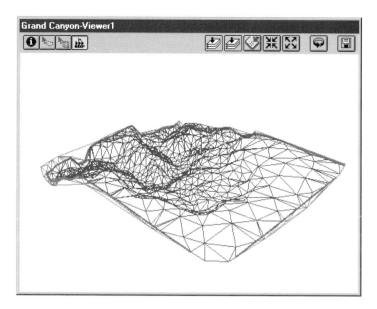

 13 On the viewer control bar, select the Identify tool. Identify a few locations inside and outside the zone of interpolation. (When triangle faces are turned off, you need to click precisely on a line to get a result.) When you're finished, close the Identify Results window.

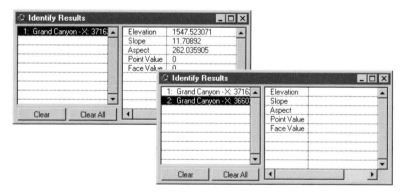

Every identified location within the zone of interpolation returns elevation, slope, and aspect values. Locations outside the zone of interpolation return empty values.

14 From the File menu, choose Close All. Again from the File menu, choose Close Project. Click No when you're prompted to save your changes.

In this exercise, you created a TIN data set called crtin1 in your c:\temp directory. Use the Source Manager to delete this data set. (If ArcView GIS continues to reference the file after the project is closed, delete the data set at another time.)

If you want to go on to the next exercise, leave ArcView GIS running. Otherwise, choose Exit from the File menu.

Creating a TIN from elevation contours

In this exercise, you'll use contour lines, rather than points, to create a TIN theme of an area in Canyonlands National Park in southeastern Utah.

◆ *E x e r c i s e   2 0 b*

1 If necessary, start ArcView GIS. Navigate to the \extend\3d\ch20 directory and open the project "ex20b.apr."

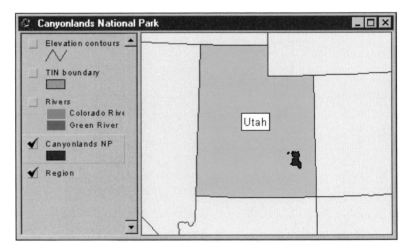

When the project opens, you see a view of Utah. Canyonlands National Park occupies 527 square miles (848 square kilometers) in the southeastern part of the state.

2   With the *Canyonlands NP* theme active, click the Zoom to Active Theme(s) button. Turn on the *Rivers* theme.

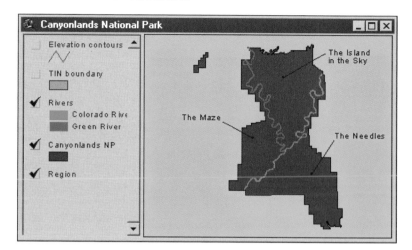

The Colorado and Green rivers run through the park, dividing it into the districts labeled in the view.

3   Make the *TIN boundary* theme active and turn it on.

The *TIN boundary* theme represents a 5-square-kilometer area in the park district known as the Maze. You'll create a TIN theme from elevation contours of this area.

4   With the *TIN boundary* theme active, click the Zoom to Active Theme(s) button. Turn on the *Elevation contours* theme.

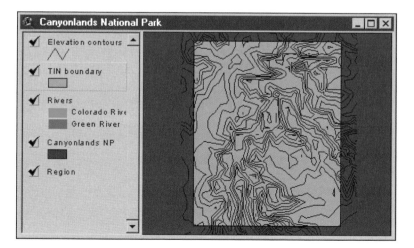

The lines have been clipped from a theme of elevation contours for the entire park.

 5   Make the *Elevation contours* theme active and click the Open Theme Table button. The theme is a 2D theme. The elevation values are stored in the Contour field and mark 20-meter changes in elevation. Close the table.

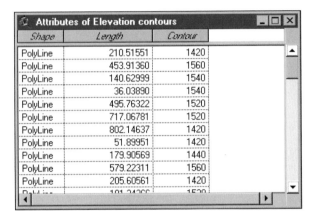

6   With the *Elevation contours* theme active, hold down the Shift key and make the *TIN boundary* theme active as well. From the Surface menu, choose Create TIN from Features.

Because it's a line theme, the *Elevation contours* theme is set to be input as hard breaklines with no height source. You need to change the settings so that the TIN theme gets its z values from this theme.

7   In the *Active feature themes* scrolling list, make sure the *Elevation contours* theme is highlighted. In the *Input as* drop-down list, choose "Mass Points."

The height source defaults to the Length field in the theme table. 3D Analyst is looking for z values in the wrong place.

In the *Height source* drop-down list, choose "Contour."

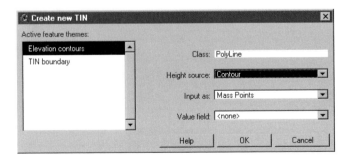

Every vertex in every contour line feature will become a triangle node. All vertices belonging to the same line feature will have the same z value.

8   In the *Active feature themes* scrolling list, click on the *TIN boundary* theme to highlight it. The theme is set correctly to be input as soft clip polygons with no height source.

Click OK. In the Output TIN Name dialog, accept the default name of crtin1 (or crtin2 if you haven't deleted the TIN from the previous exercise). Click OK to save the new TIN to your c:\temp (or working) directory.

The new TIN is created and added to the view.

9   Make the *Crtin1* theme active. From the Theme menu, choose Properties to open the Theme Properties dialog. Rename the theme **Maze** and click OK. Turn the theme on.

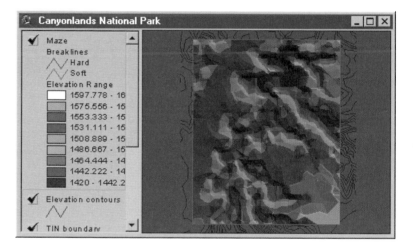

10 Make sure *Maze* is the only active theme. From the Edit menu, choose Copy Themes. Close the view.

11   From the Project window, open the Utah 3D scene. From the Edit menu, choose Paste. Select the Navigation tool and navigate to different perspectives.

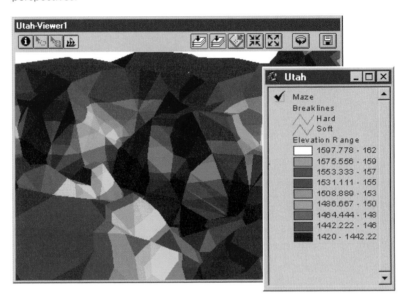

12   From the File menu, choose Close All. Again from the File menu, choose Close Project. Click No when you're prompted to save your changes.

Converting grids to TINs. In addition to creating TIN themes from feature data, you can convert grids to TINs with the Convert Grid to TIN choice on the Theme menu. One reason to convert a grid is for better zoomed-in display in 3D scenes. Another is that TINs have editing options (like the ability to add breaklines) that grids lack. When you convert a grid to a TIN, you specify the degree of accuracy you want with a z-tolerance setting. The z-tolerance defines the maximum allowable difference in elevation between each cell center in the input grid and its corresponding location on the TIN. (TIN locations that don't correspond to cell centers may lie outside the z-tolerance.) Once a z-tolerance is set, 3D Analyst calculates how many triangle nodes are needed, and in which locations, to satisfy the tolerance. You can also convert a TIN theme to a grid. The accuracy of the output grid is determined by the cell size you choose. In the online help, use the Find tab to locate the topics *Creating a TIN from a grid* and *Convert to Grid.*

In this exercise, you created a TIN data set called crtin1 in your c:\temp directory. Use the Source Manager to delete this data set.

If you want to go on to the next exercise, leave ArcView GIS running. Otherwise, choose Exit from the File menu.

Modifying TINs

Earlier in this chapter, you learned that there are different ways to influence the surface structure of a TIN with points, lines, and polygons. In addition to mass points, breaklines, clip polygons, and erase polygons, there are also replace polygons and fill polygons.

Replace polygons replace interpolated values on a TIN surface with a single constant value. The area covered by the surface of a lake, for example, should have a single value, but the interpolation process (based as it is on sample data points) may not give it one.

Fill polygons assign numeric attribute values to triangles, allowing you to symbolize a TIN theme by land cover, zoning, land use, ownership, or some other attribute.

Breaklines and all polygon types can be either hard or soft. The distinction is a conceptual one between features that mark pronounced changes in slope (like a road that runs along the side of a hill) and features that don't (like a change in vegetation type or land ownership). Whether features are "hard" or "soft," the effect on triangulation is the same.

Input type	Purpose	Accepts	z values
Mass points	Primary source of elevation values	● ∿ ☐	Required
Breaklines	Enforce changes in slope	∿ ☐	Optional
Clip polygons	Define zone of interpolation	☐	Optional
Erase polygons	Define zone of interpolation	☐	Optional
Replace polygons	Replace areas with constant z value	☐	Required
Fill polygons	Assign attributes to triangles	☐	Optional

In this exercise, you'll add a replace polygon to a TIN theme of the Big Bear Lake area. Then you'll use fill polygons to assign land cover attributes to a TIN theme of Canyonlands National Park.

◆ *E x e r c i s e   2 0 c*

1   If necessary, start ArcView GIS. Navigate to the \extend\3d\ch20 directory and open the project "ex20c.apr."

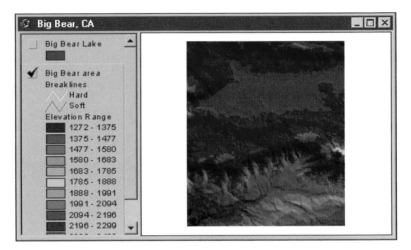

When the project opens, you see a view of Big Bear. The view contains a TIN theme of the terrain and a polygon theme of the lake.

In this exercise, you'll make permanent edits to the TIN data sets called "bbeartin" and "the_maze." To preserve the original data sets for future use, make backup copies now with the Source Manager.

---

2   Turn on the *Big Bear Lake* theme. Make sure the Identify tool is selected. With the TIN theme active, identify some of the locations within the lake.

The slope values are low and the elevation values are close together, ranging from about 2,055 to 2,058 meters. Nevertheless, a lake surface should not have changes in slope, aspect, or elevation. You'll use the *Big Bear Lake* theme to apply a constant elevation value to all areas on the TIN that lie within its boundaries. The lake boundary itself will become a hard breakline on the TIN.

3   Close the Identify Results window. In the view, make the *Big Bear Lake* theme active. Click the Open Theme Table button.

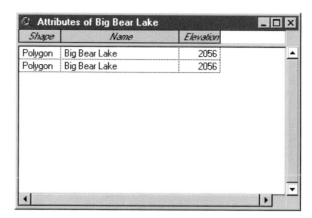

The table contains two records because a small land bridge at its eastern end separates the lake into two polygons. The constant elevation value of 2,056 meters will replace the existing elevation values for all parts of the TIN covered by the lake.

4   Close the theme table and turn off the *Big Bear Lake* theme. Make the *Big Bear area* theme active. From the Theme menu, choose Start Editing. Hold down the Shift key and make the *Big Bear Lake* theme active as well.

5   From the Surface menu, choose Add Features to TIN.

In the Create new TIN dialog, the active feature theme is *Big Bear Lake*. By default, it will be input as soft clip polygons.

6   In the Create new TIN dialog, change the *Input As* drop-down list setting to "Hard Replace Polygons." Make sure the *Height source* drop-down list is set to "Elevation."

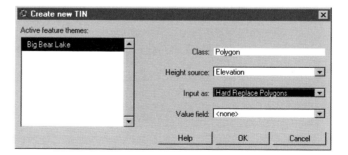

7   In the Create new TIN dialog, click OK. When the polygon features have been added, click on the *Big Bear area* theme to make it the only active theme. From the Theme menu, choose Stop Editing. At the prompt, click Yes to save your edits.

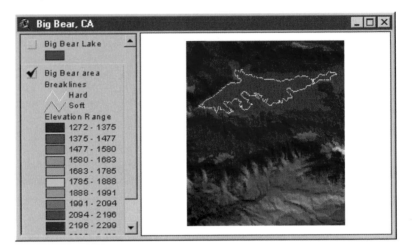

A hard breakline identifies the boundary of the lake. The TIN contains triangles within the lake and triangles outside the lake, but no triangles that cross the breakline.

8   Use the Identify tool to identify some locations within the lake boundary. When you're finished, close the Identify Results window.

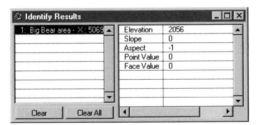

Each identified location has an elevation value of 2,056, a slope of 0, and an aspect of −1 (flat).

9   Close the view and open the Canyonlands National Park view.

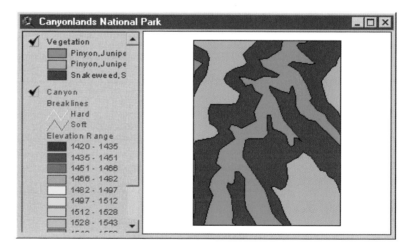

This view contains a TIN theme like the one you created in the previous exercise and a feature theme of vegetation.

10   Make the *Vegetation* theme active and turn it on.

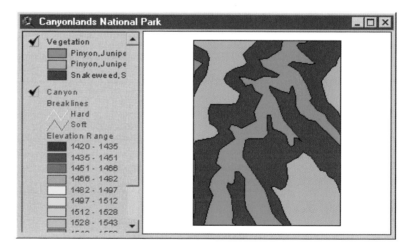

The theme identifies three types of land cover in the area.

11   Click the Open Theme Table button. In the table, scroll all the way to the right.

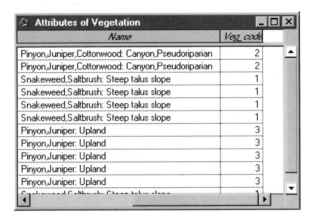

The Name field lists the dominant vegetation types in each area, with a brief description of the landform. The Veg_code field assigns a number to each unique value in the Name field.

You'll add these vegetation codes to the TIN so that you can display the TIN theme according to vegetation type.

12   Close the theme table and turn off the *Vegetation* theme. Make the *Canyon* theme active. From the Theme menu, choose Start Editing. Hold down the Shift key and make the *Vegetation* theme active as well.

13   From the Surface menu, choose Add Features to TIN.

In the Create new TIN dialog, the active feature theme is *Vegetation*.

14   In the dialog, change the *Input As* drop-down list setting to "Soft Fill Polygons." Change the *Value field* drop-down list setting to "Veg_code." The *Height source* drop-down list should still be set to <none>.

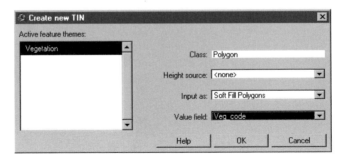

The TIN will be retriangulated, with soft breaklines marking the boundaries of the vegetation polygons. Because no triangles will cross these boundaries, every triangle in the edited TIN theme can be assigned an appropriate vegetation code.

15 In the Create new TIN dialog, click OK. When the polygon features have been added, click on the *Canyon* theme to make it the only active theme. From the Theme menu, choose Stop Editing. At the prompt, click Yes to save your edits.

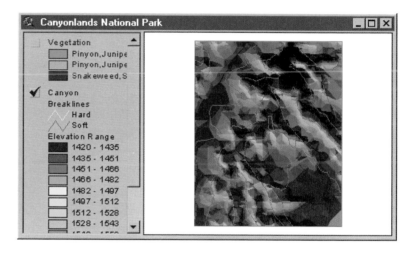

Soft breaklines identify the vegetation boundaries.

16 Make sure the *Canyon* theme is the only active theme. From the Edit menu, choose Copy Themes. Close the Canyonlands National Park view.

17 From the Project window, open the Utah 3D scene. From the Edit menu, choose Paste.

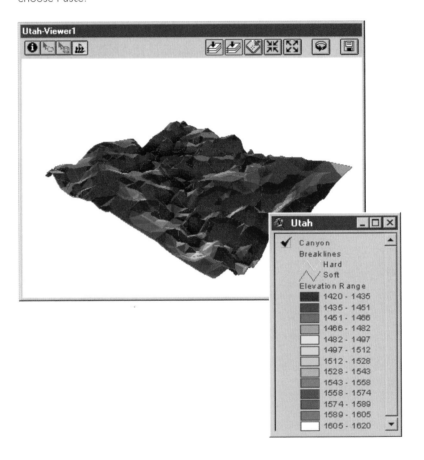

18   Double-click on the *Canyon* theme to open the TIN Legend Editor. In the
Faces panel, set the *Legend* drop-down list to "Value" and click the Edit button to open the embedded Legend Editor.

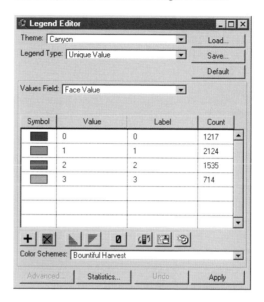

Randomly selected colors are assigned to the three vegetation
codes (1, 2, and 3). The number of triangles with each code is
listed in the Count column. The value 0 is not a vegetation code.
It's the default value assigned to triangles that lie outside the zone
of interpolation.

If you wanted, you could replace the numeric values in the Label
column with descriptions.

19 Double-click on the polygon symbols and assign the vegetation codes what-ever colors you like in the Color Palette. When you're finished, click Apply in the Legend Editor. Close the Legend Editor, the Symbol Palette, and the TIN Legend Editor.

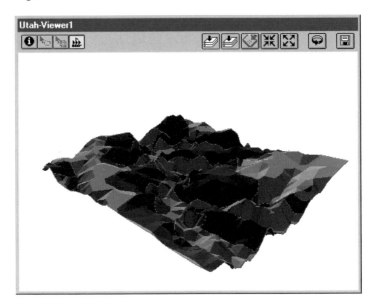

20 From the File menu, choose Close All. Again from the File menu, choose Close Project. Click No when you're prompted to save your changes.

If you're going on to the next chapter, leave ArcView GIS running. Otherwise, choose Exit from the File menu.

21

Analyzing paths

Finding steepest paths

Profiling lines

3D ANALYST IS IDEAL
for understanding paths through terrain, whether you want to predict the downhill course of water (or a chemical spill), or whether you're assessing the steepness of a planned road.

Finding steepest paths

The Steepest Path tool finds the steepest path from any point in an active TIN theme. The path continues downhill until it reaches the perimeter of the TIN, or until it comes to a sink, which is a point that all surrounding areas flow into.

In this exercise, you'll use the Steepest Path tool to draw 3D graphics that follow the steepest downhill path from each of three points on a TIN surface. You'll paste 3D graphics into a 3D line theme and display the theme in a 3D scene.

◆ *E x e r c i s e   2 1 a*

1   If necessary, start ArcView GIS. Navigate to the \extend\3d\ch21 directory and open the project "ex21a.apr."

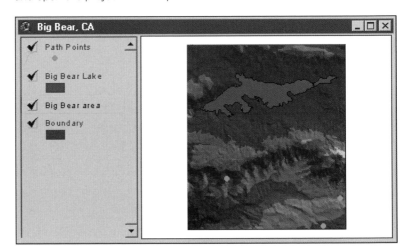

When the project opens, you see a view with a TIN theme of the Big Bear area. The *Path Points* theme contains three locations from which you'll draw steepest paths.

2   Turn off the *Big Bear area* theme, but leave it active.

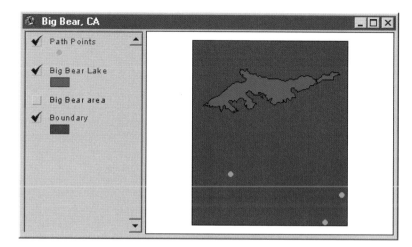

The TIN theme must be active when you draw steepest paths, but you'll be doing a fair amount of zooming in and out and there's no reason to wait for the TIN theme to redraw each time.

3   Select the Zoom In tool and zoom in on the westernmost point. Your map scale should be about 1:2,000 or less. From the *Contour tool* drop-down list, select the Steepest Path tool and click on the point.

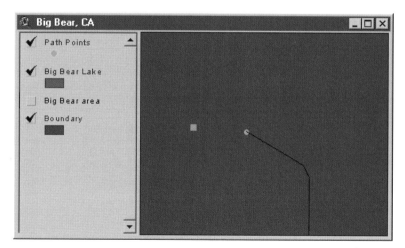

A black 3D line graphic traces the steepest downhill path from the point. The pink selection handle tells you that the graphic is selected.

4   Click the Zoom to Active Theme(s) button. Select the Pointer tool and click somewhere away from the graphic to deselect it.

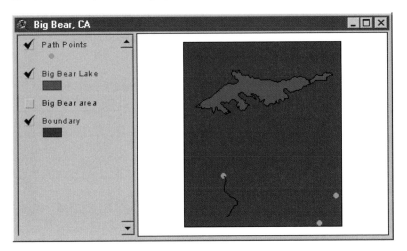

If a 3D line theme is being edited, the path will be written as a feature to the theme.

5   Use the Zoom In and Steepest Path tools to draw paths from the two remaining points.

6   When you're finished, click the Zoom to Active Theme(s) button. Select the Pointer tool and deselect all selected graphics.

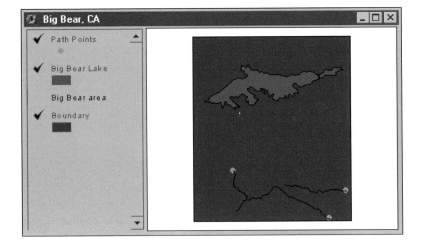

You now have three graphics tracing the steepest paths from three different points. These points weren't randomly selected, but mark points on the flow paths of streams in the area. You'll load a streams theme to see how closely the steepest paths (derived from the elevation values on the TIN surface) conform to the streams data (obtained independently).

7   Click the Add Theme button and navigate to the \extend\3d\ch21 directory. Make sure the *Data Source Types* drop-down list is set to "Feature Data Source." Add the theme *Streams.shp*.

8   Double-click on the *Streams.shp* theme to open the Legend Editor. In the Color Palette, change the line color to white. Click Apply in the Legend Editor, then close the Legend Editor and the Symbol Palette. Turn the theme on in the view.

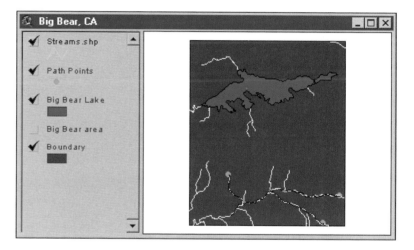

Superficially, the correspondence looks good.

9   Select the Zoom In tool to zoom in for a closer look.

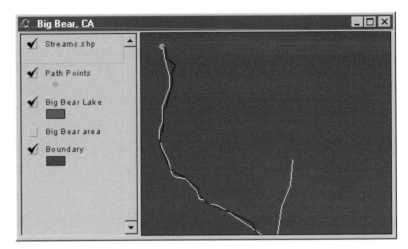

Even at close zoom levels, the stream features and steepest path graphics correspond pretty well. These results should give you confidence in the quality of your TIN surface.

You'll resymbolize the steepest path graphics to make them stand out better. Then you'll display them in a 3D scene.

10 Click the Zoom to Active Theme(s) button. From the Edit menu, choose Select All Graphics.

From the Graphics menu, choose Properties to open the Symbol Palette. In the Pen Palette, set the size to 2. In the Color Palette, choose a bright blue color. Close the Symbol Palette.

11 The graphics should still be selected in the view. From the Edit menu, choose Copy Graphics. Close the view.

12   In the Project window, click on the 3D Scenes icon and open the Big Bear 3D
      scene. From the Edit menu, choose Paste to paste the 3D graphics into the
      viewer.

The graphics appear in white bounding boxes because they're still
selected. Offset values can't be applied to graphics, so a negative
offset has been applied to the TIN theme to make the graphics
stand out from the surface.

13   On the viewer control bar, choose the Select Graphic tool and click in an
      empty area of the scene to deselect the graphics.

14   Select the Navigation tool and look at the paths from different perspectives.

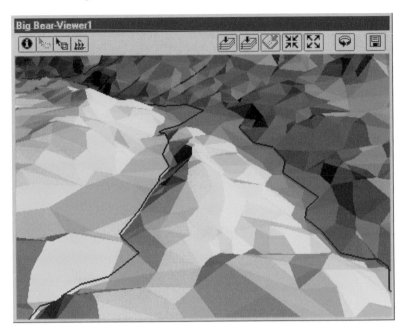

15   From the File menu, choose Close All. Again from the File menu, choose Close Project. Click No when you're prompted to save your changes.

If you want to go on to the next exercise, leave ArcView GIS running. Otherwise, choose Exit from the File menu.

Profiling lines

A profile graph is a side view of a 3D line drawn on the surface of a grid or TIN theme. The graph plots elevation on one axis and distance on the other. Profile graphs are created in Layout documents.

Any 3D line, whether a theme feature or a graphic, can be profiled. If the line is a theme feature, the theme must be active in a View document. If the line is a graphic, it must be selected in the view.

In this exercise, you'll draw a profile graph of a hiking trail in Canyonlands National Park.

◆ *E x e r c i s e   2 1 b*

1   If necessary, start ArcView GIS. Navigate to the \extend\3d\ch21 directory and open the project "ex21b.apr."

When the project opens, you see the boundary of Canyonlands National Park. A TIN theme called *Trail area* is located in the part of the park known as the Needles.

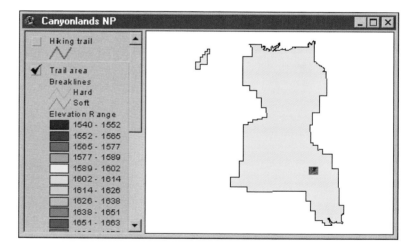

2   With the *Trail area* theme active, click the Zoom to Active Theme(s) button.
     Make the *Hiking trail* theme active and turn it on.

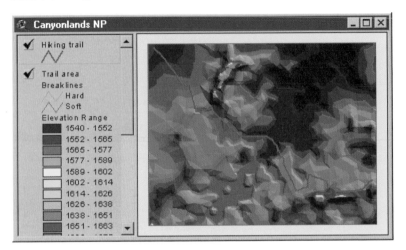

Profiling this trail, which is named the Peekaboo Trail, will show
you how steep it is.

3   Close the view. Make the Project window active and click on the Layouts
     icon. Open the Trail Profile layout.

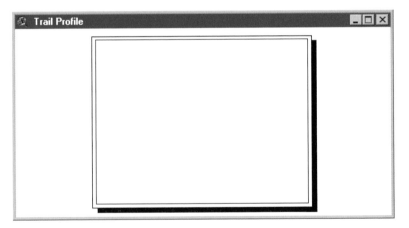

4   Select the Profile Graph tool. On the layout page, draw a large rectangle.
     Leave room on all four sides for things like titles and axis labels.

When you finish drawing the rectangle, the Profile Graph Properties dialog opens.

5   In the dialog, change the title to **Profile of Peekaboo Trail**. Leave the other settings as they are. 3D Analyst will choose elevation and distance intervals and a vertical exaggeration factor. (You can also set these values manually.) Click OK.

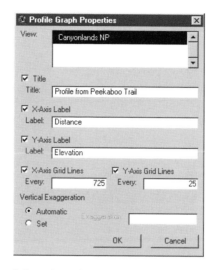

6   Select the Pointer tool and click on an empty part of the Layout window to deselect the profile graph.

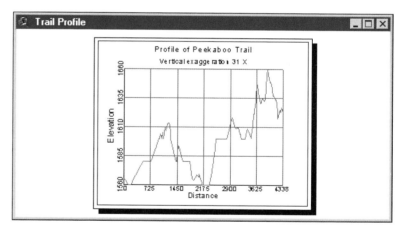

Depending on the rectangle you drew, your graph may look a little different.

The Peekaboo trail is not quite as steep as it appears. Note that 3D Analyst has applied a vertical exaggeration factor to the profile graph. Zooming in on the distance and elevation values will show that the trail rises altogether 100 meters over a distance of about 4,300 meters, with a lot of uphill and downhill on the way.

You can profile several lines at once. The profile graph will apply whatever line symbology is used in the view.

7   From the File menu, choose Close All. Again from the File menu, choose Close Project. Click No when you're prompted to save your changes.

If you're going on to the next chapter, leave ArcView GIS running. Otherwise, choose Exit from the File menu.

22

Analyzing visibility

Drawing lines of sight

Creating a visibility surface

you can find out what an observer can and can't see from a particular point on a landscape. Line-of-sight analysis tells you whether a specific object or location is visible. Viewshed analysis shows you all visible areas on the surface.

Drawing lines of sight

A line of sight is a 3D graphic drawn from an observation point to a target point on an active TIN or grid theme in a view. The line of sight not only tells you whether the target is visible, it shows you which parts of the terrain along its length lie within the observer's field of view. Green line segments indicate visible terrain; red line segments indicate terrain that can't be seen.

If the target isn't visible, a blue dot is placed on the line of sight at the obstruction point, and the coordinates of this point are displayed in the ArcView GIS status bar.

In this exercise, you'll draw lines of sight, paste them into 3D scenes, and profile them in layouts.

◆ *Exercise 22a*

1   If necessary, start ArcView GIS. Navigate to the \extend\3d\ch22 directory and open the project "ex22a.apr."

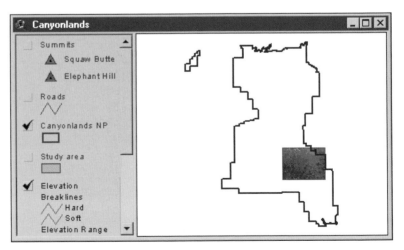

When the project opens, you see the boundary of Canyonlands National Park. A TIN theme of elevation, located in the Needles district of the park, is also turned on.

2   With the *Elevation* theme active, click the Zoom to Active Theme(s) button.

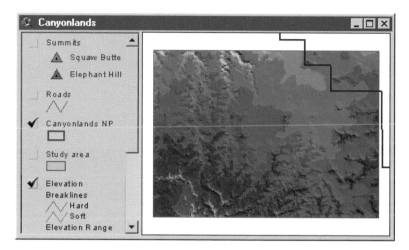

The view zooms in on the TIN theme. The theme is slow to redraw because it's quite detailed, containing more than thirty thousand triangles. It will be more efficient to turn off the TIN theme and work with the *Study area* theme, which has the same boundaries.

3   Turn off the *Elevation* theme, but leave it active. Turn on the *Study area* theme, the *Roads* theme, and the *Summits* theme.

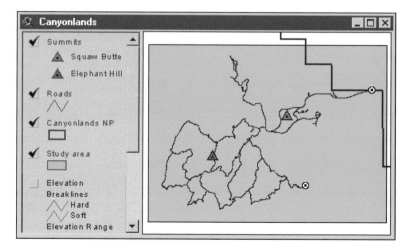

The *Roads* theme includes paved roads, two-wheel-drive and four-wheel-drive roads, and hiking trails. The *Summits* theme shows the location of two hills in the area. There are also two white graphic dots, one at the border of the park where a paved road begins, and the other at the end of the Peekaboo hiking trail you profiled in the previous chapter.

You'll draw lines of sight from these two graphic points to the hills to see whether or not they're visible. The active theme must be a surface theme (TIN or grid) of elevation.

4   Turn off the *Canyonlands NP* theme. Make sure the *Elevation* theme is still active (although turned off). From the *Contour tool* drop-down list, select the Line of Sight tool. Click OK to accept the default values of zero for observer and target.

5   Place the mouse pointer on the white dot that marks the beginning of the paved road. Click and drag a line to Squaw Butte.

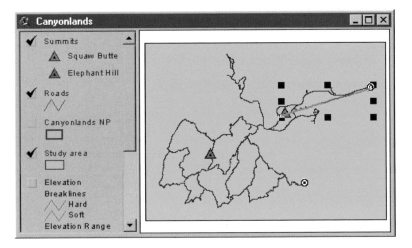

The line of sight is a 3D graphic. Its exact appearance will depend on where you start and stop drawing, but you should find that Squaw Butte is visible from the observation point. A message in the ArcView GIS status bar tells you whether or not the target is visible.

Target and offset values. The Line of Sight dialog allows you to set offsets for observers and targets to account for their heights above the surface elevation. For example, if the observer is standing on a 10-meter platform, you'd set an observer offset of 10 (assuming your map units are meters). In fact, you'd probably set an offset of 11.5 or 12 to include the personal height of the observer. If the target is a ten-story building, you'd need to add a target offset value corresponding to the height of ten stories. In the online help, use the Find tab to locate the topics *Determining line of sight* and *Calculate multiple lines of sight around an observer.*

6   Press the Delete key on your keyboard to delete the line of sight. The Line of Sight tool is still active, so click and drag a line of sight from the same observation point to Elephant Hill. When you finish the line, use the Pointer tool to deselect it.

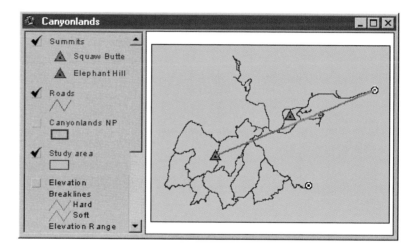

Depending on just where you start and end your line, the target may or may not be visible. If it's not visible, a blue dot will mark the position where the line of sight is blocked. The status bar will give you the coordinates of this obstruction point.

7   Use the Pointer tool to select the line of sight, then delete it with the Delete key.

After you use the Pointer tool, you need to reselect the Line of Sight tool.

8   Click on the Line of Sight tool to select it. Click OK in the dialog to accept the default offset and target heights. Draw a line of sight from the Peekaboo Trail observation point to Squaw Butte.

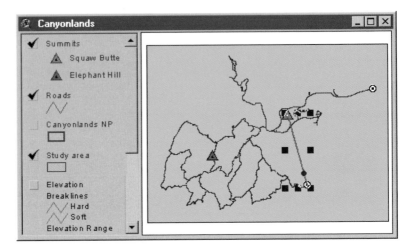

You'll probably (though not necessarily) find that the target is blocked. In any case, most of the terrain along the line of sight won't be visible.

9   Delete the line of sight. The Line of Sight tool is still active, so click and drag a line of sight from the same observation point to Elephant Hill.

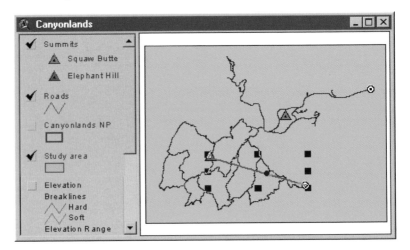

Again, you may or may not find your view blocked. If it is blocked, a blue dot will mark the first obstruction point.

In this exercise, you're working with fairly long distances at a small map scale. For more exact results, you'd zoom in on your observation and target points.

10   The line of sight graphic should be selected. From the Edit menu, choose Copy Graphics.

You'll paste the line of sight into a 3D scene, but first you'll see how it looks as a profile line in a layout.

11   Close the Canyonlands view. In the Project window, click on the Layouts icon and open the Line of Sight layout. A line of sight from Peekaboo Trail to Elephant Hill has already been profiled for you. (It may be different from your line.)

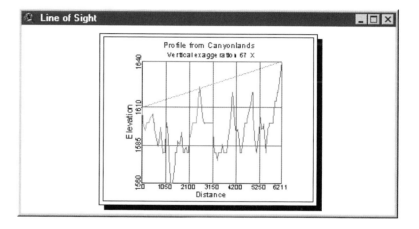

The profile shows the line of sight as a dotted gray line. The green and red line segments show which parts of the terrain are within the observer's field of view. In this particular case, the line of sight is obstructed.

12   Select the Zoom In tool and zoom in on the area where the gray line is intercepted by the green line.

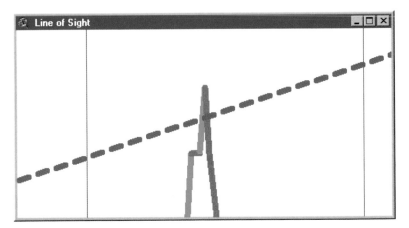

13   Close the layout. In the Project window, click on the 3D Scenes icon and open the 3D scene called The Needles.

You see the same *Elevation, Roads,* and *Summits* themes from the view. (The summits appear as dots because marker symbology isn't preserved in 3D scenes.) From the Edit menu, choose Paste.

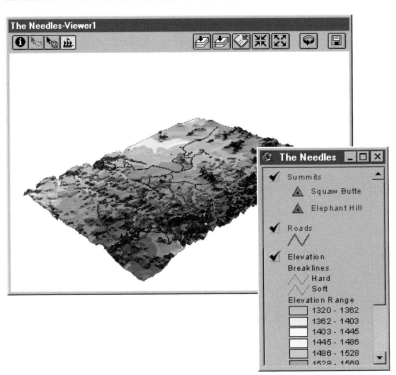

The line of sight is pasted into the 3D scene. It's bounded by a white selection box.

14 On the viewer control bar, choose the Select Graphics tool. Click in an empty area to deselect the graphic.

15 Select the Navigation tool. Examine the line of sight from various perspectives.

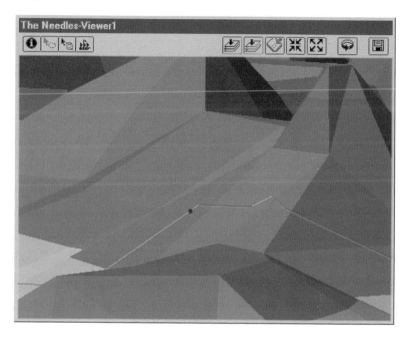

The blue dot marks the first obstruction point in the line of sight.

16 From the File menu, choose Close All. Again from the File menu, choose Close Project. Click No when you're prompted to save your changes.

If you want to go on to the next exercise, leave ArcView GIS running. Otherwise, choose Exit from the File menu.

Creating a visibility surface

Viewshed analysis calculates the areas on a grid or TIN surface that are visible from one or more observation points. The results are stored as a temporary integer grid in which the value of each cell is the number of points from which it can be seen. Cells with a value of 0 can't be seen from any of the observation points.

By default, observation points are positioned one z-unit above the surface. It's assumed that observers can see to the extent of the surface theme in all directions with an unlimited vertical angle of view.

Visibility analysis can be done on both grid and TIN themes, although the output is always a grid theme.

In this exercise, you'll create a visibility grid from a TIN surface and a theme of observation points. You'll symbolize the grid according to how many observers can see each cell, then you'll display the grid in a 3D scene.

◆ *E x e r c i s e   2 2 b*

1   If necessary, start ArcView GIS. Navigate to the \extend\3d\ch22 directory and open the project "ex22b.apr."

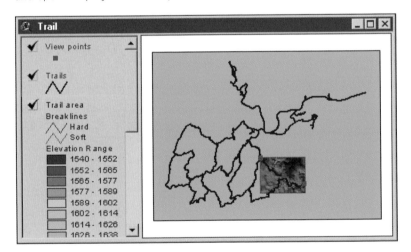

When the project opens, you see the study area boundary from the previous exercise. *Trail area* is an elevation TIN theme of the area around Peekaboo Trail.

2   With the *Trail area* theme active, click the Zoom to Active Theme(s) button.

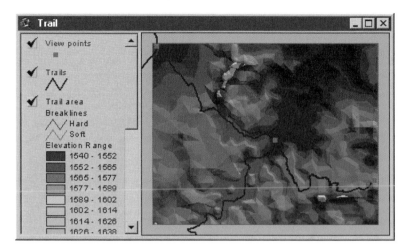

Three observation points are placed at locations where trails inter-sect. You'll create a visibility surface using the TIN theme and these points.

3   Make sure the *Trail area* theme is active. Hold down the Shift key and click on the *View points* theme to make it active as well. From the Surface menu, choose Calculate Viewshed.

In the Output Grid Specification dialog, set the output grid extent to "Same As Trail area." Set the output grid cell size to 10. Click OK.

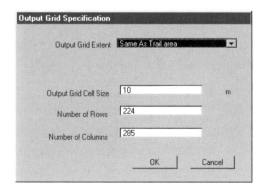

Viewshed calculations take some time, depending on the number of observation points, the spatial extent of the surface elevation theme, and the cell size of the output grid.

Line themes can also be observation themes. When a line theme is used, each vertex becomes an observation point.

4 When the *Visibility of View points* grid theme is added to the view, make it active and turn it on.

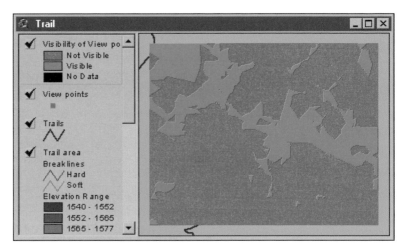

By default, visibility grids are symbolized in red and green. Red areas can't be seen by any observation point. Green areas can be seen by at least one observation point.

Visibility parameters.   You can set a number of visibility parameters by adding specially named fields to the theme table of the observation theme.

SPOT defines an absolute height for the observation point (for example, 3,000 meters for an airplane). If no SPOT field is used, the observation points are assumed to be located one z-unit above the surface.

OFFSETA adds an offset height to the observation point.

OFFSETB adds an offset height to the cells of the surface grid.

AZIMUTH1 and AZIMUTH2 set horizontal angle limits to visibility, proceeding clockwise from AZIMUTH1 to AZIMUTH2. Values are set in degrees from 0 to 360, with 0 being due north. (An AZIMUTH1 value of 0 used with an AZIMUTH2 value of 90 would confine the observer's field of view to the northeast.)

VERT1 and VERT2 set vertical angle limits to visibility. VERT1 sets the upper limit (maximum 90 degrees) and VERT2 sets the lower limit (maximum –90 degrees). The horizontal plane (0 degrees) is defined by the z value of the observation point plus the value of OFFSETA.

RADIUS1 and RADIUS2 limit the visible distance from each observation point. Areas outside the RADIUS2 search distance or inside the RADIUS1 distance can't be seen. By default, RADIUS1 and RADIUS2 values are interpreted as 3D line-of-sight distances. Their values can be made planimetric by the insertion of a minus sign in front of the numbers.

Different values for the same parameter can be applied to different records in the observation theme table. In the online help, use the Find tab to locate the topic *Grid Visibility Discussion*.

5   With the *Visibility of View points* theme active, click the Open Theme Table button.

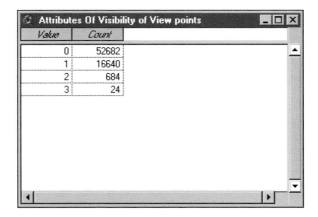

The table shows you how many cells in the grid can't be seen from any observation point and how many can be seen from one, two, or all three observation points. You'll symbolize the grid according to the number of points that can see each cell.

6   Close the theme table. With the visibility grid active in the view, double-click to open the Legend Editor. In the Legend Editor, click the Load button and navigate to the \extend\3d\ch22 directory. Load the "visible.avl" legend file, making sure that in the Load Legend dialog, *Field* is set to "Value." In the Legend Editor, click Apply. Close the Legend Editor.

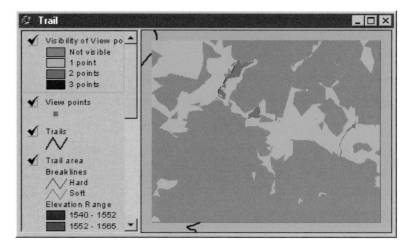

Now you'll display the grid in a 3D scene.

7   Make sure the *Visibility of View points* theme is active. From the Edit menu, choose Copy Themes. Close the view.

8 From the Project window, open the Visibility from Trail Points 3D scene. From the Edit menu, choose Paste. On the viewer control bar, click the Zoom to Full Extent button.

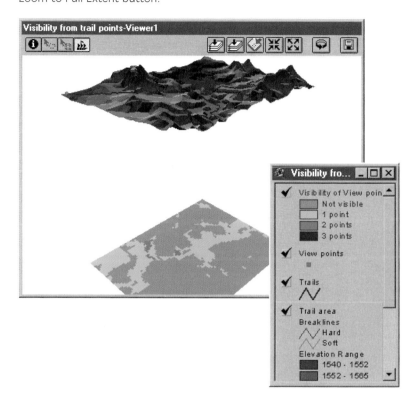

The visibility theme, being a grid theme, is assigned base heights of zero by default. Because its cell values don't represent elevation, you'll need to set its base heights to the surface of the TIN theme to display it in correct 3D perspective.

9 Turn off the *Trail area* theme. Click on the *Visibility of View points* theme to make it the only active theme.

10 From the Theme menu, choose 3D Properties to open the 3D Theme Properties dialog.

In the *Assign base heights* panel, click the Surface radio button. In the drop-down list, change the referenced data set from c:\temp\vwshd1 (the data source of the visibility theme) to c:\extend\3d\ch22\trailtin (the data source for the *Trail area* theme).

At the bottom of the dialog, click the "Show shading for features" check box to turn it on.

11 Click OK to apply the changes and close the 3D Theme Properties dialog. On the viewer control bar, click the Zoom to Active Theme(s) button.

The visibility grid is displayed according to the TIN theme's elevation values.

12 Make sure the Navigation tool is selected in the viewer control bar. Navigate to different perspectives in the 3D scene.

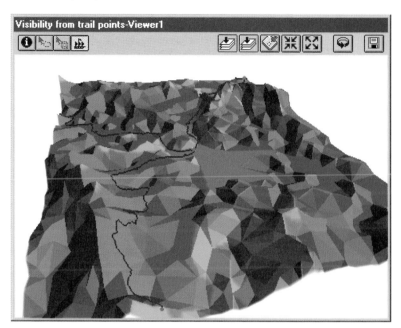

13 From the File menu, choose Close All. Again from the File menu, choose Close Project. Click No when you're prompted to save your changes. From the File menu, choose Exit.

23

More extensions

Optional extensions

Core extensions

Sample extensions

As ARCVIEW GIS SOFTWARE'S

power and versatility have grown, so have the power and versatility of its extensions. The result is a list as varied as it is long.

Some extensions are small utilities that perform one function, while others are full-blown programs that perform many tasks and require considerable processing power. Some come free with ArcView GIS, while others are sold separately. For many extensions, but not all, ESRI provides technical support. Still another group of extensions has been created by third parties, and of those, some got help from ESRI and some didn't. Extensions available in one release of ArcView GIS may not be found in another. Some extensions are designed for developers, others for users.

The following list includes only extensions created by ESRI. They're grouped into three categories: optional extensions, which may be purchased separately; core extensions, which come built into ArcView GIS and for which technical support is available; and sample extensions, which come with ArcView GIS for free, but that technical support people won't be able to help you with.

To use a sample extension, you must use your operating system's file manager to copy it from your $AVHOME\Samples\ext directory to your $AVHOME\Ext32 directory. This process is explained in detail in chapter 3.

Also noted here are those extensions that must run under the Microsoft® Windows® operating system as well as those that must run concurrently with another extension.

For up-to-date information about a particular extension, call your ESRI reseller, or in the United States only, call ESRI at 800-447-9778. For further information about installing extensions, please see your ArcView GIS online help guide.

Many user-written extensions and utility programs are available at ESRI's ArcScripts page on the World Wide Web. While many useful extensions are posted there, ESRI assumes no responsibility for their reliability or quality and recommends that you test them thoroughly before using them.

Optional extensions

ArcPress

The ArcPress™ extension lets you print large, detailed, high-quality maps, including those containing images, by allowing ArcView GIS to take over this processing-intensive task. ArcPress will convert the graphic information to the native format of an individual printer, saving time in printing and money in upgrading your system. It will also convert your maps to common graphic file formats such as TIFF.

Business Analyst (Windows)

Business Analyst is a complete GIS package for large and small businesses. It includes the core ArcView GIS software; two other optional extensions, ArcView Network Analyst and ArcView StreetMap™; and more than 40 gigabytes of comprehensive national business, household, street, demographic, and marketing data from information specialists such as Dun & Bradstreet and MetroMail.

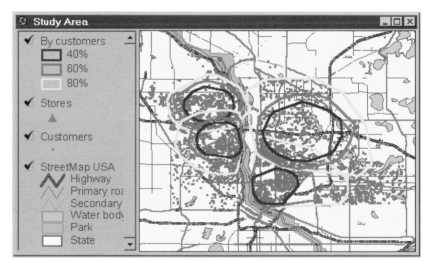

This Business Analyst screen shows an analysis of complex market areas defined by number of customers.

Designed for the business professional who needs the power of GIS without delay, the Business Analyst extension uses wizards to perform a wide range of business analysis functions. You can analyze market areas, locate customers by address, produce detailed reports, analyze customer profiles, find people for target marketing, create simple or complex ring analysis for locations, generate desire lines from your retail locations, compute equal competition areas, conduct drivetime analysis, and perform site prospecting.

**ArcView
Image Analysis**

The ArcView Image Analysis extension, developed by ERDAS, Inc., and ESRI, offers a range of tools for analyzing aerial photography and satellite imagery in a desktop GIS. Designed primarily for natural resources management, this extension is invaluable for such tasks as identifying the extent and degree of environmental change over time, and studying the effects of environmental disasters, natural or man-made.

Data that comes from satellites and aircraft—known as remotely sensed data because it's measured from a distance—brings unique benefits and problems to GIS.

Remotely sensed data, like this Space Shuttle shot of the island of Kauai, is made up of thousands of square cells called pixels, shown in the inset. Each holds data about the light reflected and absorbed from features on the earth's surface.

A notable benefit is the ability to acquire large amounts of data about features on the ground more quickly and easily than would be possible close up. Remotely sensed images are derived from both the visible and invisible parts of the electromagnetic spectrum that are reflected and absorbed by objects on the ground; data of this kind can give you more information about objects than simple shape and general appearance. The wavelengths of those objects, particularly vegetation, have unique characteristics that make them easier to identify and categorize. The ArcView Image Analysis extension provides tools to help in this process, allowing you to distinguish among ground features that, to the unaided, untrained eye, might just look like dark blotches.

Among the problems to be overcome is the fact that a satellite taking a picture from hundreds of miles above the earth is capturing huge amounts of raw data; often, an image will encompass many square miles of complex urban and rural landscape. Processing so much specialized data requires tools of the kind ArcView Image Analysis provides.

A Space Shuttle view of Miami, Florida, before and after ArcView Image Analysis enhancement.

It's not easy to pick out individual features in a landscape from far above, so ArcView Image Analysis uses different kinds of filters to refine and enhance the image. Accessible from a drop-down menu and through the Legend Editor, these filters let you sharpen dull images, smooth out rough ones, and adjust brightness and contrast. Controls to enhance colors and shading with even finer detail are also available from the Legend Editor.

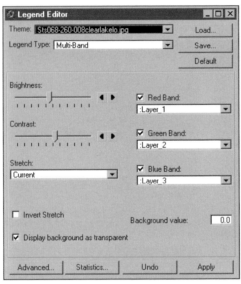

The ArcView Image Analysis Legend Editor gives you several ways to adjust an image's appearance.

Often you'll be interested only in one portion or feature of a remotely sensed image, such as an oil spill, or an area where fire has destroyed a forest. ArcView Image Analysis lets you isolate these and turn them into shapefiles you can use in other ArcView GIS projects.

You could simply draw an outline around the figure manually using the standard ArcView GIS drawing tools. A better way is to use an ArcView Image Analysis utility known as the Seed Tool. It works by sampling the spectral characteristics of a small number of the pixels that represent that feature; it then creates a graphic outline that includes similar, adjacent pixels. This procedure gives you a good representation from which accurate dimensions can be derived and which you can copy into a new feature theme.

This polygon outlining the boundaries of Clear Lake in northern California was created using the ArcView Image Analysis Seed Tool. The graphic can now be used in another theme or application.

ArcView Image Analysis will also find other features of the type the Seed Tool has isolated—such as other oil spills or other burn areas—that aren't adjacent to the original polygon, but rather scattered throughout the image. This is helpful when those other areas are small and hard to see.

ArcView Image Analysis is well suited for natural resource applications because of the distinctive spectral characteristics of chlorophyll in plants and trees.

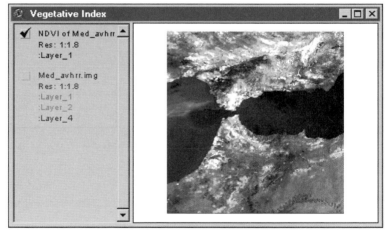

Areas of healthy vegetation show as bright white in this satellite image.

If you have images of the same area at different times, ArcView Image Analysis and its Vegetative Index can calculate the difference in the amount and health of vegetation. This can be useful in measuring the growth rates of forests, or the destructive effects of a storm on agricultural production. Since the software can distinguish between healthy and stressed vegetation, it's also useful for environmental studies or crop management.

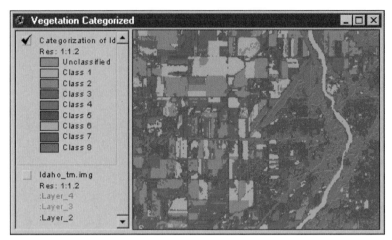

An ArcView Image Analysis categorization of land in Idaho. Class 1 is water and Class 5 is urban area. You can use the Legend Editor to label them appropriately.

ArcView Image Analysis can help in areas beyond natural resource management. You may, for instance, want to match your aerial images with real-world map coordinates, perhaps to assess the accuracy of those maps or to use an image as a backdrop to a feature theme. ArcView Image Analysis provides a tool for doing this matching, a process known as image rectification.

Image rectification with ArcView Image Analysis is done here on an aerial photo and a theme of Seattle streets. The red dot is one of several control points used in the process to make the two themes line up exactly.

You can use a limited number of image data formats with core ArcView GIS software, but ArcView Image Analysis will let you work with a much broader array. Included on the format list are most of those in the Landsat system; the Satellite Pour l'observation de la Terre (SPOT); the Indian Remote Sensing Society (IRS); Digital Ortho Quad (DOQ); ERDAS IMAGINE, ERDAS LAN and GIS; ArcGrid™; TIFF; JPEG; and MrSID™ files.

Internet Map Server

The Internet Map Server takes maps that you create in ArcView GIS and puts them on your Web site, giving Web surfers and potential customers the benefits of GIS power on your Web site at no cost to them.

Its uses are virtually limitless. Local government agencies can use the extension to publish maps of service areas, road closures, or emergency conditions; businesses can use it to help customers find retail outlets, authorized repair shops, or delivery areas.

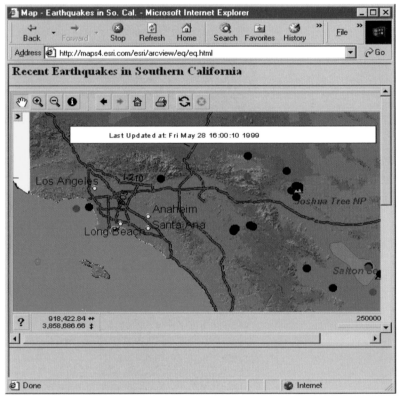

The Internet Map Server interface.

The extension is easy to use, and requires no programming skills to get up and running, although it has considerable potential for customization. Once installed, Internet Map Server puts the map of your choice on the Web server that you designate, inside a default interface. The interface is run by a Java applet called MapCafé™ that's packaged with the extension. It presents Web surfers with an ArcView GIS window of your map and lets them immediately use several standard ArcView GIS display tools, such as pan, zoom, and feature identification.

With a little programming knowledge, you can expand and customize your map-focused Web pages any way you want. For example, you can use Avenue, the ArcView GIS programming language, to control how the extension responds to user requests, or to customize MapCafé by adding your own buttons and tools to the interface. MapCafé is also easily integrated with popular Web page authoring programs.

StreetMap and StreetMap 2000 (Windows)

StreetMap and StreetMap 2000 give you detailed street maps of the entire United States, and software to view and use this data.

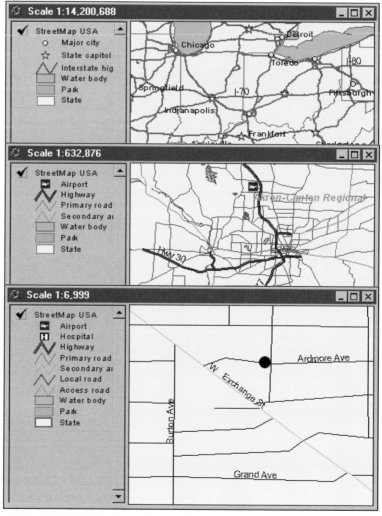

As you zoom into StreetMap, more details become visible.

If you type the address of any place in the country, StreetMap will find it for you, zooming in to show the exact street location you entered. If you geocode addresses, the software will produce a point theme of the matched addresses.

The *StreetMap USA* theme contains four levels of information: national, state, regional, and local. As you zoom to each level, more map detail is revealed. At the national level, the map shows major cities, interstate highways, bodies of water, and state boundaries. At the state level, state capitals and parks are added to the view. At the regional level, you see all those details, plus the location of airports, highways, and primary, secondary, and connecting roads. At the local level, hospitals and local and access roads are added. The extension lets you adjust to a considerable degree the appearance of these default views.

StreetMap 2000 has a more recent and complete database and more robust geocoding capabilities.

Tracking Analyst

The ArcView Tracking Analyst extension, a joint development of ESRI and Litton/TASC, puts maps into motion.

Using this extension, you can track the path of anything that moves across geographic space. The list is almost limitless: forest fires, fire engines, birds, space shuttles, tornadoes, smog, pizza deliveries, swarms of killer bees.

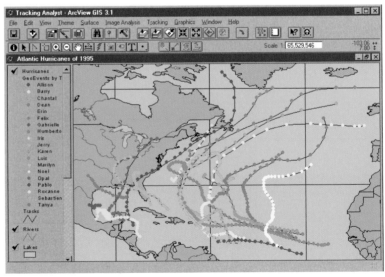

Natural phenomena such as hurricanes are among the diverse objects that can be mapped with the Tracking Analyst extension.

Tracking Analyst is most useful for spotting patterns of events or of movements over time. Tracking tornadoes over an extended period of time can show you whether a "tornado alley" is developing in a new and unexpected area. Tracking lightning strikes could show you places where it might be dangerous to locate new construction. Tracking the paths that wildlife follows during the course of a migratory season could provide new insights into the species' interaction with man.

Tracking Analyst is not limited to keeping tabs on physical objects. With the appropriate data, it's possible also to study more intangible things: the spread of an epidemic disease, for example, or the development of a demographic or economic trend.

With the help of global positioning system (GPS) units and Tracking Analyst software, you can also monitor the progress of moving objects, such as a fleet of delivery trucks winding around city boulevards.

To do all this, Tracking Analyst introduces a new kind of shapefile to an ArcView GIS project, a GeoEvent. A GeoEvent is essentially a point with a time attribute attached to it. A theme table in Tracking Analyst is based not only on the familiar points, lines, and polygons, but also on GeoEvents.

Shape	Track_id	Id	Date	Time	Lc	Lat	Lon	Edate
GeoEvent	5695	5695	19940831	18:19:43	0	65.439	-141.824	8/31/94, 18:19:43
GeoEvent	5695	5695	19940831	18:50:08	A	65.709	-142.270	8/31/94, 18:50:08
GeoEvent	5695	5695	19940831	19:58:20	0	65.462	-141.916	8/31/94, 19:58:20
GeoEvent	5695	5695	19940831	20:28:40	A	65.311	-141.702	8/31/94, 20:28:40
GeoEvent	5695	5695	19940831	22:09:22	0	64.773	-141.235	8/31/94, 22:09:22
GeoEvent	5695	5695	19940831	23:14:50	0	64.413	-140.863	8/31/94, 23:14:50
GeoEvent	5695	5695	19940831	23:48:19	0	64.218	-140.832	8/31/94, 23:48:19
GeoEvent	5695	5695	19940901	00:52:11	0	63.841	-140.621	9/1/94, 00:52:11
GeoEvent	5695	5695	19940901	01:32:15	0	63.835	-140.625	9/1/94, 01:32:15
GeoEvent	5724	5724	19940902	10:49:26	0	67.103	-50.951	9/2/94, 10:49:26
GeoEvent	5724	5724	19940902	11:42:50	0	67.052	-50.896	9/2/94, 11:42:50

Attributes of per1994.shp

This tracking theme table of bird migration indicates a time and geographic position for each GeoEvent on the map.

At the heart of Tracking Analyst is the Playback Manager, accessed from the Tracking menu.

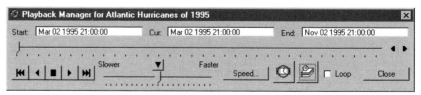

The Tracking Analyst Playback Manager.

Working like a VCR, the Playback Manager allows you to play tracking themes—that is, make the objects you're tracking move across your map—at any speed you want. It also allows you to fast-forward and rewind them, to put them on a loop, or isolate and stop movement so you can study them further. You can enter a particular time in a window to see what's happening to your objects at that moment.

Tracking Analyst offers a wide range of tools with which to display themes, so that in presentations you can emphasize certain objects, tracks, or GeoEvents. In addition, you can define the specific period of time for tracking. In the hurricane example, for instance, you might be interested in what the storm's been doing in the last twenty-four hours, not what it was doing last week. Tracking Analyst lets you customize the data and display to do just that.

Core extensions

CAD Reader

This extension allows ArcView GIS to use Computer Aided Design files, including Microstation Design (.dgn) and AutoCAD® and AutoCAD 2000 (.dwg, .dxf) files. When the extension is loaded, ArcView GIS will include these files in its search when you browse for feature themes.

Database Access, Database Access 2

Database Access links ArcView GIS to relational databases such as Oracle®. Using a relational database with a GIS brings exponential increases in data capacity and in the number of users who can access the data.

Loading the extension lets you add a database table from the Project window, or a database theme from the View menu. From there, dialogs prompt you to make the connection to the database. In the case of the database theme, this is accomplished through ESRI's Spatial Database Engine™ (SDE™) technology, which is required to store and work with spatial data in a relational database. Dialogs further prompt you to build standard SQL statements in order to identify which records you want to work with.

Database Access 2 increases the flexibility of these connections, as well as the connections between ArcView GIS and industry-standard ODBC-compliant databases. It also strengthens the link between records in a database table and geographic features in a database theme.

Dialog Designer

Avenue programmers can use this extension as a way to build new applications within ArcView GIS through the use of customized interface elements such as dialogs and list boxes. The extension allows for considerable modification of the standard ArcView GIS interface.

Digitizer (Windows)

This extension provides support in digitizing maps.

Geoprocessing Wizard

The Geoprocessor lets you create new feature themes through overlay analysis.

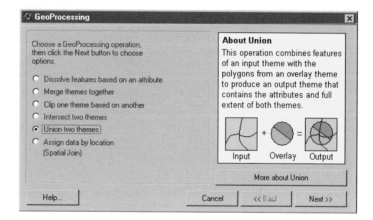

The extension will prompt you to choose which method you want to use, then help you through each step. The *Intersect* method lets you integrate two feature themes and preserve only the features falling within the spatial extent common to both themes. The *Union* method lets you combine two feature themes into a new theme that contains all the features from both. The *Dissolve* method combines features within a theme based on attribute value; it's a way to simplify your database for faster display and query. The *Clip* method cuts out a piece of one theme using another theme as a "cookie cutter." The *Merge* method appends the features of two or more themes into a single theme.

Graticules and Measured Grids

This extension gives your map layouts extra polish and precision by letting you place a grid over the top of your map and set it either to lines of latitude and longitude (a graticule) or to some other scale of measurement.

Image Support

ArcView GIS can read images from several formats, including several used for military applications, if the specific extension for each format is loaded. In addition to those mentioned under the ArcView Image Analysis category in this section, they include: ARC Digitized Raster Graphics (ADRG); Compressed ARC Digitized Raster Graphics (CADRG); Controlled Image Base (CIB); and National Image Transfer Format (NITF).

Legend Tool

The Legend Tool extension lets you customize map layouts with a wide variety of typefaces, border styles and sizes, shapes, and special effects.

Report Writer

Report Writer eliminates the need to export ArcView GIS project data to outside graphics and word-processing software to assemble a professional-looking printed report. Those functions are integrated within ArcView GIS itself.

The extension gives you the choice of formatting a quick, basic report from the data in a view, or using the Report wizard. The Report wizard lets you create a more detailed and sophisticated presentation than the quick report, using data from a wide range of sources, including popular contact managers such as ACT!® and relational databases such as Oracle.

A series of screens in the wizard prompts you for the kinds of data you want to include in the report, then helps you with overall report design, including formatting and layout; text placement, size, and font; and insertion of graphic elements, including OLE objects.

VPF Viewer

This extension lets you work with Vector Product Format data in ArcView GIS directly, adding VPF themes without first having to convert them to shapefile format.

Sample extensions

ArcView Connect for R/3 (Windows)

This extension helps establish communication between ArcView GIS and SAP™ R/3®, the enterprisewide information and management software. The extension is accessed from the Project window. From there, a dialog box guides you through the steps needed to complete the default function, which downloads customer information to ArcView GIS from R/3. Other functions are also available using the Microsoft Visual Basic® source code included with this extension.

Cell Tools

This ArcView Spatial Analyst extension is useful for understanding and analyzing grids at the cell level of detail.

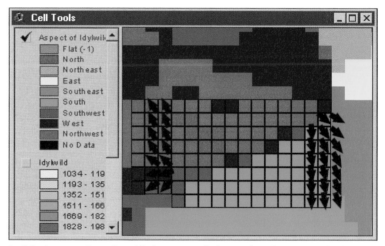

In this close-up view of a grid, the Draw Cells button has drawn several adjacent nine-cell matrices; the Direction Arrow graphics point in the appropriate compass direction.

When installed, the extension adds four new buttons to the ArcView Spatial Analyst interface: Row&Column, Draw Cells, Cell Values, and Direction Arrows. Each button triggers a different action when you click on an individual cell. The Row&Column button identifies the row and column location of a particular cell, and gives you the value of that cell. The Draw Cells button draws a matrix of nine cells: the one you select at the center and its eight immediately adjacent neighbor cells. The Cell Values button brings up the value of the selected cell. Clicking the Direction Arrow button when an aspect theme is active draws arrows that reflect the compass direction of an individual cell within a grid.

Class Browser

This extension gives you additional flexibility when working with Avenue, the ArcView GIS programming language.

Extension Builder

This tool helps you assemble scripts, documents, and GUI elements into your own custom-made extension.

Graphic Labels, Load & Save

This tool lets you save the graphic labels in a theme to a separate file for later use.

Hydrological Modeling, Hydrological Modeling 1.1

This ArcView Spatial Analyst extension provides tools for measuring and analyzing hydrologic processes.

The Hydro menu from the interface offers you the choice of completing several common hydrological modeling tasks individually, or of starting a wizard that will take you through the steps required to delineate watersheds from Digital Elevation Models.

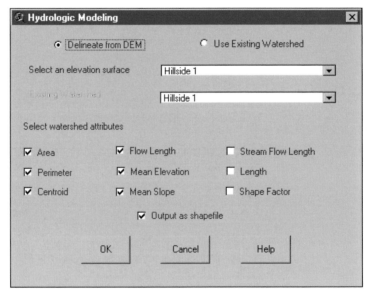

The opening screen of the Hydrological Modeling extension wizard.

Among the tasks available individually or through the wizard are calculation of flow direction, flow length, and flow accumulation; identification of sinks; sink filling; and creation of stream networks and pour points.

MGE Viewer (Windows)

This extension lets you read Intergraph's MGE and Bentley's MicroStation GeoGraphics™ data directly into ArcView GIS. You can symbolize, query, and analyze this data as you would any other, without needing to convert to shapefile format. Loading this extension also loads the CAD Reader extension.

Multi-Theme Auto Labeler

Instead of labeling themes in a layout one at a time, you can use this extension to bring up a dialog box that helps organize the feature labels of several different themes at once. The box allows you to pick type-faces, sizes, and colors of theme labels; to manipulate their placement; and to categorize them according to importance.

Named Extents

When zooming in and out of a large geographic area in your view window, you can use this extension to name a zoomed view. ArcView GIS will remember the name so you can go back to it quickly, rather than hunting for the previous magnification.

ODB Table Extension

This tool lets you make changes to the fields and field aliases of tables, and keep those changes attached to the table when it's used in another project.

Overview Utility

When this extension is loaded and turned on, a new window pops up on your ArcView GIS screen and gives you a miniaturized overview of what you're doing within the active, full-sized view.

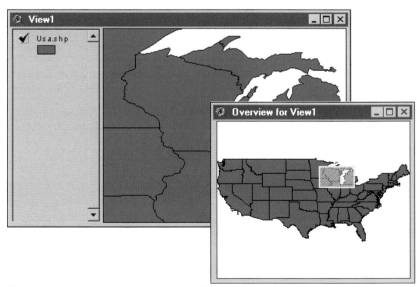

This overview reminds you that your overall theme is the United States.

Point Dispersion	This extension is useful for tasks such as geocoding by ZIP Code, when you need to separate points that normally land on top of each other because you're working in a small area.
Port Project Utilities	If you need to move an ArcView GIS project from one computer to another, this extension provides tools to make the job easier. It adds a new menu to the Project window.
Projector!	This extension provides a way to align two or more data sets that are not in the same coordinate system. An updated projection utility is included in ArcView GIS 3.2. See appendix B, "Aligning your data."
SDE 3 Tools, SDE Edit, SDE 3A Edit	These utilities perform several functions that help with processing relational databases through the Spatial Database Engine (SDE), which is required to work with spatial data in a relational database. Each tool requires that the Database Access extension run concurrently. If it isn't already running, loading each of these tools will also load Database Access.
	SDE 3 Tools provides information about those columns in the database that contain spatial data. SDE Edit lets you import and export spatial database shapes for editing within ArcView GIS. SDE 3A Edit adds a button that allows you to click on a database shape and edit its attributes.
Script Editor Utilities	Avenue users can load this extension to access a variety of tools to aid in script writing and editing.
Samples Browser	The Samples Browser makes it easier to load and unload sample extensions.
Shapefile Description Dialog	This extension opens an information box that gives you additional details about the shapefiles in the active theme. Among these are their type, their number, and a listing of all the shapefile attribute field names and types.
Speed Limit Calculator	The Speed Limit Calculator is a Network Analyst extension used to help estimate driving times along roads according to their speed limits. Its use is demonstrated fully in chapter 3.

Virtual Document Utilities

By default, the ArcView GIS document listing in the Project window is grouped by View, Table, Chart, Layout, and Script. This tool lets you customize that arrangement, arranging documents in any number of ways.

Visibility Tools

This ArcView Spatial Analyst extension allows you to ascertain where one point on a grid surface is visible from another. It also allows you to determine the extent of an observer's view of the terrain from any point on the grid.

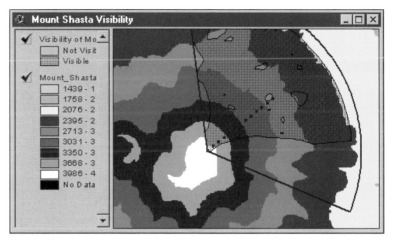

Visibility tools in use on a grid of Mt. Shasta. Even though the observer is near the top of the mountain, the unshaded areas indicate that some places still can't be seen.

The extension adds two buttons to the ArcView Spatial Analyst interface. The Line of Sight button lets you draw a line from one point, the observer's, to the point being observed. The line tells you whether or not the target is visible and shows which parts of the terrain along the line of sight are visible to the observer. The information is also drawn as a profile graph in a layout. The Visibility button produces a new theme and graphic that overlays all the visible and nonvisible areas within an angle of sight.

Warp Environment

This ArcView Spatial Analyst extension lets you overlay one set of grid data onto another grid data set that's from the same geographic location but which has come to you in a different coordinate system from the first. Load this extension and you'll be able to transform the coordinates of one grid to the coordinates of another, and to see both data sets in the same view and in the same coordinate system.

The extension gives you a new drop-down menu, a new button, and two new tools on the ArcView GIS interface. After you designate one grid data set as the one that will be moved, you may use the tools to draw and then link points from one data set to another. As with image georeferencing, the more points you designate, the more accurate your coordinate transformation will be; you also have the option of writing in specific numeric coordinates directly.

Network Analyst pathfinding algorithm

THE OBVIOUS APPROACH

to finding the shortest path between an origin and a destination is to examine all the possible paths. This isn't practical, however. A large network contains so many possibilities that a method has to be used to exclude most of them. Several algorithms have been developed for finding the shortest (or least-cost) path through a network. Network Analyst uses the most well-known of these, developed by E. W. Dijkstra ["A Note on Two Problems in Connexion with Graphs," Numeriske Mathematik, 1 (1959)].

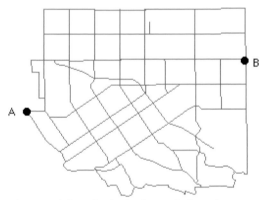

Given an origin and a destination node, how does Network Analyst find the shortest path from A to B?

Executing the algorithm

This appendix contains a step-by-step execution of Dijkstra's algorithm. The following diagram shows a network in which the algorithm will find the shortest path from node A to node G. A node exists wherever line segments connect.

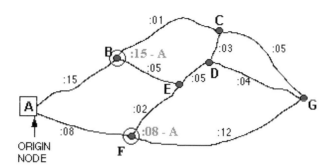

The algorithm begins at the origin node, A. When it determines the node that has the lowest cumulative travel time from the previous node, the node becomes "reached." Since there's no previous node for node A, it's reached and so is placed in a table of reached nodes.

The algorithm then considers all nodes adjacent to the last reached node. (One node is adjacent to another if it's connected by a line segment.) These adjacent nodes are placed in a table of scanned nodes. At each step of the algorithm, the node with the lowest cumulative travel time in the scanned table is deleted from the scanned table and placed in the reached table. The process continues until the destination node is reached.

This process isn't yet constructing the actual path. Rather, it's establishing the connectivity and travel cost relationships among the nodes. Once it has this information, it derives the shortest path from the information in the reached table.

Step 1 The algorithm sets the origin node as reached and places it in the reached table. Then it scans the adjacent nodes (B and F) and places them in the scanned table.

REACHED TABLE

NODE	CUMULATIVE COST	PREVIOUS NODE
A	:00	none
B		
C		
D		
E		
F		
G		

SCANNED TABLE

NODE	CUMULATIVE COST	PREVIOUS NODE
B	:15	A
F	:08	A

The cost to get to node B is 15 minutes and to node F, 8 minutes. Nodes B and F are placed in the scanned table with their cumulative cost and previous node.

Step 2   **Picks the scanned node with the lowest cumulative cost and puts it on the reached table.**

Of the currently scanned nodes, node F has the lowest cumulative cost. Node F is moved to the reached table with its cumulative cost (8 minutes) and previous node (A). Node F is deleted from the scanned table.

REACHED TABLE

NODE	CUMULATIVE COST	PREVIOUS NODE
A	:00	none
B		
C		
D		
E		
F	:08	A
G		

SCANNED TABLE

NODE	CUMULATIVE COST	PREVIOUS NODE
B	:15	A
F	:08	A

Step 3   **Scans the nodes adjacent to the node just reached and puts them on the scanned table.**

The nodes adjacent to node F are nodes E, G, and A. Node A has already been reached, leaving nodes E and G as scanned. On the scanned table, the cumulative cost to reach these nodes is the cost to reach node F (8 minutes), plus the cost of the connecting line segments (2 minutes for node E and 12 minutes for node G).

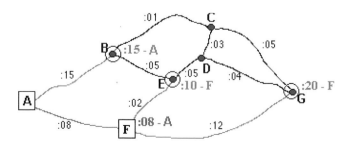

The results after node F is reached and the adjacent nodes have been scanned:

SCANNED TABLE

NODE	CUMULATIVE COST	PREVIOUS NODE
B	:15	A
E	:10	F
G	:20	F

Node B remains in the table because it hasn't yet been reached.

Step 4   **Picks the scanned node with the lowest cumulative cost and moves it to the reached table.**

Node E has the lowest cumulative cost, so it's moved to the reached table and deleted from the scanned table.

REACHED TABLE

NODE	CUMULATIVE COST	PREVIOUS NODE
A	:00	none
B		
C		
D		
E	:10	F
F	:08	A
G		

SCANNED TABLE

NODE	CUMULATIVE COST	PREVIOUS NODE
B	:15	A
E	:10	F
G	:20	F

Step 5   Scans the nodes adjacent to the node just reached and puts them on the scanned table.

The nodes adjacent to node E are nodes B, D, and F. Node F has already been reached, which leaves nodes B and D. On the scanned table, the cumulative cost to reach these nodes is the cost to reach node E (10 minutes) plus the cost of the connecting line segments (5 minutes for node B and 5 minutes for node D).

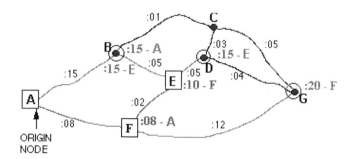

The results after node E is reached and the adjacent nodes scanned:

SCANNED TABLE

NODE	CUMULATIVE COST	PREVIOUS NODE
B	:15	A
G	:20	F
B	:15	E
D	:15	E

Node B has been scanned twice—once from node A and once from node E. The cumulative cost is the same in both cases (15 minutes). Node D also has a cumulative cost of 15 minutes. The algorithm will arbitrarily choose one of these three options.

Step 6   Picks the scanned node with the lowest cumulative cost and puts it on the reached table.

In this example, the algorithm chooses node D.

REACHED TABLE

NODE	CUMULATIVE COST	PREVIOUS NODE
A	:00	none
B		
C		
D	:15	**E**
E	:10	**F**
F	:08	**A**
G		

SCANNED TABLE

NODE	CUMULATIVE COST	PREVIOUS NODE
B	:15	**A**
G	:20	**F**
B	:15	**E**
D	:15	**E**

Step 7   Scans all the nodes adjacent to the node just reached and puts them on the scanned table.

Node D was just reached. Disregarding node E (already reached), the adjacent nodes are nodes C and G. The cumulative cost to reach node C is 18 minutes and to reach node G, 19 minutes.

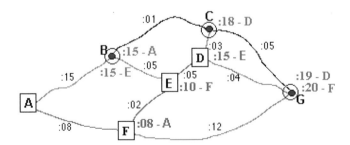

The results after node D is reached and the adjacent nodes scanned:

SCANNED TABLE

NODE	CUMULATIVE COST	PREVIOUS NODE
B	:15	A
G	:20	F
B	:15	E
C	:18	D
G	:19	D

Node G now appears in the scanned table twice. It has a cumulative cost of 19 minutes (from node D) and a cost of 20 minutes (from node F).

Step 8   **Picks the scanned node with the lowest cumulative cost and puts it on the reached table.**

Node B is now the scanned node with the lowest cumulative cost. Node B was reached from two different nodes (A and E) with the same cumulative cost. In this case, the algorithm arbitrarily chooses the entry with node E as the previous node.

REACHED TABLE

NODE	CUMULATIVE COST	PREVIOUS NODE
A	:00	none
B	:15	E
C		
D	:15	E
E	:10	F
F	:08	A
G		

SCANNED TABLE

NODE	CUMULATIVE COST	PREVIOUS NODE
B	:15	A
G	:20	F
B	:15	E
C	:18	D
G	:19	D

Step 9   **Scans all the nodes adjacent to the node just reached and puts them on the scanned table.**

Node B was just reached. Disregarding nodes A and E (because they've been reached), the adjacent node is node C.

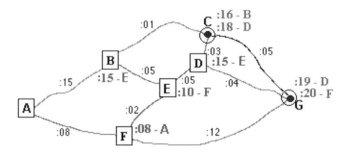

The results after node B is reached and the adjacent node has been scanned:

SCANNED TABLE

NODE	CUMULATIVE COST	PREVIOUS NODE
B	:15	A
G	:20	F
C	:18	D
G	:19	D
C	:16	B

Step 10   **Picks the scanned node with the lowest cumulative cost and puts it on the reached table.**

Node B is on the scanned table with a cumulative cost of 15 minutes (from node A). But node B has been reached; it already has an entry on the reached table, so the algorithm disregards the entry for node B in the scanned table.

SCANNED TABLE

NODE	CUMULATIVE COST	PREVIOUS NODE
~~B~~	~~:15~~	~~A~~
G	:20	F
C	:18	D
G	:19	D
C	:16	B

Node B has been reached. Disregard this entry.

Node C has the lowest cumulative cost (16 minutes), so it's moved to
the reached table.

REACHED TABLE

NODE	CUMULATIVE COST	PREVIOUS NODE
A	:00	none
B	:15	E
C	:16	B
D	:15	E
E	:10	F
F	:08	A
G		

SCANNED TABLE

NODE	CUMULATIVE COST	PREVIOUS NODE
G	:20	F
C	:18	D
G	:19	D
C	:16	B

Step 11   **Scans all the nodes adjacent to the node just reached and puts them
on the scanned table.**

Node C was just reached. Disregarding nodes B and D (because they've
been reached), the adjacent node is node G.

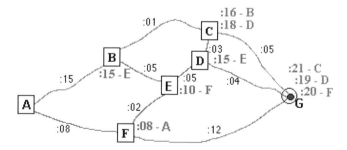

The results after node C is reached and adjacent nodes are scanned:

SCANNED TABLE

NODE	CUMULATIVE COST	PREVIOUS NODE
G	:20	F
C	:18	D
G	:19	D
G	:21	C

Step 12 **Picks the scanned node with the lowest cumulative cost and puts it on the reached table.**

Node C is on the scanned table with a cumulative cost of 18 minutes from node D. But node C has been reached; it has an entry on the reached table. The algorithm disregards the entry for node C in the scanned table.

SCANNED TABLE

NODE	CUMULATIVE COST	PREVIOUS NODE
G	:20	F
~~C~~	~~:18~~	~~D~~
G	:19	D
G	:21	C

Node C has been reached. Disregard this entry.

This leaves only entries for node G on the scanned table. The entry with the lowest cumulative cost is 19 minutes from node D. This entry is placed on the reached table.

REACHED TABLE

NODE	CUMULATIVE COST	PREVIOUS NODE
A	:00	none
B	:15	E
C	:16	B
D	:15	E
E	:10	F
F	:08	A
G	:19	D

SCANNED TABLE

NODE	CUMULATIVE COST	PREVIOUS NODE
G	:20	F
G	:19	D
G	:21	C

Step 13   Scans all the nodes adjacent to the node just reached and puts them on the scanned table.

The only entries left on the scanned table are for node G. There are no nodes adjacent to node G that haven't been reached. There's nothing left to scan, and this phase of the pathfinding algorithm is complete.

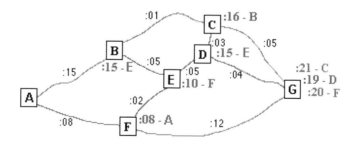

Using the results

The algorithm has now determined the travel cost relationships among the nodes.

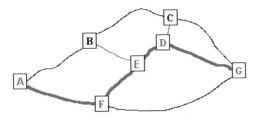

REACHED TABLE

NODE	CUMULATIVE COST	PREVIOUS NODE	
A	:00	none	[5]
B	:15	E	
C	:16	B	
D	:15	E	[2]
E	:10	F	[3]
F	:08	A	[4]
G	:19	D	[1]

To derive the shortest path from node A to node G, use the reached table and work backward from the destination node G by looking at its previous node, D; then the previous node of D, which is E; then the previous node of E, which is F, and finally the previous node of F, which is A. The path from A to G is {A, F, E, D, G}, with a travel time of 19 minutes.

To find the shortest path from the origin to any node, use the same procedure. For instance, to get the shortest path from A to C, you'd work backward from C and derive {A, F, E, B, C}. This route takes 16 minutes. Note that the possible path {A, B, C} is also 16 minutes. The path that's chosen as the actual route depends on the arbitrary choices made during the scanning process.

Aligning
your data

DIFFERENT DATA SETS
often have different map projections. Vector data sets are usually distributed in unprojected format (decimal degrees). However, because surface analysis isn't valid on unprojected data, most grid, image, and TIN data sets are projected. If some of your data is projected and some isn't, or if some is in one projection and some in another, the themes won't align properly in a view. All your theme data needs to be in the same coordinate system (either decimal degrees or a map projection) to display properly.

What ArcView GIS projects

ArcView GIS can't project grids, TINs, or images. It can, however, project feature data. When your feature and surface themes don't align, it's always the feature theme that must be changed to match the projection of the grid or TIN theme.

ArcView GIS projects feature data by applying a projection to the view in which the theme is displayed. This "on the fly" projection is specific to the view to which it's applied and doesn't change the feature data set's underlying coordinate system. You can, however, make the projection permanent by converting the feature theme to a new shapefile while it's in a projected view.

ArcView GIS can also reproject feature data—that is, change projected data to a new projection—with the ArcView Projection Utility (available in ArcView GIS 3.2) or the Projector! sample extension (in ArcView GIS 3.1). This appendix shows you how to align unprojected feature data with a grid and how to use the ArcView Projection Utility to reproject a projected feature theme.

When data doesn't align

In this example, you have an elevation grid theme of a portion of the Santa Ynez Mountains north of Santa Barbara, California. The grid is in a UTM projection. When you add it to a new view, it displays properly.

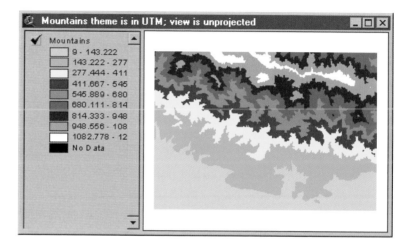

When you add an unprojected feature theme of roads for the same geographic area to the view, the two themes don't align. In fact, their coordinate systems are so different that neither theme is visible.

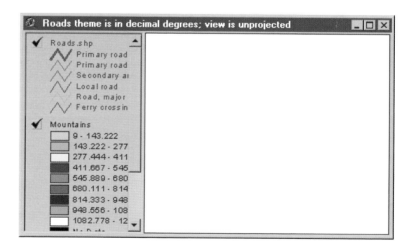

Since ArcView GIS can't change the grid theme's projection, you must project the feature theme to match the grid. This means that you need to find out what projection the grid data is in.

Determining the grid projection

Projected data is normally distributed with metadata describing its projection. If the grid was projected in ArcInfo, there should be a file called prj.adf in the grid file directory (see appendix C, "Data file structures"). If there's no projection file, you'll need to look for a Read Me file, a data dictionary, or a similar source.

In this case, the grid's projection information is stored in a prj.adf file. You can navigate to the location of the grid on disk and open this file in a text editor.

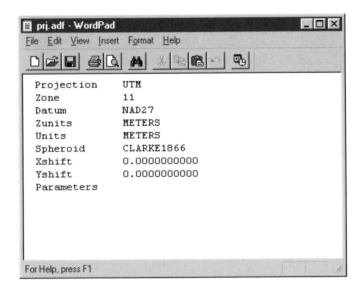

Displaying unprojected data in a projected view

The *Mountains* grid uses the UTM Zone 11 projection and the NAD27 datum. Because the *Roads.shp* theme is unprojected, you can align it with the grid by projecting the view.

Click the Projection button in the View properties dialog. In the *Category* drop-down list, choose the appropriate projection—in this case, "UTM - 1927." In the *Type* drop-down list, choose the appropriate zone—"Zone 11."

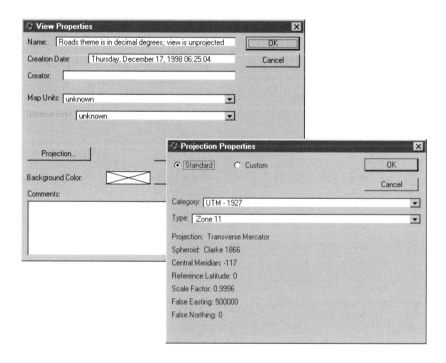

Information on map projections and datums is available in the ArcView GIS online help. Refer to the topic *Map projections* or to the names of individual projections, such as *UTM*.

When the projection properties have been set correctly, the feature theme and the grid theme align. The coordinate system of the *Roads.shp* theme is still decimal degrees, but the data displays as if it were projected.

Projecting data permanently

If you regularly use a set of unprojected feature data with a projected grid or TIN theme, you may want to set a permanent projection for it. When you make a feature theme active in a projected view and choose Convert to Shapefile from the Theme menu, ArcView GIS will ask you if you want to save the converted shapefile in the projected units of the view.

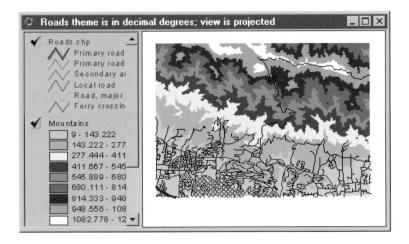

Reprojecting data

A more complicated situation arises when your vector data is already projected, but the projection is different from the one your grid is in. To solve this problem, you can use the ArcView Projection utility. In this example, your roads theme is in a State Plane projection and is called *roads_sp*. The grid is again in UTM. When both themes are added to the same view, they don't line up.

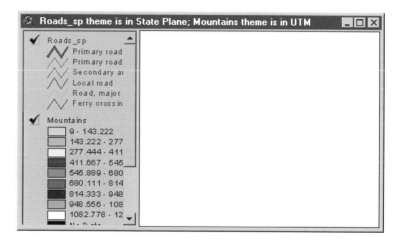

The ArcView Projection Utility is available in the $AVHOME\bin32 directory and is called projutil.exe. To use it, press your operating system's Start button. From the Programs menu, go to the ESRI menu, then to the ArcView GIS 3.2 menu. Choose Projection Utility. The first panel of the ArcView Projection Utility wizard displays.

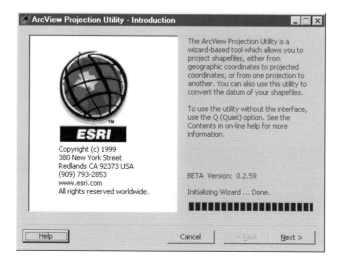

Click the Next button to view the Step 1 panel of the ArcView Projection Utility. Use the Browse button to locate the shapefile Roads_sp.shp.

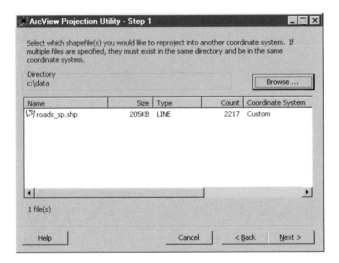

The dialog shows you the name of the shapefile, its size, its type, and other information. Click the Next button to display Step 2.

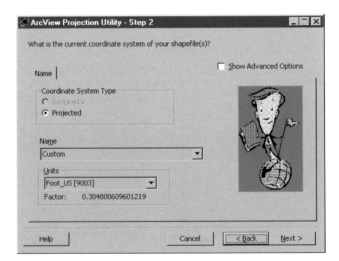

This panel is used to define the current coordinate system of your shapefile. If your shapefile has an associated projection file, the utility will set the information automatically. Otherwise, you can use the drop-down lists to set the information manually.

In this case, the ArcView Projection Utility reads the projection information from the roads_sp.prj file and automatically updates the current coordinate system information. Click the Next button to display Step 3.

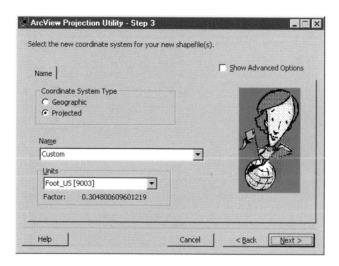

This panel is used to define the output projection. In the *Name* drop-down list, you choose "NAD_1927_UTM_ZONE_11N." The units are automatically updated to "Meter."

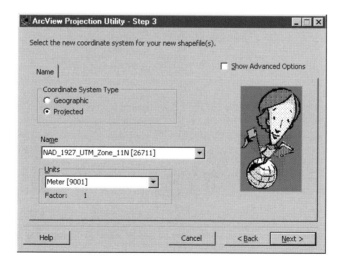

Click the Next button to display Step 4. In this panel, you specify an output location and file name for the reprojected shapefile. Click the Next button to display the Summary panel.

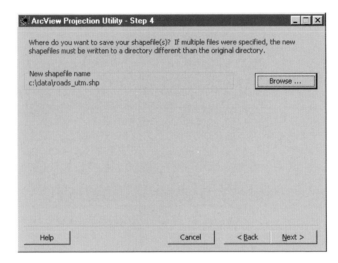

The final panel shows a summary of the input file name, the input coordinate system, the output file name, and the output coordinate system.

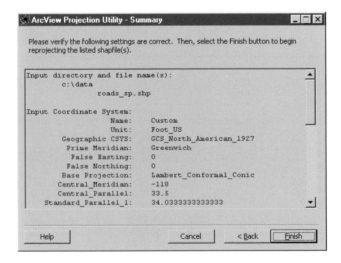

Click the Finish button to create the new shapefile. Once the process is complete, you add the new shapefile to the view.

The new projected shapefile lines up with the grid theme because both belong to the same planar coordinate system.

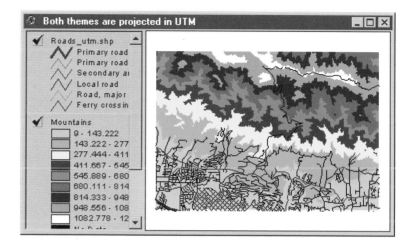

In the online help, use the Find tab to locate the topics *Aligning your raster data with vector data in a view* and *How projections affect analysis.*

Data file structures

IN THIS BOOK,
you've worked with shapefiles, grids, and TINs. The file structure of each of these data source types is described in this appendix.

Shapefiles

Shapefiles store the geographic location and attribute information of point, polyline, and polygon features. A shapefile is composed of three files, each with its own file extension.

The **.shp** (shape) file stores each geographic feature in its own record as a list of x,y coordinate pairs. Since each feature (except point features) may contain a different number of coordinate pairs, each record in the .shp file may be a different length. Variable-length records take a long time to process and draw on screen, so the .shp file is indexed with the .shx file.

The **.shx** (shape index) file contains one fixed-length record for each record in the .shp file. Each record in the .shx file contains the record number and the length in bytes of the corresponding record in the .shp file. Since the records in the .shx file are all the same length, they can be read quickly and so serve as a lookup table for the records in the .shp file.

The **.dbf** (dBASE file) file stores attribute information for the features in the .shp file. The .dbf file contains one record for each feature in the .shp file.

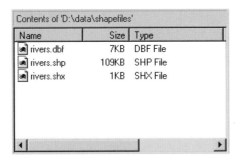

The shape index (.shx) file speeds the drawing of all features in a shapefile. You can hasten the query and selection of individual features by creating spatial and attribute indexes.

Spatial indexes

ArcView GIS creates a spatial index whenever you perform a spatial join or a theme-on-theme selection. You can also create this index by highlighting the Shape field in a theme's attribute table and choosing "Create Index" from the Field menu. The index consists of two files:

The **.sbn** (spatial bin) file divides the area containing the geographic features of the .shp file into rectangular areas called bins. Each bin contains the record numbers of the features in the .shp file that fall within its area. When you make a spatial query, the records in the .sbn file are read first, and only the features that intersect the bins specified by the query are considered. This greatly speeds processing. Since a different number of features may fall within each bin, however, bin records vary in length and need an index of their own.

The **.sbx** (spatial bin index) file contains one fixed-length record for each of the records in the .sbn file. Each record in the .sbx file contains the record number and the length in bytes of the corresponding bin record in the .sbn file. Since the records in the .sbx are all the same length, they can be read quickly and so serve as a lookup table to the variable-length records in the .sbn.

Attribute indexes

Whenever you perform a link on a table, ArcView GIS creates an attribute index. You can also create this index by highlighting any field other than the Shape field in a theme's attribute table and choosing "Create Index" from the Field menu. Attribute indexes can be created for theme attribute tables, .dbf tables, or ASCII text tables. The attribute index consists of two files:

The **.ain** (attribute index) file contains one index for each field involved in a link or that has had an index created for it by the method described above. These indexes improve the performance of data retrieval operations such as join and link, and speed simple queries such as [Name] = "Ohio". An attribute index won't improve performance on queries that involve string matching, such as [Name] = "Oh*", or comparisons, such as [Population] < 250000.

The **.aih** (attribute index header) file contains the name of each field that's been indexed. It serves as a directory to the values contained in the .ain file.

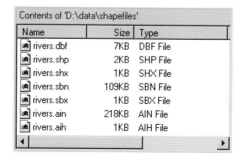

Contents of 'D:\data\shapefiles'		
Name	Size	Type
rivers.dbf	7KB	DBF File
rivers.shp	2KB	SHP File
rivers.shx	1KB	SHX File
rivers.sbn	109KB	SBN File
rivers.sbx	1KB	SBX File
rivers.ain	218KB	AIN File
rivers.aih	1KB	AIH File

3D shapefiles

3D shapefiles have the same file structure as ordinary shapefiles, with the addition of elevation, or z values, for all points defining a feature. The z values are stored in the .shp file along with the x and y coordinates. Feature types include pointZ, polylineZ, and polygonZ.

Grids

A grid data set is split into two directories, one called by the grid name and one called INFO.

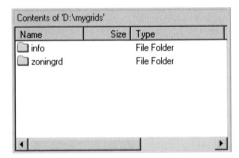

The INFO directory may be shared by several grid directories in a single folder.

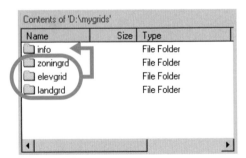

All files in a grid directory except the LOG file have a .adf extension, which stands for "arc data file."

dblbnd.adf: stores the rectangular boundary of the grid

hdr.adf: stores the type of grid (integer or floating point) and its cell resolution

prj.adf: stores the map projection information of the grid (optional)

sta.adf: contains statistics (minimum, maximum, mean, and standard deviation) for the cell values in the grid

vat.adf: stores unique cell values and a cell count for each value (integer grids only)

w001001.adf: stores the cell data for the grid

w001001x.adf: indexes the values in w001001.adf

log: records the history of the grid, including the date of its creation and a list of the ArcView Spatial Analyst commands performed on it (for instance, SPLINE, FLIP, HILLSHADE)

Contents of 'D:\mygrids\zoningrd'

Name	Size	Type
dblbnd.adf	1KB	ADF File
hdr.adf	1KB	ADF File
log	1KB	File
sta.adf	1KB	ADF File
vat.adf	8KB	ADF File
w001001.adf	984KB	ADF File
w001001x.adf	19KB	ADF File

The vat.adf, sta.adf, and dblbnd.adf files in a grid directory each have a pair of corresponding INFO files, the .nit and .dat pairs, in the INFO directory. In each case, the grid file contains the raw data values. Its corresponding .dat file (e.g., arc0001.dat) contains a relative path to the grid data file (e.g., d:\mygrids\zoningrd\vat.adf). Its corresponding .nit file (e.g., arc0001.nit) contains the definitions of the items, or column headings, in the grid file. For example, a vat.adf file will contain at least two items, VALUE and COUNT. The type, width, and name of each item are stored in the .nit file.

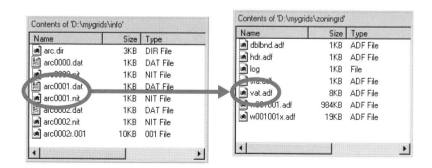

Grid naming conventions

No folder that's part of the path to a grid folder should contain spaces or periods. Only alphanumeric characters should be used. It's recommended that folder names that appear in the path to a grid be no longer than eight characters.

TINs

A TIN data set is stored as a folder of binary files, each with a .adf extension.

tdenv.adf: stores the range of z values and the spatial boundary of the data

tnod.adf: identifies the nodes that comprise each triangle

tnxy.adf: stores the x,y coordinates of the nodes

tnz.adf: stores the z value at each node

tedg.adf: identifies the edges of adjacent triangles

thul.adf: identifies the nodes that are part of the TIN hull (The hull is formed by one or more polygons containing the entire set of data points used to construct the TIN.)

tmsk.adf: defines the zone of interpolation

tmsx.adf: indexes the tmsk file

prj.adf: stores the projection information of the TIN (optional)

tnval.adf: stores user-defined values for nodes (optional)

tndsc.adf: stores internal, unique ID values for nodes (This file is automatically created to accompany the tnval.adf file.)

ttval.adf: stores user-defined values for triangles (optional)

ttdsc.adf: stores internal, unique ID values for triangles (This file is automatically created to accompany the ttval.adf file.)

```
Contents of 'D:\tin_data\elev_tin'

Name            Size    Type
tdenv.adf       1KB     ADF File
tedg.adf        77KB    ADF File
thul.adf        1KB     ADF File
tmsk.adf        1KB     ADF File
tmsx.adf        1KB     ADF File
tnod.adf        77KB    ADF File
tnxy.adf        51KB    ADF File
tnz.adf         13KB    ADF File
ttdsc.adf       1KB     ADF File
ttval.adf       26KB    ADF File
```

Network index directories

When you create a result theme for a network problem, Network Analyst creates and maintains a directory of index files for the network data. Unlike most directories, the network index directory name has an extension appended to it. The extension name reflects the type of network data you're using. For a line shapefile called Streets, the network directory would be streets.nws. For an ArcInfo line coverage called Pipes, the directory would be pipes.nwc. Any other data source will have the extension .nwo.

These naming conventions apply only if you have write access to the directory where your network data is stored. If you don't, the network index directory will be created in your project's working directory, and will be called xxnet<n> followed by the appropriate extension, where n is a number distinguishing the index directory from others that may already exist in your working directory.

The network index directory contains the following files:

id: stores User-IDs for edges (line segments), junctions, and turns

nodes.dbf: stores node topology

elem and **ov:** store network topology

weight: stores impedance values for the network

ini: stores metadata about the network such as the layer name, weight name, and data source

net: header file for the network index directory

eix and **jix:** lookup indexes for the network index directory

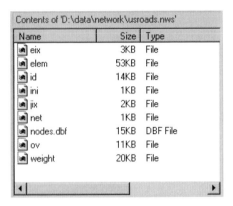

Resources

ESRI OFFERS A VARIETY OF RESOURCES

to help you get the most out of your software. You may be looking for spatial data, like a street network of Boston. Or you may want a script to perform a special function, like converting a TIN to a polygon shapefile.

You may have a question that no one in the office can quite figure out ("How do I use this elevation grid to find the average elevations of my soil polygons?"). You may want to build new software skills, like Avenue programming. Or you may be interested in learning about a GIS application area, such as hydrology.

The following list of resources contains ideas to help you keep extending your ArcView GIS knowledge once you've finished this book.

www.esri.com

For company news and information about products, services, or support, visit us on the Web at www.esri.com. Our Web site is a comprehensive source of GIS information. Link to the ARCVIEW-L discussion list, ArcScripts, ArcData℠ Online, and the GIS Jump Station.

ARCVIEW-L is a discussion list for ArcView GIS and its extensions. You can post questions and get fast answers from experienced ArcView GIS users.

ArcScripts is a source of Avenue scripts and ArcView GIS extensions created by ESRI employees and developers in the ArcView GIS community.

ArcData Online is a site where you can create maps interactively and download the spatial data used to make them. Much of this data is free, some can be licensed from commercial vendors.

The GIS Jump Station is a catalog of GIS Web sites organized by category (government, educational, and so forth). Many of these sites offer downloadable spatial data.

campus.esri.com

ESRI Virtual Campus delivers self-paced, online courses in ESRI software products, GIS application areas, and GIS science. ESRI Virtual Campus courses include conceptual material, exercises, challenges, quizzes, and more. Most courses provide downloadable software and free introductory lessons. Taking a course makes you part of a worldwide GIS learning community where you can share ideas with other students.

Training

ESRI instructors teach classes at scheduled locations around the country and at customer sites. ESRI courses are written and taught by the people who know the software best. For more information, contact ESRI at

ESRI Learning Center
Telephone: 909-793-2853, extension 1-1585
Fax: 909-335-8233
E-mail: learnGIS@esri.com
Internet: www.esri.com/training

In addition to ESRI's own teaching staff, a network of ESRI authorized instructors teaches ESRI courses in 49 states and U.S. territories. To find an ESRI authorized instructor or learning center near you, contact

ESRI Authorized Teaching Program
Telephone: 909-793-2853, extension 1-2111
Fax: 909-307-3050
E-mail: atp@esri.com
Internet: www.esri.com/training

Contact us

For more information, give us a call at 1-800-GIS-XPRT (1-800-447-9778). Outside the United States, call 909-793-2853, extension 1235. You can also e-mail us at info@esri.com.

Corporate headquarters

ESRI
380 New York Street
Redlands, CA 92373-8100 USA
Telephone: 909-793-2853
Fax: 909-793-5953

Regional offices

Alaska
Telephone: 907-344-6613
Fax: 907-344-6813

Boston
Telephone: 978-777-4543
Fax: 978-777-8476

California
Telephone: 909-793-2853
extension 1906
Fax: 978-307-3025

Charlotte
Telephone: 704-541-9810
Fax: 704-541-7620

Denver
Telephone: 303-449-7779
Fax: 303-449-8830

Minneapolis
Telephone: 651-454-0600
Fax: 651-454-0705

Olympia
Telephone: 360-754-4727
Fax: 360-943-6910

St. Louis
Telephone: 636-949-6620
Fax: 636-949-6735

San Antonio
Telephone: 210-499-1044
Fax: 210-499-4112

Washington, D.C.
Telephone: 703-506-9515
Fax: 703-506-9514

International offices

ESRI–Australia
Telephone: 61-89-242-1005
Fax: 61-89-242-4412

ESRI–BeLux
Telephone: 32-2-460-7480
Fax: 32-2-460-4539

ESRI Canada Limited
Telephone: 416-441-6035
Fax: 416-441-6838

ESRI–Europe
Telephone: 31-10-217-0690
Fax: 31-10-217-0691

ESRI France
Telephone: 33-1-46-23-6060
Fax: 33-1-450-70560

ESRI–Germany
Telephone: 49-8166-677-0
Fax: 49-8166-677-111

ESRI Hong Kong Limited
Telephone: 852-2730-6883
Fax: 852-2730-3772

ESRI Italia
Telephone: 39-06-40696-1
Fax: 39-06-40696-333

ESRI Korea, Inc.
Telephone: 82-2-571-1101
Fax: 82-2-571-1311

ESRI Nederland B.V.
Telephone: 31-10-217-0700
Fax: 31-10-217-0799

ESRI Polska
Telephone: 48-22-825-9836
Fax: 48-22-825-5705

ESRI–South Asia
Telephone: 65-735-8755
Fax: 65-735-5629

ESRI Espana
Telephone: 34-91-559-4375
Fax: 34-91-559-7071

ESRI Sweden
Telephone: 46-23-84090
Fax: 46-23-84485

ESRI–Germany (Swiss Regional Office)
Telephone: 41-1-360-2460
Fax: 41-1-360-2470

ESRI–Thailand
Telephone: 66-2-678-0707
Fax: 66-2-678-0321-3

ESRI (UK)
Telephone: 44-1-923-210450
Fax: 44-1-923-210739

ESRI de Venezuela, C.A.
Telephone: 58-2-285-1134
Fax: 58-2-285-0714

ESRI also has more than sixty distributors in other countries worldwide. For more information, contact ESRI at 909-793-2853, extension 1235. Or visit our Web site at www.esri.com and click on Third Party Solutions.

Using
the CD

CD contents

The *Extending ArcView GIS* CD contains ArcView GIS project files and approximately 90 megabytes of spatial data used in the exercises. It also contains installation software to copy the projects and data to your computer's hard drive.

Installing the exercise data

Insert the CD and navigate to your D: drive (or the drive letter assigned to your CD–ROM).

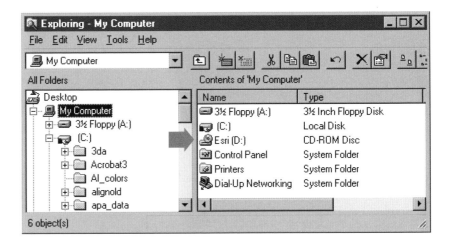

Double-click on the CD–ROM icon to display the contents of the CD. Locate the Setup.exe file.

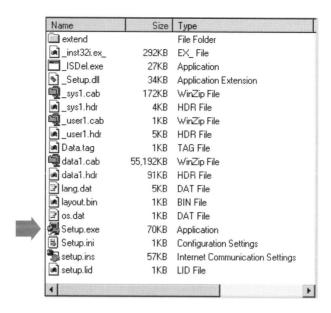

Name	Size	Type
extend		File Folder
inst32i.ex	292KB	EX_ File
_ISDel.exe	27KB	Application
_Setup.dll	34KB	Application Extension
_sys1.cab	172KB	WinZip File
_sys1.hdr	4KB	HDR File
_user1.cab	1KB	WinZip File
_user1.hdr	5KB	HDR File
Data.tag	1KB	TAG File
data1.cab	55,192KB	WinZip File
data1.hdr	91KB	HDR File
lang.dat	5KB	DAT File
layout.bin	1KB	BIN File
os.dat	1KB	DAT File
Setup.exe	70KB	Application
Setup.ini	1KB	Configuration Settings
setup.ins	57KB	Internet Communication Settings
setup.lid	1KB	LID File

Double-click on the Setup.exe file, then follow the wizards to install the software.

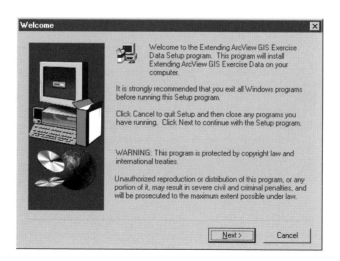

Welcome

Welcome to the Extending ArcView GIS Exercise Data Setup program. This program will install Extending ArcView GIS Exercise Data on your computer.

It is strongly recommended that you exit all Windows programs before running this Setup program.

Click Cancel to quit Setup and then close any programs you have running. Click Next to continue with the Setup program.

WARNING: This program is protected by copyright law and international treaties.

Unauthorized reproduction or distribution of this program, or any portion of it, may result in severe civil and criminal penalties, and will be prosecuted to the maximum extent possible under law.

Next >   Cancel

The exercise data can be installed all at once or separately for each section of the book. The default is all at once. If you're working with one or two extensions rather than all three, you may want to download only the relevant spatial data.

The Network Analyst data uses 14 megabytes of hard disk space. The ArcView Spatial Analyst data uses 31 megabytes. The 3D Analyst data uses 44 megabytes.

The default data installation folder is c:\extend. If you install to a folder other than c:\extend, it's recommended that no folder names in the full path to the root folder contain spaces or have more than eight characters.

It's possible to load exercise projects and data directly from the CD while ArcView GIS is running. But some exercises require you to edit data, and data sets can only be edited if they're installed on your computer's hard drive.

Removing the exercise data

To remove all exercise data and projects from your hard drive, use the Add/Remove Programs function in your operating system's Control Panel. The data will be listed in the Add/Remove Programs Properties dialog as "Extending ArcView GIS Exercise Data."

Alternatively, you can drag the data folders (such as "extend" or "network" or "ch01") to the Recycle Bin. To copy, delete, or move individual data sets within a chapter folder, use the ArcView GIS Source Manager (described in chapter 9).

Index of topics

ArcView Network Analyst

ArcView 3D Analyst

Books from ESRI Press

GIS for Everyone
Now everyone can create smart maps for school, work, home, or community action using a personal computer. Includes ArcExplorer geographic data viewer and more than 500 megabytes of geographic data.   ISBN 1-879102-49-8

Enterprise GIS for Energy Companies
A volume of case studies showing how electric and gas utilities use geographic information systems to manage their facilities more cost effectively, find new market opportunities, and better serve their customers.   ISBN 1-879102-48-X

Transportation GIS
From monitoring rail systems and airplane noise levels, to making bus routes more efficient and improving roads, this book describes how geographic information systems have emerged as the tool of choice for transportation planners.   ISBN 1-879102-47-1

Serving Maps on the Internet
Take an insider's look at how today's forward-thinking organizations distribute map-based information via the Internet. Case studies cover a range of applications for Internet Map Server technology from ESRI. This book should interest anyone who wants to publish geospatial data on the World Wide Web.
ISBN 1-879102-52-8

Managing Natural Resources with GIS
Find out how GIS technology helps people design solutions to such pressing challenges as wildfires, urban blight, air and water degradation, species endangerment, disaster mitigation, coastline erosion, and public education. The experiences of public and private organizations provide real-world examples.
ISBN 1-879102-53-6

Getting to Know ArcView GIS
A colorful, nontechnical introduction to GIS technology and ArcView GIS software, this workbook comes with a working ArcView GIS demonstration copy. Follow the book's scenario-based exercises or work through them using the CD and learn how to do your own ArcView GIS project.   ISBN 1-879102-46-3

ArcView GIS Means Business
Written for business professionals, this book is a behind-the-scenes look at how some of America's most successful companies have used desktop GIS technology. The book is loaded with full-color illustrations and comes with a trial copy of ArcView GIS software and a GIS tutorial.   ISBN 1-879102-51-X

Zeroing In: Geographic Information Systems at Work in the Community
In twelve "tales from the digital map age," this book shows how people use GIS in their daily jobs. An accessible and engaging introduction to GIS for anyone who deals with geographic information.
ISBN 1-879102-50-1

ARC Macro Language: Developing Menus and Macros with AML
ARC Macro Language (AML™) software gives you the power to tailor workstation ArcInfo software's geoprocessing operations to specific applications. This workbook teaches AML in the context of accomplishing practical workstation ArcInfo tasks, and presents both basic and advanced techniques.
ISBN 1-879102-18-8

Understanding GIS: The ArcInfo Method (workstation ArcInfo)
A hands-on introduction to geographic information system technology. Designed primarily for beginners, this classic text guides readers through a complete GIS project in ten easy-to-follow lessons.
ISBN 1-879102-00-5

*ESRI Press publishes a growing list of GIS-related books. Ask for these books at your local bookstore or order by calling **1-800-447-9778**. You can also shop online at **www.esri.com/gisstore**. Outside the United States, contact your local ESRI distributor.*

ESRI Press ▪ **380 New York Street** ▪ **Redlands, California 92373-8100**

SPECIAL OFFER

Order

- **ArcView Network Analyst**
- **ArcView Spatial Analyst**

or

- **ArcView 3D Analyst**

now

**and get $100 off
the suggested list price.***

Order direct:

1-800-GISXPRT

(1-800-447-9778)

or ask for the ESRI reseller nearest you

* Offer good in the United States only. Can be used for any or all of the
extensions listed above. Not good with any other discount or promotion.

SPECIAL OFFER

Order

- **ArcView Network Analyst**
- **ArcView Spatial Analyst**
  or
- **ArcView 3D Analyst**

now

and get $100 off the suggested list price.*

Order direct:
1-800-GISXPRT
(1-800-447-9778)

or ask for the ESRI reseller nearest you

* Offer good in the United States only. Can be used for any or all of the
  extensions listed above. Not good with any other discount or promotion.